Sayles on Sayles

Sayles on Sayles

by John Sayles and Gavin Smith

faber and faber
BOSTON · LONDON

First published in 1998
by Faber and Faber Limited
3 Queen Square London WC1N 3AU

Photoset by Stanton Publication Services, Inc., St. Paul, Minnesota, U.S.A.
Printed in England by Clays Ltd, St Ives plc

A CIP record for this book
is available from the British Library

ISBN 0-571-19280-7

2   4   6   8   10   9   7   5   3   1

Contents

List of Illustrations

Introduction

In this era of twin movie industry Holy Grails—the blockbuster that grosses three or four times its cost at the world boxoffice on the one hand, and the independent film that earns ten times its production cost on the other—perhaps only John Sayles has worked both ends. One of the quintessential independent filmmakers of contemporary American cinema, the only one to combine longevity and high productivity, Sayles has a unique ability to work both inside and outside the Hollywood system. Within the space of one year he went from rewriting Ron Howard's 1995 blockbuster *Apollo 13* (uncredited) to writing, directing, and editing his own independent film, *Lone Star*, his most successful film to date at the boxoffice. Why begin discussing Sayles's career in terms of budgets and grosses? Because Sayles's singular position between the commercial mainstream and the specialty margins is the result of economic necessity. In the tradition of John Cassavetes, who financed his independent films in the sixties and seventies by acting in mainly minor Hollywood pictures, Sayles works as a journeyman writer for hire, ploughing his earnings back into his own personal projects. In this way he continues to ensure his creative freedom and commercial survival. And it's fitting to begin with the economic bottom line, a fact of life that all of Sayles's films insist upon.

The work ethic is deeply ingrained in Sayles. In the past twenty-five years he has written, directed, and edited eleven feature films, written or rewritten eighteen produced features and made-for-TV films, and published three novels, one work of nonfiction, and twenty-two short stories. In addition to directing three music videos and two self-penned plays, and creating a TV drama series, he has also acted in seventeen films, including six of his own. (He may be the only director in history to cut himself out of his own movie, as he did in *Lone Star*, in which he played a Texas border patrolman.) Although he received a prestigious five-year MacArthur "Genius" Grant in 1983, Sayles is a notably down-to-earth, unassuming figure—though, at six foot four, a physically imposing one. With typical flippancy in his *Contemporary Theatre, Film, and Television* entry he describes his politics as "survivalist" and his religion as "Roman Catholic Atheist." He keeps Hollywood at a healthy distance, working out of a small downtown New York office on the borders of Little Italy and Soho. He has lived in New Jersey and upstate New York since the early eighties—that is, after an obligatory spell in southern California spent establishing himself as a screenwriter in the late seventies.

Born in 1950, he grew up in and around the blue-collar town of Schenectady in upstate New York, the son of school teachers. A self-admitted academic underachiever and "subverbal" personality, his passions were sports and fiction—he read and began writing from an early age. He went to college in the late sixties, at the height of the student movement, but kept his distance from campus radicalism and spent his time reading, hitchhiking around the country, and latterly acting and directing in college theater. Although not a joiner, he was a keen observer of people and he put this to use in his writing. After graduation, he continued to lead a life of casual nonconformism, working as a day laborer, medical orderly, and meat packer, and moving to Boston in the mid-seventies. Via college theater connections, he began performing with the Eastern Slope Playhouse, a New Hampshire summer stock theater, while pursuing short story writing. His first novel *Pride of the Bimbos*, published in 1975, was followed by a number of short stories and then, in 1977, his second novel *Union Dues*. *Pride of the Bimbos* is an almost allegorical portrait of masculinity in crisis that follows a tour of the South by a team of ill-assorted baseball players, the Bimbos, who play in women's drag. The team is tracked by a black pimp seeking revenge against one of the players, a midget. *Union Dues*, conceived on a larger scale than the earlier novel, is an ambitious, multicharacter portrait of America and its social divisions in the late sixties. It follows a middle-age West Virginia coal miner to Boston in search of his teenage son, who has left home to find his older brother, a Vietnam veteran, who has fallen in with a radical, would-be revolutionary political group planning a political action.

Jean Renoir's dictum that "everyone has their reasons" is at the heart of Sayles's approach as both a writer and a director. His first two novels (as well as his third, *Los Gusanos*) pay particular attention to the nuances of point of view, which shifts from character to character, encompassing the perspectives and world views of main protagonists and minor bystanders alike. This mosaic narrative effect and sense of an ensemble cast of characters begins to emerge in Sayles's later films; in fact, many of the themes, preoccupations, and attitudes that have characterized Sayles's subsequent work can be found in *Pride of the Bimbos* and *Union Dues*: an unsentimental view of everyday life; a keen sense of the price characters pay for knowledge; questions of loss of innocence, compromise, and redemption; the interplay of personal and political/social spheres; the centrality of unresolvable father-son conflicts; and a sense of fatalism or pessimism about the prospects for change for the better at the end of the day.

Moving to California after the success of *Union Dues*, Sayles set out to break into screenwriting, following the traditional route from fiction to screenwriting to directing. He found work writing three exploitation films for Roger Corman's New World Pictures, bringing invention and subversive humor to pop genre chores. *Piranha* (1978) was a memorable *Jaws* knock-off with an antimilitary spin, directed by Joe Dante who would go on to a notable career in Hollywood; *The Lady in Red* (1979), an uneven but vigorous depression-era feminist crime picaresque directed by Lewis Teague, followed the fortunes of a young woman who would eventually gain notoriety as the woman who was at bank robber John Dillinger's side when the FBI gunned him down outside a Chicago movie theater; and the sci-fi yarn *Battle Beyond the Stars* (1980) spliced together *Star Wars* and *The Magnificent Seven*. His knack for witty dialogue, realistic characters, and playful, intelligent genre revisionism—and his ability to deliver fast—quickly established Sayles as an in-demand rewriter. Joe Dante brought him in to write *The Howling* (1980), a lively, intriguing, contemporary werewolf shocker that relocated lycanthropy to southern California in the era of media saturation and self-help groups. And Lewis Teague got him hired to write *Alligator* (1980), a droll, effective B-movie mix of *Jaws* and the alligator-in-the-sewer urban legend, about which Sayles once remarked, "My original idea was that the alligator eats its way through the whole socioeconomic system."

At this point Sayles seemed poised to segue into directing genre/

exploitation films of his own, in the tradition of Jonathan Demme. Instead, following the Cassavetes example, he cashed in what he had learned about the economic realities of low-budget film-making and the money he'd made writing *Piranha* to do what he'd planned all along—make a self-financed, 16 mm independent film with his summer stock theater collaborators back at the Eastern Slope Playhouse. A generous-spirited, affectionately observed ensemble drama about the weekend reunion of a group of friends (all former student activists), *The Return of the Secaucus Seven* (1980) was an unpretentious attempt to acknowledge the diminished expectations and adjusted ideals of a generation whose values and beliefs were now all but dismissed by Reagan-era America. Inspired partly by Swiss filmmaker Alain Tanner's 1975 film *Jonah, Who Will Be 25 in the Year 2000*, and despite the film's technical limitations, it's a remarkably fresh, clear-headed portrait of Sayles's contemporaries. A number of his collaborators would go on to form a core of Sayles regulars: Sayles's partner and producer Maggie Renzi, composer Mason Daring, actors David Strathairn and Gordon Clapp. A milestone in the ongoing history of American independent filmmaking, *The Return of the Secaucus Seven* was a critical and commercial success and established Sayles as one of the most promising writer-directors of his generation.

If Sayles was unmistakably portraying a group of people and a world of which he knew personally in his first film, his subsequent two independent films, *Lianna* (1982) and *The Brother from Another Planet* (1985), might be said to be explorations of the experiences of two distinct Others. In contrast to the warmth and community of the group in *The Return of the Secaucus Seven*, both films emphasize the isolation and alienation of being an outsider and the difficulties of negotiating some form of social integration. It is no coincidence that these are the only Sayles films in which a single protagonist's point of view predominates. *Lianna* is a drama about the struggle for self-definition of a middle-class wife and mother who realizes she is a lesbian and is unprepared for the emotional and practical consequences of coming out. *The Brother from Another Planet* might be a comic rejoinder to Steven Spielberg's *E.T.: The Extra-Terrestrial*. (Sayles wrote an extra-terrestrials-on-earth script for Spielberg called *Nght Skies*.) The fish-out-of-water premise—what if E.T. were a mute telepathic black man and he landed in inner city Harlem instead of suburban

California?—provided a pretext for an exploration of the black urban experience compressed into a series of emblematic incidents and encounters.

In between these two low-budget independent films, Sayles was hired by producers Amy Robinson and Griffin Dunne to write and direct *Baby, It's You*, to be released by Paramount Pictures. Charting the diverging courses of a middle-class, college-bound, Jewish, high school senior and her working-class, Italian-American boyfriend amidst the social and cultural upheaval of the mid-sixties, this coming-of-age story conveys a vivid sense of both the heightened romance of adolescent experience and the poignant loss of illusion that comes when confronted with the compromises and defeats of the real world. His most accessible and mainstream work, *Baby, It's You* gave Sayles the chance to utilize the production values and technical sophistication of a Hollywood studio film—and to experience firsthand the ordeal of having a studio interfere with the film's editing and then abandon it after release. While Sayles's version of the film ultimately prevailed and was distributed, the whole episode served to confirm Sayles as an independent filmmaker who would only work on his own creative terms. Although *Eight Men Out* was distributed by Orion, known to be the most hands-off studio of the time, Sayles has otherwise never directed another studio release. Indeed, his there-and-back studio experience seemed to validate him as a model of independent integrity and commitment for a subsequent generation of young writer-directors who have emerged in the current independent film boom, which began in the mid-eighties.

Financing has never been easy to come by for Sayles and he has tended to be his own first investor. He has raised money from a variety of sources: a five-year MacArthur Grant in 1983; directing three music videos for Bruce Springsteen in 1984; and, above all, taking sometimes uncredited and often unproduced writing assignments from Hollywood such as *The Challenge* (1982), *The Clan of the Cave Bear* (1986), and most recently *Apollo 13* and *Mimic* (1997). He has also worked as a dayplayer actor in a number of films, including *Hard Choices* (1986), Jonathan Demme's *Something Wild* (1986), Spike Lee's *Malcolm X* (1991), and for former collaborators like Joe Dante (*Matinee*, 1993) and actors Perry Lang (*Little Vegas*, 1990) and Vondie Curtis-Hall (*Gridlock'D*, 1996). Moreover he has appeared in small roles in his own films, usually for pragmatic reasons, but often with an air of ironic countercasting—as a well-meaning sexist film professor in *Lianna*, as one-half of a duo of comically sinister extraterrestrial "Men in Black" in *The Brother from Another Planet*, as a hard-shell Baptist preacher holding forth on the evils of Communism in *Matewan*, as a cynical crippled loan shark and arsonist in *City of Hope*.

The sheer diversity of Sayles's cinematic output cannot be overstated. He does not work in the major movie genres, and so for all their thematic echoes and links, his films do not bear much resemblance to each other in subject matter or style. They are unified chiefly by a realistic, unsentimental sympathy; a rational, almost-journalistic sensibility; an animating spirit of inquiry; and by a shrewd underlying awareness of the political implications of his material. If Sayles has an overarching impulse, it is to investigate the complex, shifting relationship between individuals and their communities and social orders, or put another way, the dynamic between the personal and the political in ordinary life.

Exemplifying this, his next three films, *Matewan* (1987), *Eight Men Out* (1988), and *City of Hope* (1990), and his third novel, *Los Gusanos* (1991), manifest an increasing ambition in terms of scale and density of material, and their innocence-lost scenarios assume an overtly political focus. *Matewan* chronicles the conflict between striking miners and the pit owners' hired enforcers in a remote West Virginia community in the 1920s, and the efforts of an itinerant labor organizer to unite local workers with Italian immigrants and black workers brought in to break the strike. *Eight Men Out*, an adaption of Eliot Asinof's account of the Chicago Black Sox scandal, could almost be *Matewan*'s counterpart, set as it is in 1919 and concerning the grievances of exploited workers—the baseball players who conspire with gamblers to throw games in the World Series. With its muscular, continuous camera movement and busy, intensified visual style, *City of Hope* is perhaps Sayles's most formally compelling film. Its cause-and-effect, multi-character depiction of the almost Darwinian ecosystem of a modern American city is unique and distinctive, interweaving personal and civic dilemmas, social and political divisions, and a nagging moral tension between idealism and cynicism, optimism and despair, that permeates all strata of society. *Los Gusanos*, Sayles's contemporaneous novel set in the world of Miami's Cuban exiles, was a similarly multicharacter, multiperspective narrative, but the pressures and tensions facing the community originate not in the territorial imperatives of the urban immediate present, as in *City of Hope*, but in the seemingly irreconcilable reversals and displacements of decades-old history, with its burden of loss, betrayal, and denial.

At the end of the eighties, Sayles's attention to the ethical and moral dilemmas and complications of modern life also found its way to the small screen with a short-lived, hour-long TV series, "Shannon's Deal," which he created and for which he wrote the pilot and initial episodes. In a sense the show was a reconsideration of the values and attitudes of the characters in *The Return of the Secaucus Seven*—from the point of view of a corporate sellout now looking for redemption, former corporate lawyer Jack Shannon, who uses his gambler's wits and legal expertise in defense of the underdog. Its premise—the economically marginal lawyer who can't be bought, winning small but honorable victories against the system and living to fight another day—invites itself to be read as a reflection on the precarious position of the independent filmmaker, just as *Lianna* and *Matewan* concerned themselves with the high price of even qualified independence. After all, just as the individuals in Sayles's films and novels are defined by and reliant upon community, even the most "independent" filmmaker is dependent on the structures of the film industry—financiers, banks, agents, actors, distributors, exhibitors, audiences, to name only the obvious instances. Independence is a state of mind and dependency is its flip side.

It seems natural, then, that Sayles's next film, *Passion Fish* (1992), should probe the dynamics and faultlines of dependency, incarnated in the relationship of a paraplegic soap opera actress and her nurse, a recovering drug addict trying to make a new start in small-town Louisiana. Breaking with Sayles's recent phase of hard-edged, large-cast, broad canvas subjects, *Passion Fish* is lyrical, intimate, and domestic, intent on excavating painful personal truths and confronting inner demons, offsetting the unsentimental sympathy with which the characters are scrutinized with a light, sensuous style and comedic observation. After the bleak impasse of *City of Hope*'s last moments, with no prospect of help for a desperate father and his dying son, and the nightmarish awakening to reality of *Los Gusanos*'s final pages as a Cuban would-be Joan of

Arc finds herself "lost on the dark island," Sayles's films demonstrate a real will to come to terms with the loss or regret that seem to be the common lot of most of the characters in his *oeuvre*. The recovery of some sense of possibility and growth is at the heart of *Passion Fish*'s enterprise. The children's tale *The Secret of Roan Inish*, set on the Irish coast in the early fifties, is informed by an adult sense of loss—of connection from ancestral land and of family—yet finds redemption and regeneration through the determined efforts of a young girl who locates truth in myth, with the intercession of supernatural forces.

Likewise, loss and redemption figure prominently in *Lone Star* (1996), a counterpart to *City of Hope* in that both films are readings of the state of America at its racial, political, and sociological ground zero, but with the added dimension of a sense of history. Ostensibly it's a mystery in which a small-town sheriff must face down his past and the myth surrounding his dead father in order to solve a murder committed thirty years previously. But it goes a step further to anatomize how the oppressive weight of unexamined and repressed history underwrites the film's multiple instances of father-son estrangement, racial tension, and thwarted romantic hopes, then to envisage the possibility of both personal and social reconciliation. In *Lone Star*, whose title again, perhaps ironically, evokes a spirit of independence, Sayles tries to find a way to free the present from a past whose secrets and falsehoods serve only to perpetuate division and denial.

Sayles's latest film, *Men With Guns*, completes a gravitation toward an interest in America's backyard, apparent in *Los Gusanos* and *Lone Star*. A contemporary road movie set in an unnamed Central American country, it concerns a benevolent, patrician city doctor who travels to his country's interior to visit his former students, graduates of a program to train doctors and set up clinics in indigent Indian communities. One by one he discovers his students have been killed, victims of an endless war of attrition between a ruthless military and elusive guerrilla fighters. The doctor is the latest in a long line of Sayles characters who find their most basic beliefs and assumptions crumbling, to be replaced by brutal new truths about themselves and their worlds. At times recalling a spiritual allegory or parable—the doctor gradually acquires as traveling companions a young orphan boy, a soldier, a priest, and a mute woman—*Men With Guns* presents the inadvertent, systemic complicity of progressive humanism with right-wing genocidal militarism as a horrific, bitter, historical irony. Shot in Mexico and once again partly financed by Sayles himself, it is filmed entirely in Spanish and native Indian dialects, subtitled in English.

Sayles remains an unapologetic specialist in life's inconvenient truths and hard facts—things which remain as unfashionable as ever. Accordingly, he has invariably demonstrated how little the work of making entertainment, particularly the kind that seeks to expand or extend the cultural discussion, need be about enlisting viewers in a pleasing escape into the reassuring satisfactions of glamour, fantasy, or contrivance—which, to be sure, have their place. To the charge of being a worthy-but-dull message movie-maker: not guilty. His filmmaking is plainly concerned with description and commentary, not invention and prescription. And if his first five or six films can be located more or less in the formally straightforward naturalistic/realistic tradition of the classic message film, his work since has evolved steadily toward the more subjective stylings and intricate narrative construction of his novels and short stories; with greater formal and technical control comes an inevitable tilt toward a more stylized aesthetic. At the same time, in Sayles's sensibility, this inclination to enter and shuffle the subjective points of view of his characters is offset with an overarching, engaged objectivity. Put another way, his films function both as windows and mirrors—giving us an objective view of the world but also a subjective view of ourselves.

For Sayles the satisfactions of narrative and fiction are never ends in themselves, but his films are not message movies: they are opportunities for inquiry, attempts to find illumination through staging dialogues across the faultlines of society and culture. The characteristic pressures of authorial privilege and will-to-resolution in fiction never quite overcome Sayles's determination that his stories contribute to and become a forum for the push and pull of diverse points of view, beliefs, and interests. Just as his films embrace alike art's capacity to function as window and mirror, his films are energized by the struggle to reconcile the impasse between the one and the many, between storytelling and conversation.

Thanks to: Dan Weaver, Tara M. Padykula, Mark Olson, Ray Privett, Dan Rybicki, Melissa Rubin, Rodney Hunter, Ted Pankin, Sara Bensman, Richard T. Jameson, Christine Spines, Jeffrey Nelson, Howard Mandelbaum at Photofest, Alissa Simon at the Chicago Film Center, and Herbert Klemens at Filmbild Fundus.

Sayles, Stephen J. Lang, and Anthony John Denison
on the set of *City of Hope* (1990).

CHAPTER I

Background and Early Years

Tell me about your background.

I was born in 1950, September 28th. I grew up in and around Schenectady, in upstate New York, the town where General Electric was originally based. It was a mixed, ethnic, working- to middle-class city, a factory town. My parents were both teachers. My mother taught elementary school and my father taught math and science and eventually got into school administration. Both of their fathers were cops. A lot of relatives were police and firemen—the Irish American thing of coming over and getting on the force. My parents were the first generation to finish high school and go to college. My father was an MP in World War II, mostly in Italy, and he went to college on the GI Bill, which was the big break for an awful lot of people in that generation who ordinarily wouldn't have gone to college.

We were raised Catholic, which is definitely an influence. We went to church every Sunday. It's a belief system, a mythology that you're given. Every Sunday there's a sermon based on the Gospel of that week, and if it's the first week of January, it's going to be the same Gospel. You're constantly being given simile and metaphor. Christ is always talking in parables and the punchline is always a simile or an allegory. I still think of myself as Catholic, as an ethnicity. I studied to be an altar boy but I never actually served—it was the first time I had to learn lines and I actually have a good short-term memory for that kind of thing. I learned all the Latin for the Catholic Mass in one night, got a hundred on the test the next day and forgot it within a week, I'm sure.

We moved a lot when I was a kid, even though it was a small area, so I went to six or seven different schools within the twelve years I was in public school. The first one I went to was out in farmland that was gradually turning into a suburb, near an atomic power laboratory. There was this whole "Why Ivan Is Better than Johnny" thing going on because of Sputnik, so there was a lot of emphasis on math and science when I was a little kid. We moved back into Schenectady in my sixth grade and I went to a city school that had much bigger classes and was more ethnic—there were a lot of Jewish kids. In ninth grade I went into a special program, what was called a Technical Electrical Program, where you could go to high school a year early. The main reason I went was that I knew I would face a line-up of real Fellini teachers—really odd, strange, awful teachers—if I stayed in my junior high school ninth grade. Even though I wasn't that interested in the technical stuff and in being an electrical engineer, I could qualify, so I got out and went to high school early. I was probably the least serious student they had in that program but I could get by because of that good short-term memory—I could memorize all the formulae five minutes at lunch before the test, not knowing at all what they meant, come back from lunch and write them all down. Eventually some of the smart guys who used to help me at lunch wouldn't do so anymore because I was getting better grades than them and they knew that I didn't know anything.

Did the instability of changing schools make you particularly adaptable to different situations?

Yeah, I'd say there was a lot of perspective. Often in that situation you were inventing yourself again and you had a whole new ecosystem to make your place in. If you grow up and go to the same school with the same kids year after year, you're never the new kid.

I really didn't like school. I didn't care about getting A's, I just wanted to keep people off my back. There wasn't anything that interested me except sports. As far as I was concerned, school wasn't a job, they weren't paying me to be there, they were supposed to be teaching *me* something. When I was in college I really had that attitude, when it was probably more accurate, because actually I was paying *them*.

I wasn't great at sports but I was okay at them. I played baseball, football, and basketball, and track for a couple of years. That was the world I lived in. It's time consuming—from the time I was in junior high until I graduated there might have been three weeks

at the most of every school year where I went home at three
o'clock after school. The rest of the time I was in practice or had a
game. The school had a very serious football program; we were
probably the best team in the state, so when I went to college, it
was kind of small and it had a football team but it was like going
back to the boy scouts after you've been in the marines.

You were fairly gregarious?

No. I was subverbal until I was out of college for a couple of
years. My brother was one year ahead of me and he was much
more gregarious, a much more high-profile athlete and student. I
was out of it quite a bit, just oblivious to a certain extent. I had in-
somnia as a kid so I would stay up late watching TV or listening to
baseball games on my transistor, then try to get weird rock and
roll from far away because the wave band is much clearer late at
night. I'd be tired in the morning, so I'd really be out of it at least
until lunch. I slept in class a lot. My father's doctoral thesis when
he was trying to get himself upgraded into administration was on
the underachiever, and he used my brother and especially me as
his examples.

   I read a lot. As a child I liked stories about animals, especially
stories by James Farley, who wrote *The Black Stallion*, and (Jim)
Kjelgaard, who wrote a lot of dog stories, and Jack London. At
the same time that I was reading kids' books, I was reading Her-
man Wouk's *The Caine Mutiny*, then later I saw the film. I was always interested in books that got made into movies and what was
different about them. I remember reading *Catcher in the Rye*
when I was eleven. When I was in high school, as well as reading
fiction like Thomas Pynchon's *V.* and *The Crying of Lot 49*, I
started reading a lot of nonfiction, like *The Autobiography of
Malcolm X* or Tom Wolfe. I read all kinds of stuff that sounded interesting. My parents had not been English majors. They didn't
know that much about literature, but they'd get, literally, a box
full of books from friends or relatives and they'd be a real mixed
bag. I didn't take English courses in college so I have these huge
gaps. I've never read any of the Russian or French or British guys.
My interest started with Mark Twain and went forward from that.

   When we lived in the country we went to the drive-in. Usually
the first feature was a Western and it was in color, and then the

second feature was in black and white, and as far as I was concerned it was all *The Man in the Grey Flannel Suit* kind of thing, dull and mushy and too much talk—unless it was a Hitchcock movie, which could hold your interest even though it was in black and white. There were an awful lot of Elvis movies and movies like *The Incredible Mr. Limpet* and Doris Day–Rock Hudson movies, which I didn't particularly care for but that was what was playing. Because I didn't especially do homework, when I came home I either read or watched TV. There was something called *The Early Show* at seven o'clock when we came home from practice, which showed all kinds of movies. There were genres I didn't like; I wouldn't watch a musical. I liked Westerns, some science fiction, monster movies like *Them!*. Every once in a while I'd see a movie on TV that seemed like "Jeez, that seems almost like people might actually say that." I remember William Wellman's *Wild Boys of the Road* and I talked to my father about the Depression afterwards and that film had made an impression on him when he was young too. When I was a teenager, we used to go down and see James Bond movies, or anything that had any sex at all in them. I didn't see a foreign movie with subtitles until I was in college. The first one I saw was Andzrej Wajda's *Kanal*, a really good movie. There was a thing in the Catholic church called the Legion of Decency and once a year you had to raise your hand and promise you wouldn't go to any of the movies they had condemned. There was only one place that showed those kinds of movies near us, across the river in a town called Scotia. It was called the Scotia Art Theater and it played Belmondo movies, pretty lame stuff by today's standards, but they were considered racy. We would never have gone there anyway but we had to promise not to. The local Unitarians, who were mostly nonpracticing Jews, had a film series in their basement and they showed what sounded like interesting stuff, but as a Catholic, you weren't supposed to go into a church of another denomination.

On the face of it, there's not much in your childhood or teenage years that points to a creative path.

I did pay attention and I watched people—by not being an actor in events. And I wrote a lot. Just for fun. It was kind of like seeing a baseball game and wanting to go out and play baseball. My brother and I used to watch baseball games with our gloves on and we'd watch three or four innings until we couldn't stand it anymore and then we'd go out and play for a while, then come in and watch some more of the game. I read stories and it seemed like a neat thing to do. About the third grade, eight years old, I started to write stories. They were all ripoffs of *Twilight Zone* episodes that would star kids in the neighborhood, or something like that—they were usually influenced by something I'd seen or read, and I'd do my own version. It was just something to do for myself. There wasn't any audience to speak of, I didn't show them to people, I'd show them to my parents if they asked. Once a year there'd be an assignment to write a story and that was fun, to actually do my homework happily for once. I liked to draw too, and mostly it was pretty technical—I wanted to be able to draw so that it looked like real life. I was not particularly coordinated and I was left-handed, which is always a problem, although I'm ambidextrous. I liked to draw literally, not really artistically, but representationally. Now I draw my storyboards.

What was your awareness of the political ferment in the country during those years?

It was more about race than class or international politics. The civil rights movement was very heavy. I had relatives in the South. My mother's parents lived in Hollywood, Florida, just north of Miami, so I had been going down there for years, which is one of the reasons I wrote *Los Gusanos*—I had seen that Cuban community every two years from its birth. I remember wanting to go to the colored water fountain because I thought it would be colored like Kool Aid, and being disappointed when it was just clear. And some old cracker at the train station saying, "That's the colored water fountain, you don't want to be going over there." So I thought, Okay, there are some weird rules going on in this part of the country, what is this story? Black music was really going mainstream at that point through Motown, all of the major sports had been integrated, and Roberto Clemente was my favorite baseball player, a black Puerto Rican guy. I grew up with this idea that people had serious hang-ups that I did not share and people were dying over them—people were getting lynched still and beaten with clubs and chewed by dogs nightly. And to a certain extent there was a way of saying, "Oh, that's just those people in the South." By 1968 that wasn't true anymore. Black people were not too thrilled anywhere. It was just something that was all around me. Most of the black kids I grew up with were not that politicized until my senior year. Then I could see that with the younger black kids, there were some wild-assed, angry kids who were going to end up as Black Panthers. There was a lot of very open prejudice—"nigger" and "kike" and "dago" were in the air constantly—but it wasn't as insidious as the closed prejudice that I ran into later, it didn't mean that much. If you were a smart black kid you could take any course you wanted to in my high school. There weren't the same barriers that there were in the South. There were a lot of fucked up things about being black in northern society, but if you could play you could stay. A generation earlier that wasn't true.

Do you think you developed a kind of self-sufficiency that has been beneficial in your career?

Yeah, from being on my own. Especially in not being especially other-directed or giving that much of a shit what other people felt like. I basically did better when I was on my own. Even in sports I made greater strides without somebody yelling at me. If I stopped being interested in something, I just wouldn't do it. If I made that deal with myself that this is something I wanted to do, I would figure out, What are the things you have to know to do this? When I first approached making a movie, I knew nobody in the movie industry so I went around personally to laboratories and asked, "How much does it cost to develop a film?" I felt, Who else is going to do this for me? I don't know anybody so I should do it myself. I'm not going to hope someone magically comes along. Once I bite something off, it's my responsibility and I don't expect other people to fill in for me. I don't expect magic—I'm not a magical thinker. I write fast so I don't have to worry too much about deadlines. I don't get up at a certain time in the morning and start writing, only when I have a job. I work on it until it's done. If I don't feel like working on it that day, I don't. I'm usually working on three things at the same time so if I don't feel like working on that particular thing, I'll work on another. I'm very disorganized.

Why did you go on to college given that you were completely turned off by academia?

It was a big deal and a privilege for my parents that they got to go to college and it was kind of assumed that I would go. I really had no desire to get more schooling, but Vietnam was starting and I knew that war or no war, I had no big desire to go into the army. It wasn't Vietnam that bothered me, I just didn't want to take orders anymore. I could have taken a football scholarship to a New York State school because my college boards were good enough, much better than my grades, but I didn't especially want to go as a football player with the pressure of, Yes, you have to play. I didn't want to go to college in the northeast because I don't like winter, but the reason I went to Williams was they had outlawed fraternities. I liked a lot of the people there but I didn't especially like the school. I certainly didn't like the weather.

Did you become politically active at Williams?

I went into college in 1968 with a distrust of authority and it wasn't a hippie thing—we had exactly three hippies in our high school and nobody really knew what they were, they just knew that they didn't like them. I grew up in and around Italian neighborhoods and there was a real Italian feeling of distrust of government and organized society—if you can't run it, keep it out of your life. You don't rely on or be too disappointed by government, because you know that it has limitations, it's as frail as human beings are. I didn't have the illusion that the government was our friend. I didn't think it was the enemy, I just thought, Well, they have their agenda. And then there were the fights between the IUE, the local electricians union, and General Electric. Schenectady was "the city that lights the world" and General Electric's slogan was "Progress is our most important product," but they were also those sons-of-bitches who were always trying to pull one over on the fathers of most of the kids I grew up with, and threatening to move their plants to Alabama. So you realized that politics is not an absolute thing, it's a gray area.

Because my parents were teachers, I grew up knowing that teachers were fallible. You're there while they talk about colleagues who they think are jerks or who messed up. I didn't have any feeling that those were invulnerable people. So much of the political activity of the sixties was from a fairly privileged group of kids finding out that their parents, authority figures, school, government—who they had been sold on in the fifties and had been told were there to help them—had lied to them. If you're a naive believer, you're much more betrayed when people are hypocrites. I think so much of the sixties was a reaction to hypocrisy. Personally I didn't have as many illusions, but I did have the illusion that people in college would be on a higher plane, that they'd be more free of petty prejudices. And I didn't know any rich people, so I had a prejudice toward, or a general distrust of, these guys.

Was there much student political activity there?

What epitomised Williams politically when I was a freshman was that when the black kids took over the administration building and made certain demands, the first thing the administration did was ask them if they had enough food to last for a week. I was really not involved in anything. I truly thought student activism on campus was a waste of time. There were one or two faculty members on the campus who you could probably consider war criminals but they weren't making nerve gas, they were historians who advised on foreign policy but they were pretty far removed. I always felt campus activity was off the point—why are you bothering these professors, if you really wanted to stop the war, quit school, lie down in front of a recruiting office? Or an army base, where you're closer to the real problem?

By my second year I had read enough about Vietnam to feel that it was a bullshit war. I didn't think there was a good reason for people to be killed, Americans or Vietnamese. It seemed like somebody else's agenda. I would go to the big marches, but although I might get a ride with a bunch of people, I didn't necessarily hang with them at the march. Sometimes I did, sometimes I didn't. I was truly outside college society. My attitude was, Well, these people want to join together to do things and they don't always get along, and that's their trip. If they want to get me involved in it, I'm only going to go in as far as I want to. I was very unlikely to join a group like SDS (Students for a Democratic Society), and to a certain extent I'm still unlikely to join those groups because I have a lot of suspicions about them. I really didn't buy the Amerika with a "k" thing and that this was the most oppressive regime since Nazi Germany, and I also didn't buy that any of the activists talking about The People *knew* any of the people. They were stereotyping them in a way. Those were the people in the SDS as far as I was concerned. They did some good stuff but they did some stupid stuff. I recognize that sometimes there are things you can only do by joining together, but once that specific thing is done, let's not try to keep the band together. *Matewan* is a good example of that. When the workers had a common enemy that was so nasty, they were able to forget for a little while about race and ethnicity. The minute they got the union, those things came back in and the black coal miners got pushed out and it became a club.

I didn't get politicized through a group, I got politicized through paying attention. The thing that the people on the left wanted to do, which was end the war, I was for wholeheartedly. It was a very uneasy coalition. You'd go to those marches and the people there were all over the place—there were Yippies, and Dave Dellinger, and Mothers for Peace, and people who didn't have one other thing in common either in personal style or world belief, and there were fascistic personalities up there who I wouldn't want to spend three minutes with and certainly wouldn't ever want to have any position of power over me—but they were against that war, so, Okay, you're invited to the coalition. The energy went from the civil rights movement to the antiwar movement and for a while to the women's movement, and then it dissipated.

There's a belief that if we're all against the war, we should believe in the same things—we should also be for the civil rights movement, for sexual liberation. But in the civil rights movement, those guys are not just kidding about being ministers—half the shit you do as a young college student is stuff they condemn. But you've got to be on the same bus with them when you're trying to integrate the schools. They've got to be open to that too. There are people who are truly kind, open, and generous but who hate black people. And you've got to deal with that somehow. That complexity of human behavior makes storytelling much more difficult. That's one of the reasons why my secondary characters tend to be three-dimensional and come close to the foreground. If there're just good guys and bad guys, you can make genre pictures. The minute that the good guys are a little more complicated, your stuff starts to fall in between genres.

Was there an experience for you in this period that summed all this up?

I had never been west of Buffalo, New York, until I started hitch-hiking in college. During breaks and sometimes during school I would skip classes for a couple of days and start hitchhiking west or down to Florida. And so you're riding with somebody who's a KKK guy for eight hours. When you're hitchhiking you generally get people who want to be entertained or who want to tell you shit. You're the shrink they never have to go back to. I had people confess murders to me. People assume that because they're talking to you that you share certain ideas with them, so I've had people explain the difference between Italians and white people and they're assuming that I'm somewhere in the same conversation. Because I wasn't especially crazy about myself or committed to myself, generally I would become whoever they wanted me to be. So if they wanted somebody to entertain them, I'd make up a lot of shit. I could make up a better story than the one I was living. It might be something that the last guy who picked me up told me. So even before I was on stage, I was acting to a certain extent. I'd just wing it, and then if it was a long ride, try to remember what I'd said at the beginning of the conversation so that I could be somewhat consistent. It was just being bored with yourself, just reinventing yourself for the duration of a ride, to see how far you could get.

Most people would say that was a pretty strange thing to do.

Yeah. I'd say it's a weak link not only to reality but to who you are. It's always seemed easier for me to let somebody else break the ice. Certainly interpersonally I wish I had been better at talk-ing to people, less shy. It seemed fascinating to me that some peo-ple could walk into a situation and just chat up anybody they wanted to, whether it was for a political reason or to get a girl-friend. I certainly didn't have a clue about who or what to talk about. I wasn't much of an actor in college. I didn't go to many classes or belong to any organizations. I played sports for about one year and then pretty much disappeared: I realized I didn't re-ally like them and wasn't especially great at them, or didn't like the teams, didn't feel like playing organized sports anymore. I didn't talk in class. If I wasn't interested in a class, I didn't go. You only had to keep a C-minus average to stay in and not go to Vietnam. I only took writing classes to get my grade point average up—I would hand in my six pounds of fiction or whatever and they'd give me an A and that would counterbalance the D-minus I'd gotten in psych, my major. For me, it was like a four-year, semi-paid vacation. I could watch movies all night long.

In my last year of college I got involved with theater. In my junior year, Gordon Clapp, who has been in some of my films and is now on TV's *NYPD Blue*, was directing *Of Mice and Men* and asked me to read for Slim, I think because I was tall and thin. I asked if I could read for the old guy because I'd worked in all these nursing homes and I knew all these old guys that I could draw on and I ended up playing Candy. It was fun being in a play. There wasn't a drama major at Williams but it offered a Winter study course where all January you took one course and concentrated on it. You could do a theater course or an independent study. I took an independent study and wrote a movie in about a week, then went to Florida. The next year I directed a play, Bruce J. Friedman's *Steambath*, about a bunch of guys sitting around in a steambath who realize they've all died and God is a Puerto Rican bath attendant. It seemed funny and had a lot of different characters and it seemed right for a school that was mostly still all men. For me, directing for theater was a form of storytelling where you didn't necessarily provide the story but you controlled it. Then I was in a couple of plays in my senior year.

Isn't directing an unlikely choice for someone who, as you put it, was a subverbal loner?

All of a sudden there was a reason for me to talk about something. But to a certain extent it wasn't me directing—it still isn't me directing. Every day when you go onto the set to direct, it is a performance. There are certain things that you want to get done, you come in with a script of what you want to do that day, and there's a certain amount of freeform to it, when somebody comes back at you with something—a need, a question, whatever—and you wing it. The winging is the part that's interesting.

Did you know that at the outset, when you decided to direct the play?

Yeah. Because who am I to tell everyone what to do? But it was also on a level where they didn't know that much more than me. I didn't cast all the people who usually got the leads, I cast people who had only done small things or who had never acted before. I knew as much as they did. I was fairly confident—not that I was good at it but that if I wasn't, what did it matter? I wasn't a hard-core hanging-out-at-the-theater-workshop person but it was fun. What was fun about acting was that in real life, being subverbal, I didn't know what line came next. I was never nervous acting. You know what is going to happen next, you are in control of the situation and it is a lot like sports. In sports, if you're really breaking through, if you're in the Zone as they say, you've done all this technical work and you've trained certain parts of your body and certain parts of your mind to react well, so it's second nature and you don't have to think about it anymore and there is an existential, just-reacting-to-the-moment kind of thing when you're really doing it well. And there's a back-and-forth thing that is in improvisatory jazz. One of my short stories, "Hoop," is about these basketball players playing with each other like soloists jamming and it turns into music at one point. In theater, you've done the work, learned the lines and the blocking, but when you're in front of the audience you adjust your performance to them. And you have to react to your co-players, otherwise you're gonna miss the pass. So it was a kind of sport to me.

It was also interesting that you could be emotional and get really upset and live those emotions, yet you didn't have to live with them. Just like when I was hitchhiking, a Vietnam vet could tell me all the awful things he'd done and been through, unload all this shit and then never see me again. A lot of people would say, "I've never told this to anybody before," and they got to say it, wrap it up and throw it away, because I got off. "Have a nice life," that's what people used to say when they let you out of their car. In theater, you did that in the part—it wasn't even you. You could say and feel and do all these things—it was an interesting game, an edge you could walk on. Out in the world, every ride you got, somebody else had a different perception of the world, whereas in college, there were some differences, but it is a kind of closed group. It was out in the boonies and to a certain extent it was a dreamworld. And it was nice there. I had a good time inasmuch as I had a good time. It was a vacation from life, but I always knew it was.

Frances McDormand and Sayles on the set of *Lone Star* (1996).

CHAPTER 2

Pride of the Bimbos and *Union Dues*

What happened when you graduated from Williams?

I wasn't shocked and depressed when I graduated and nobody was waiting for me with a great job. I knew a lot of people, like my brother, who hung around for another year or two and lived in that college community because they didn't want to leave the womb. I wasn't trained to do anything. I was a psych major and we used to joke that there were the pre-meds and the pre-patients, and I was one of the pre-patients. I had this worthless degree in economic terms and I got out of college right when it was very hard to get hired doing anything unless you were willing to sign up for more school. I didn't, so I said, "Okay, I'm on my own now," and I went and got a job. I worked in hospitals for a while. I liked working with the patients—as an orderly you did quite a bit of that. It was mostly geriatrics and some car crash victims, mostly poor people who ended up there because they couldn't get homecare. I put catheters in and took blood now and then and gave postmortem care and some physical therapy, and I kind of liked that. If I'd continued, I would have probably become a physical therapist.

Were you happy and fulfilled?

Not especially. I didn't have any illusion that there was any deal where you were supposed to be happy. Mostly what I felt was fairly cut off. I had a few friends from college but I hadn't bonded deeply. I didn't feel like I'd been singled out for any special lack of connection so it wasn't like I felt sorry for myself, but I wanted to be more connected than I was and I wasn't exactly sure how to do that. I continued to write stories for myself and started sending them out the year after I got out of college. In the back of the O. *Henry* collection they gave the addresses of the magazines that they looked at to pick the best short stories of the year and I started sending my stories to them. I would get these letters back saying, "*Ararat* is the Armenian National Quarterly. We liked the story but there are no Armenians in it. Why are you sending us this?" I was working in a nursing home in Albany in 1973, living in a crummy little apartment and nobody was writing me letters, but I would get mail. It was this weird connection with the world outside—rejection slips! It was kind of cool. So then I actually looked for some of these quarterlies and magazines to try to figure out what kind of stories they published. I didn't know any professional writers, I hadn't taken literature courses, and I wasn't a literary groupie. I didn't even know that you got paid—most of them didn't, they just sent you copies of the magazine. That was great. I had this circuit of about eight monthly magazines and I had a little chart and when it would come back from *The Atlantic* I would send it to *Esquire* or *Playboy* or *Harpers*, and then I would start on the bigger quarterlies and then move down to the smaller ones, who had nice rejection slips. I had a wall with all the rejection slips on it. I got an acceptance from a quarterly that folded, so they never published the story.

Winter came and winter in the northeast is one of my least favorite things. I was in a car crash, my car was totalled, and for a couple of weeks I had to walk to work in the snow. I got sick of winter so I gave notice and when my car got out of the shop I started driving south. I thought I was going to find work in Florida and I got as far as Atlanta. I stayed there for almost a year and did day labor, digging red clay rainpipe ditches and swimming pools. And I was selling my blood. Writing and doing as little work as possible. When I came back east in 1974 I had an envelope full of money and didn't feel like working in hospitals again. I knew these people from college who lived in East Boston and I liked them okay so I figured, I'll try living in a city.

I was working as a meat packer. I got into the union, the Amalgamated Butcher Workers and Meat Packers of North America, and was making much better money than I had working in hospitals. I sent out a fifty-page short story called "Men" to *The Atlantic*. The woman in an apartment above me got evicted and came back the next day and took the trap from under the sink and turned the faucets on and totally ruined the apartment. All the water collected over the chair where the carbon copy of my fifty-page short story was and dripped on it all day long while I was at work making salami. I came back and it was totally sodden. I hadn't heard from *The Atlantic* in a month, who usually gave me a good two-week turnaround on my rejection slip. I called up, which I had never done before, and said, "I'm just wondering how come I haven't got my rejection slip yet." And they had no record of any story called "Men." I thought, I'm fucked. What can I remember? I had my notes, but I really just sat down and wrote it on the typewriter. About two days after that when I was feeling really down I got a call from Atlantic Press and they said, "We have your novella, we're really interested and we'd like you to meet an editor." Apparently somebody hefted fifty pages and said, "This isn't a short story, this is a novella," and sent it over to the Press. I went and met this editor, a woman named Peggy Yntema, and she suggested I make it into a novel—and that became *Pride of the Bimbos*. She said you've got great characters and interesting situations, what you need is a plot. I thought, Good idea, this is what editors are for. Almost one week later I got laid off, which was not bad because since it was a union job I could get unemployment. I think I got twenty-one weeks at $48 per week and that was my grant to the arts. So I made the story into a novel, the editor liked it, sent it upstairs and they said, "We're going to publish it," which was pretty incredible. What Peggy did as an editor was just ask questions. She'd say, "I don't understand this," or, "Why that?" And sometimes when I explained it she'd say, "Oh right, yes, that's there," and other times she'd say, "I don't see it." I did one more pass and that was it. At the same time they asked if I had any short stories around and I gave them this hitchhiking story, "I-80 Nebraska," and it was published as an "Atlantic First," a first story by an unknown writer, and it got into the *O. Henry* collection. They asked if I had any more so I sent them two stories they had already rejected, not telling them they'd rejected them, figuring that different people would read them, and they published them.

Pride of the Bimbos *is a study of masculinity in crisis and its tone and style seem very distinct from your films.*

Somebody once asked me to characterize my novels as movies and I said, "*Pride of the Bimbos* is a Fellini and *Union Dues* is a De Sica and Zavattini." I had two things going on in *Pride of the Bimbos*. Having been a jock and having done day labor, having worked with guys who drank their lunch and went back to furnished hotel rooms, I had seen all kinds of masculinity, as you said, in crisis. And who would have to be more macho than a bunch of straight guys who had to dress up like women for a living in an athletic, jock setting. Also, I had spent a lot of time in the South, I had cousins who lived in different parts. The South was changing rapidly and having an identity crisis—there was a huge amount of tension in those years, not just about civil rights but about, "Are we going to give in and do things the way those Yankees do and become part of the twentieth century?" In the book what happens is that everybody—the ball players—who is looking for the Old South finds the New South. It's unfamiliar, where do they fit? And then the guy who would be the most happy to find the New South, the six-foot-eight black Dred, all he finds is the Old South, which is like a nightmare to him.

Dred's journey south is fascinating—it assumes an allegorical quality as he's gradually stripped of his identity, until he's finally reduced to a primeval state.

Dred wasn't in the original story. He became the parallel plot, using the idea of two forces parallel to each other, which I've used in a lot of my novels. I was thinking about how people define themselves. Very few people can define themselves outside of the small world that they live in. He's a guy who is able to carry this definition of himself outside his neighborhood. He's lost his own street credibility, he doesn't believe in himself anymore—until he can revenge himself on this little white guy. There are certain things that he carries with him that signify his world, and they get stripped away and there's still somebody there—he doesn't get that until the last scene, the only time when he has any perspective and can see himself from the outside. Most of the characters in the book don't ever get to see themselves from the outside—they're totally trapped in those roles. Dred gets taken so far out of his context that eventually he can see the ridiculousness of his own actions.

How did things change after the publication of your first novel?

What they paid first-time writers back then was $2,500, which was less than I was getting working in the sausage factory. On an hourly basis it was less than minimum wage. I went back to labor work for a while as a carpenter's assistant, nothing very permanent. I had just enough to live on and I was living communally in East Boston—eight people shared two floors of a tenement building on the docks and everyone paid according to their ability, so some people were paying nothing and one guy who worked in housing for the city was paying a third of the rent. I started to get to know more people who had been politically active in the sixties. The people in *The Return of the Secaucus Seven* were based not necessarily on people I knew in college but people I met afterwards, who had been in VISTA (Volunteers in Service to America), the domestic peace corps. VISTA kids had made the choice to be downwardly mobile, to do something more interesting. What I think was important about it was that you had to deal with people. You might be helping them build a rec center or get food stamps, but you also had to deal with the fact that they might be fundamentalist Christians. You had to deal with the real world whereas in the SDS you didn't necessarily. You had marches where people threw shit at you but the organization of the SDS tended to stay on campus in that specialized, hothouse world.

I'd been working for a long time on a big novel about Brian McNeil, a character who's in a bunch of the *Anarchists' Convention* hitchhiking stories, who's involved with a Vietnamese woman. She has a cat and as the relationship gets worse this very symbolic cat gets fatter—like in a Stephen King book or a David Cronenberg movie it had ingested all the bad shit in their relationship. He ends up getting burned really bad. Dred and Pogo Burns from *Pride of the Bimbos* were also in it. I had 250 pages written and I realized, I'm only a third of the way through this, and it's about everything—I'm never going to finish it. So I put it aside, and just so I wouldn't get too depressed that night I stayed up and developed the idea for *Union Dues*. I outlined the whole novel until about four in the morning. Later I went back to the unfinished novel and chainsawed a couple of good short stories out of it. *Union Dues* is about a kid who's destined to be a coal miner but just can't see any future in it and goes to find a brother in Boston who's disappeared after Vietnam. And his father, who's a widower, goes after him. The structure was based on *Heidi*—whenever Heidi goes out the front door, her grandfather comes in the back door. These two guys would have parallel experiences in the same place but would never meet and were being pulled in different directions. And it was set in and about the polarization of the sixties.

What brought me to it was having been on the road in all those different places in the late sixties and early seventies. It didn't take you more than ten minutes outside of a college town to run into people who, if you didn't look like a hippie, which I didn't, would start talking about those hippies. In high school when I transferred to the Technical Electrical Program, I went to school across town from where I had gone to school before, and the people in this school said, "Oh, they're just like that over there," they would see them in some stereotyped way, whereas I had just been over there and I knew that wasn't true. And I had heard what the people over there had said about them and now I was here and I knew that what they had been saying wasn't true. That's what *Union Dues* is about. In the sixties there were all these armed camps and I wanted to take the reader into them. They had very little useful interface with each other—it was mostly confrontation and prejudice. In those few years, it was possible to really believe that it was all coming apart and you were part of it, if you were in one of those coteries. Whereas if you went just three blocks away and hung out on a porch with somebody, they'd say, "What are these people doing?" And I had this idea of two people, father and son, bobbing on the surface of a flood, being swept this way and that. There is an incredible lack of connection not just between groups but between individuals in the whole book. There's the scene between Hobbie and the other working-class kid where the group puts them together and expects sparks to fly because finally they have these two working-class kids together—and they talk about old *Twilight Zone* episodes together. That's their common language. The idea that the working class has some kind of cohesion had been real at one point but it was gone by then. And *Union Dues* is like a documentary: if it rains on a Thursday in Boston, it rained on that Thursday. I would read the *Boston Globe* and the alternative papers for every day that I was writing about.

The story Hobie tells the group ten years later becomes part of the plot of Matewan. *When did it occur to you that it could be the basis of a film?*

When I was hitchhiking through West Virginia and Kentucky, there was a power struggle for the control of the UFW between Yablonsky and Boyle, which is an element in *Union Dues*. All you heard was these two guys butting heads. I got rides from people on both sides who were really upset and almost all of them would say, "It's almost like the days of the Coal Wars and the Matewan Massacre." I got intrigued and started reading about it and came upon this story. Things were simpler in a way, and they were worse, more polarized, but there was no ambivalence in being a union member. It was a life-threatening decision because it was so violent in that part of the South. I was interested in that stark polarity in the context of *Union Dues*, where things are more ambiguous and there's more baggage to everything. The kids in the political group are inventing themselves and are there by desire, not necessity, whereas nobody wanted to be in the Matewan Massacre, nobody was there for romantic or even altruistic reasons. There's a kind of purity that is attractive in Hobie's story. And I thought it would make a great movie—here's a whole area of labor history that I'm learning more about but it also has this absolute movie structure, like a gunfighter movie with these mounting confrontations that all lead to a showdown on main street at high noon.

While you've often said you try to give every character his or her day in court and not divide the world into black and white, it's still clear in Union Dues *that your sympathies are with certain characters more than with others. The depiction of the student radical group is more or less satirical.*

The group in *Union Dues* is based on groups that went beyond cadre into cult. The people who fall away from that group are going to be the lucky ones. Mark Frechette, who was in Antonioni's *Zabriskie Point*, got into one of the Boston groups this is based on. Eventually they robbed a bank and an employee got shot. Frechette went to jail and somebody dropped a barbell on his neck in the gym. A bunch of groups ended badly like that. More and more they narrowed their focus as to who was an acceptable person. At first you say, "Well, we're for the people, the proletariat." But then you start running into the American proletariat and they don't want anything to do with you. Then you start having self-criticism sessions and start to sharpen and sharpen your definitions until you have this tiny nugget and you can't see anybody else's point of view. It's beyond an elite—it becomes a pathology. You're so pure that you can't really act in the world anymore, except destructively. It happened to the Symbionese Liberation Army, where they began by saying, "Well, we're going to kill liberals first, number one because they're easier to kill but number two because we want to distance ourselves further from them. We're going to kill the people who are actually making things better, because they're not going to make it better enough to change the world the way we want it to be changed." What has to happen first is that the world has to get so bad that everyone will rise up. The people I have the least emotional interest in are the people who have no perspective, who should have more. They've come from the outside world and have chosen to limit their perspective. That's an important thing to me. Some people have a limited perspective because they grew up in the 'hood and they've never been three blocks away. And then there are people who've been there and then chose to narrow it, maybe because it makes the world a safer place to live in emotionally.

Do you see that amongst filmmakers?

Yeah, and sometimes that's because they've just given up and sometimes it's because that's happened to the filmmaker. Sometimes there's some distance between the filmmaker and the films, like, "Well, that's what they want, that's what I'll do." Other times it's because those values have been internalized.

Union Dues *and* Pride of the Bimbos *both deal with subjects that imply a certain idealism—baseball and working-class politics—yet have very pessimistic endings in which the characters are defeated.*

Oh yeah. You don't have much hope for the kid at the end of *Pride of the Bimbos*. In *Union Dues* it's physicalized. Given where he's come from and the world he's wandered into, Hobie in *Union Dues* isn't really prepared to fend for himself—and what does he have to go home to? He was smart to run away and now he's lost his ability to, so as an adult he's stuck with certain things. He's not going to have any control, just like his father. That is finally the ceiling that is not self-imposed. Political movements and people only have so much energy. You have to be almost a kind of frightening zealot to hold out beyond a certain point. Or you have to have a lot of support. What does it mean anymore to hold out on principle? Those ceilings don't have to mean much if you have some other way around them—a spiritual or intellectual way, or whatever. These guys don't have that perspective, what political kids in the sixties would call the "analysis," to transcend them. That's a limitation within them but it's also the way society is set up—it's not set up in their favor.

Why is your approach to character behavioral rather than descriptive?

There's almost no internal description. I don't do internal monologues, I try to create character by what you hear said or what you see done. You don't get to access someone's thoughts, you access their point of view. I've written stories in the first person and it's a lot of fun, but it's too easy. Usually when I've done it, the first person is not necessarily the main actor in the story.

Point of view seems to be the key to your approach. Why does it shift so much in your novels?

It's pretty much always the way I've seen the world. What's my evidence for how this person thinks? Can I imagine from the evidence what must be going through his head, whether it's somebody I like or don't like? Where is this person coming from? How do they see the world? I was always fascinated with that question. And there's an attempt, when I go into those different points of view, to have the style of the writing be the style of the person and the scope of their vision. I sometimes write awkwardly on purpose because if I write any smoother, people will glance right over it. I've got to fuck up the frame a little bit.

When you walk into a crowded room you can either get paranoid and think, "Everybody's looking at me and they don't like me," or, like Charlie Wade in *Lone Star*, "I'd better whip these people into line so they know who the fuck I am." Or you can just read the vibe in the room, watch and feel for a while and figure out the dynamic that's going on. No species ever evolves alone— species only evolve in terms of an ecosystem. If the bugs get bigger, one of the birds is going to get a bigger beak. If it and its main competitor can't survive, one or the other of them will probably evolve to a different niche, higher or lower on the food chain. I see the same thing with any dramatic situation, which is that there is a context for action.

There was a book I read in high school, *The Presentation of Self in Everyday Life* by Irving Goffman. I saw it with cops. Many cops are one type of person without the uniform on, another type with it on, same as a bullfighter. Certain people get stuck in the presentation and that's the only way they can behave. They're no longer adaptive—like an actor who can only do one role. There are some brilliant cops who can read the situation right away and come at it with exactly the right thing. It's a joy to see them work. I've been almost busted by cops when I was hitchhiking where at the end I'd say, "You're really good at your job." Because they came at you with exactly what they should have come at you with: not too heavy, not too light; they get the information, realize you are not a danger to their community, and send you on your way without making it a nasty situation. Other guys come at you with total bullshit and you have to give total bullshit back to a certain point or else you are gonna get beat up, which also happens.

Was your use of shifting point of view and found texts like newspaper headlines and song lyrics influenced by John Dos Passos's USA Trilogy?

I still haven't read him. People keep telling me I should. I try to deal with the way the media are a very important part of so many people's lives now. That is a lot of how they see the world, so I have to get it in somewhere without crapping the book up to the point where it's just a bunch of brand names.

The short story collection The Anarchists' Convention *is like an anthology of contrasting voices and points of view.*

To me those short stories are like an album where there's some boleros and some rancheras and reels and headbanger stuff. Each one has its own emotion and rhythm. Some are very dry and distanced and others are really right down in the funk and wash over you. Each is its own world, and that's the way I think of movies. There's a thought and a feeling and you find the right form for them. The nice thing about short stories is that you can limit them to one or two feelings or ideas and really concentrate them.

David Strathairn, John Sayles, and Adam Lefevre in *One Flew Over the Cuckoo's Nest* (1974).

John Sayles, Brian Johnston, and David Strathairn in *Of Mice and Men*, directed by Adam Lefevre at the Eastern Slope Playhouse (1975).

What happened after you finished Union Dues?

In 1975 I was asked to do summerstock again—minimum money but you got free room and board. The previous year Gordon Clapp, Jeffrey Nelson, and David Strathairn, who I didn't know that well but had all gone to Williams, were all working in summerstock at the Eastern Slope Playhouse in North Conway, New Hampshire. They called me pretty much at the last minute to play the Indian in *One Flew Over the Cuckoo's Nest*—large, retarded people became a theme in my acting. This time they invited me for a whole season, and I got to do *Of Mice and Men* again, this time playing Lenny, the retarded guy. So I was in the same bunkhouse, the same play, playing a different guy—even more perspective. A totally different world. You don't even hear some things you used to be attuned to before, when you're the old guy worried about losing your job. That's so much of what you do as a director and a writer. I got to direct a couple of plays—one was *Play It Again Sam*. And we did a play by an actor we'd gone to school with, Adam Lefevre, who's in some of my films. For a summerstock theater it was probably more ambitious than the people in town wanted it to be, but it was tough. You had to work boxoffice and people would not ask the name of the play, they'd ask, "Is it air conditioned?" We usually had a pretty good house.

I sent *Union Dues* off to Atlantic Press, then I realized I wouldn't have time to come down and do the contract. A friend of mine had played poker with a guy who was a literary agent named John Sterling, who said, "Oh, you know John Sayles. I really liked his first novel, I'd really love to represent him." She said, "Well, don't call him because he doesn't want an agent." So he called. I said, "Well, you're in luck, I just sent this thing over to Atlantic, do you want to do the deal?" He got $10,000 for it. I thought, That's incredible. I didn't meet him until after he sold the book. So then I didn't have to work for a while and I started working on my short stories and did some acting.

I was pretty good at acting. I got paid as an actor before I got paid as a writer or director. But I didn't have any driving need to do it, the need to act, to get my emotional needs for approval or love or attention on a stage because I wasn't getting them in real life. Fairly early on I felt like whatever I want to get from other people emotionally, I'd rather get directly and personally and not

Jean Passanante, David Strathairn, and John Sayles in *Bus Stop*, directed by Jeffrey Nelson at the Eastern Slope Playhouse (1976).

in front of other people. I just don't have that need for attention. If I could continue to write and direct stuff with somebody else's name on it and never have to do another interview, great by me. But I understand that it's part of the price of admission.

Plus, how many things did I see that I wanted to be in? Where not only would I like the part, but also feel good about the work itself? So I would maybe be doing a good job in something that I didn't even agree with or like. That's the actor's life. So why not have more control of the storytelling and work on stuff I'm *really* interested in? Ask myself, What's going on here? How can I find out more? Well, maybe if I try to tell a story about it I can take all these disparate little scenes and make some sense out of it. To me storytelling is about making some sense out of stuff, making some kind of connection. The movies I've made and the books and plays I've written have always been about things that I feel I need

Sayles at the Eastern Slope Playhouse (1978).

to know more about and want to figure out. I want to make films that I haven't seen before, whether it is in the complexity that they're dealt with, or that I just feel like this is something that needs to be made. Even if making a movie that doesn't show in a thousand theaters is not exactly touching popular culture, it's certainly wider than writing a book or putting on a play off-Broadway. There's at least that chance to get into the conversation. There's stuff I'm interested in and I can say, "Great, I can go to Truffaut for that," or I can go to this filmmaker for this or that filmmaker for that.

I grew up in Italian neighborhoods. The closest I've come to exploring that is in *City of Hope* and *Baby, It's You,* where the experience is somewhat reflected. But I don't need to make that movie, because there's Martin Scorsese. And now a dozen other guys. *Mean Streets* was a very useful movie for me in explaining where I came from to people. I could say to them, "If that was the Minor Leagues, I was in the Triple D; we had those guys, but the stakes weren't quite as high."

Why do you factor out personal self-expression when you approach a film or book?

None of my stuff is really autobiographical. I spend twenty-four hours a day with myself. I'm not that fascinated in my own thoughts. My work is personal in that it's about what I am interested in, but it is not about how I see the world. I want to have other voices in the picture. When you put the work out, you're a little bit like a reporter, like somebody writing an editorial.

CHAPTER 3

Screenplays for Roger Corman and Beyond

How did you gravitate to writing screenplays?

Union Dues came out and my agent told me that I had *de facto* a Hollywood agent trying to sell my book as a film property. I had started thinking about doing movies, but I didn't know much about how they got made and I knew I didn't want to go out there and knock on doors—but here was an agent's telephone number. I figured a lot of people had started out as writers and became directors—John Huston was foremost in my mind. Filmmaking seemed like a natural thing. Growing up I read books, but the principal storytelling medium I was exposed to was TV and movies. Even *Pride of the Bimbos* in my mind had first been a black-and-white movie, and then I just thought, I'm going to get a six-foot-eight black guy and a midget? Come on. Every now and then I write something that turns from one thing to another. *Breaking In*, which Bill Forsyth eventually made, was based on a short story I never published because I never got it to work. I would try a different point of view, would go from first person to third person and I never liked it enough to try to get it published. And then my first agent said, "Do you have a contemporary comedy I can send out? You've got all these heavy historical things." And the minute I wrote it as a screenplay, it made perfect sense. But that's fairly rare.

I took a good film course in college from an English professor, Charles Thomas Samuels, who died the next year. It wasn't a production course, we just watched movies and then he'd go through it and talk about it. He taught that things are done for a reason in a good movie and you should learn to "read" them. I took a study course where we did nothing but watch the first fifteen movies Ingmar Bergman made, including the first five or six before he got the hang of it. I had written two film scenes based on chapters from Ralph Ellison's *Invisible Man*, just for the fun of it. And after I got out of school I read somewhere that the American Film Institute was giving money away to make movies, so I wrote a scripted documentary, and the working title was *The War Ends for Charlie*, which was the name of a guy who lost his legs in Vietnam. A film crew comes to make a documentary about him, and what happens to them is an exact parallel of what happened to the U.S. in Vietnam under Eisenhower, Kennedy, Johnson, and Nixon. So the work deteriorates and they get stuck in this awful documentary and eventually the crew revolts against the director. I figured if you could shoot it in a documentary style, then you could be really half-assed about the lighting. It would have worked. I wrote the AFI and said, "I hear your biggest award is $10,000, I can make this feature for $10,000"—and I could have. They never wrote back.

I liked to watch different kinds of movies so I figured I could write them. I had what turned out to be this totally unfounded idea that having written a novel, I would be a good candidate to adapt other people's novels. In actuality, most people who hire writers think, Oh my God, a writer—those are the bastards who, after we buy their books for too much money, insist on writing the first draft, it's terrible, and they say bad things about us in the newspaper when the movie comes out as they count their money. So being a writer of books was a negative, not a positive.

So what happened after you moved out to California?

I was still writing short stories and sending them out. About three months after I got to Santa Barbara, where we lived, Frances Doel, who was Roger Corman's right hand and the story editor at New World, called my agent to say, "Well, we've got a rewrite called *Piranha* where we want to keep the title and throw out everything else, who do you have?" And my agent gave my name. Frances had read some of my short stories so she told my agent, "Have him come over." Frances actually read literature. I always considered her the opposite of the kid who's got the comic book inside his Chaucer: She's sitting there reading *Lurid Tales* and Roger looks in and says, "How are you doing?" and she'd have John Updike inside of it. So I got that job, and had some good meetings with Roger and Frances. It was just the two of them—little did I know that in the future there would often be fifteen people in the room, and who knew if they would be there the next time you were in the room? And who you had to listen to and who you didn't have to listen to? But here was the head of the company and his only story editor—that was it. It's good that I was an actor because it makes me good at story conferences and that's a reason I got jobs as a writer. The five-minute version, the ten-minute version, the half-hour version—whatever you want. Also you draw the other person out like in improvisation—what do you like about this story, what do you want this movie to be? And you listen enough so that it's a two-way street.

What's good about working with Roger is that he's very specific, instead of, "Oh, we have problems with the second act," or whatever, it would be things like, "What we want here is something that's as close to *Jaws* as we can get, except that the menace is small, razor tooth piranha, and we want to have a situation where a few people are in danger all the way through, but at the end there's some kind of mass attack on a resort or something—so

Piranha (1978), Sayles' first produced screenplay,
directed by Joe Dante.

figure out how to get there." We were really talking about the trailer. "These are the moments I need in the movie"—and those would be the moments in the trailer. When we talked about the scripts it would be about how to space those moments out or how to build up to them. It would really be, "I think we have two attacks that are too close together. I think we should have the threat of an attack, but phew, the kid got out of the water—and then five pages after that we'll have an attack." There was a script and they didn't much care about the characters and the writer was a little too hung up on the fact that you had to be bleeding for the piranhas to sense you and attack, so hippies would be hanging out and a bear would attack them and claw them and they'd jump in the water and get eaten. . . .

I threw out the whole script basically. My model was the giant ant movie *Them!*, directed by Gordon Douglas in 1954. When I was a psych major I specialized in animal behavior, that was the only part that really interested me. So I just read monographs about piranha behavior. I read up on alligators when I wrote *Alligator*. And it has continued to stand me in good stead. I've written about wolves, cockroaches, and I'm doing *Brother Termite* now, where the aliens are based on termites. I'm very comfortable extrapolating animal behavior into movies. I actually drew a map: X is where the piranha are put into the river, Y is where the people get on the raft to go down the river, and here's the dam where they think they've stopped them, and here's the little stream that goes around the dam, and here's the resort where you have the big finale where they eat a lot of children, and here's the ocean. Roger said, "We might want a sequel." Poor James Cameron ended up directing *Piranha 2*, in which they had bred with flying fish.

Had you studied screenplay structure at all?

No. When I was still writing short stories a guy who was a cameraman took an option on my short story "I-80 Nebraska," which came out right when CB radio hit. I got about $1,000 and wrote a screenplay based on it. He had some Texans interested in financing it if Don Meredeth was the lead trucker. He gave me one screenplay to read, William Goldman's *The Stepford Wives*. So I used the form. I didn't underline or use as many exclamation points as William Goldman did. I'd seen so many movies that if I was writing a genre movie, I would think about other similar movies. Both *Alligator* and *Piranha* are monster movies, not horror movies. The suspense rests on, is it going to show up and bite your leg? In *Alligator* it's slightly tougher because you have to step on it for it to get you. And like Godzilla or Mothra, they're born knowing how to get to Tokyo somehow; they don't need directions, they just end up there. And there's confrontation building, like in *The Blob*, the first manifestation you don't even see. The next time, one person sees it and nobody believes him. The next time the hero sees it and believes the person who saw it the first time and was traumatized by it. Then the fourth time the military try to stop it and their shit bounces off it, and then somebody thinks they've stopped it and then it reappears, and then somebody has the bright idea of how to kill it.

Usually I write fast, and they were pretty happy with what they got; there were only two drafts and that was it. Roger at the time was a signatory to the Writers Guild, which meant that for a full draft and a couple of rewrites I got $10,000. I probably spent six weeks on it. I'd spent a year writing *Union Dues*, so in terms of me making a living it was, "Jesus Christ, I worked for a month and a half, I'll do more of these." Even though it was scale, writers' minimum, it was great. So very shortly after that he offered me *The Lady in Red*, then *Battle Beyond the Stars*. In the case of *Lady in Red* he just said, "I want a female *Godfather* story about the woman who was with John Dillinger when he was shot." That's all he gave me. And he said, "Maybe we should have you do a treatment and then a draft," and I said, "You know, I really don't like treatments, so what if I write you a draft and we'll call it a treatment?" He said, "Yeah!"

When did you realize you could inject social commentary and genre revisionism into the Corman scripts?

I had seen Roger's movies before, ones he produced and directed. I liked some of his Poe stuff and some of his *Jackson County Jail* funky drive-in movie stuff, and I just realized that even in something like *The Big Dollhouse*, there was some feminist stuff in there. The nice thing about Roger is that once you've hit the bases you have to hit within the genre, he gives you a lot of leeway to make it funny or good, although he isn't going to give you any

Alligator (1980), directed by Lewis Teague.

more money or time. As long as you have nudity and the heli-
copter blows up, you can do anything you want. I also realized
that there is nothing more dismal than a genre movie that is a pale
imitation of a better one, so if you're gonna remake *Them!*, you'd
better do something that *Them!* didn't do or have some kind of
perspective on it.

In *Alligator* there's a point where the game hunter, Henry Silva,
finds the alligator shit. I always figured in monster movies, there
must be monster poop! And it must be enormous! If you're looking for the monster, what would you do? You'd follow the poop,
and when it starts to be fresher, you'd know you're getting close.
It's a practical depth of feeling that I try to achieve even in those
movies. I don't like it when I see a romantic movie and the minute
the two people see each other, the next thing is three minutes of
montage where they're walking on the beach and I don't hear
what they're saying. I want to know what they're saying. How did
they get to fall in love? That's the shit that's useful if you're trying
to do it yourself. Nobody does a montage for you in real life.
Some of that was really just my resenting when movies didn't
think deeply enough and blew information by you and you just
don't buy it. The movie doesn't even live up to its own rules. The

minute you start to set something in the real world, you've got to start to live up to those rules. I never wanted it to degenerate into camp, but I thought, "What would happen if the people in a horror movie had seen a horror movie?" That was one of the concepts in *The Howling*. The characters don't go back into the place where six of their friends have been ax-murdered to find their cat like Sigourney Weaver did in her underwear in *Alien*. It takes a lot of contrivance to make the behavior somewhat believable in a regular context even though you have supernatural elements. And then, as in my novels, you have to bring in the media. If somebody discovered an alligator as big as an El Dorado, the media would be all over the place.

On all of the three movies I wrote for Roger, the director had not been chosen, much less involved, until after I was officially off the job. Each time I would get a panicked phone call from them saying, "Look, I can't possibly do something this ambitious with the money Roger's given us. Could you do a draft for free or give me some guidance?" When *Piranha* was about to be shot a drought hit in California, so they had to go to Aquarina Springs in San Marcos, Texas, south of Austin. The script calls for a brand-new resort, but they couldn't find one. There was an amusement park but it was full of really old, funky equipment, so Joe Dante said, "We'll fly Sayles down and get him to play a part. He's acted in plays, and while he's there he can see what the situation is and do a few rewrites for us." That was the first time I got on a movie set and it was the only time I'd ever looked through a movie camera until the day I actually made my first movie. Joe had started out with a $1.3 million budget, but because Roger was also making *Avalanche* and it was not going well, the day before Joe started shooting Roger yanked half a million dollars off *Piranha* and Joe only had $800,000 to make it. So I got a good front row seat as to what costs money and what doesn't, what you could make up with hard work, what was labor intensive, and what was capital intensive.

With *The Lady in Red*, Lewis Teague said, "Look, I have $800,000; this is 135 pages long, it has 70 speaking parts, it's an epic. I'm trying to recreate 1933 Chicago in Los Angeles." So I'd talk him through and say, "Okay, what's costing you the most money? Okay, I can amend that, I can cut that, I'll try and cut 20 pages." Because he said, "What's going to happen is, whatever we don't shoot during the day, we're just ripping it out of the script" and that's not going to be good for me. And as it is there are some big gaps in there. Originally there were four scenes between when the main character's friend in the factory dies and her friend who's a prostitute dies, but those four scenes didn't get shot so now there's only five minutes between two best friends getting killed. It really got squeezed out as a 90-minute movie from a 135-page script. I probably got it down to about 100 pages. So that was me learning, "Well, Roger really told me just go wild with this thing but he wanted a 90-minute movie and if I had to direct this I would want an 85-page script."

Did both Teague and Dante bring you in on Alligator *and* The Howling, *respectively?*

They inherited scripts they weren't crazy about and they had very little time to do anything with them so each one said, "Will you hire this guy, because he's fast and I've already worked with him." So in both cases I came in very late in the game. They'd already gotten the money from the foreign distributors and spent it, so it's the perfect rewrite situation. Number one, they're gonna make the movie, and number two, they can't mess around with what you do very much because they don't have time to. So almost anything you do that makes it any better is going to make it into the movie. I said, "Well, what do you like about this?" And they'd say, "I like the concept and the title and that's it. What do you want to do with it?" And then I could take it from there.

These first screenplays showcase an ability to create three-dimensional characters from generic types.

In the case of *Piranha*, I had just seen *Deathsport*, and I realized that the second lead was the stunt coordinator as well. So I decided I'd better protect myself from bad acting or nonacting, which is almost a tradition in monster or horror movies. It's not the most important thing about the movie so they don't bother to get people who have acting skill or don't give them enough time to do something good. So I wrote the main character very thin. Then I got a call from Bradford Dillman, who was playing the lead. They were going to shoot in two days, and he said, "It's a nice little

Pamela Sue Martin in *The Lady in Red* (1979),
directed by Lewis Teague.

Battle Beyond the Stars (1980), directed by
Jimmy Teru Murakami.

script but the lead character's a little thin." I said, "Thin? It's non-existent." He says, "Well, would you be interested in giving him a backstory?" I said I'd love to. I went up to his house. He happened to live in Santa Barbara, in a different neighborhood than I did—nobody kept chickens in his neighborhood. We sat down and talked and I was able to really flesh out his character. I had thought of the stuff but didn't put it in because I just figured it'd be cut or given to somebody who's no good. In *Alligator*, Robert Forster even brought some of his own stuff to it. He was having a hair problem and Lewis said, "I don't know, I don't think it looks that bad," and Forster said, "What if I start working it in?" And I gave him a few lines about it. It gives the actors something to do apart from "Look!" "Watch out!" and "Duck!"

Did you completely throw out the source novel for The Howling?

Yeah, pretty much. The many, many sequels were based on it. In the novel a woman is raped and she goes to a little town in California and she hears this howling and asks, "Did you hear that howling last night?" and everyone says, "Howling? What howling?" So of course you know they're all in on it. It's kind of Transylvania West. I just didn't buy it. So we talked about taking it back to the original shapechanger myth. And we had to have rules—if it can only become a werewolf when the full moon's out, then you have to have a month between the action. What can kill it? Can fire kill it? Can silver? The main question was, Is there free will? Even though you may have some human conception of free will, if you're part wolf, what kind of free will does a wolf have? It's more hardwired than we are. It has certain instincts that drive it forward. When you're in wolf form, do you think the way a human being does? And when you go back to being human, do you take some of that wolfness with you? We were making this kind of hokey werewolf movie but we had to have a long talk about free will.

Having been a psych student, I had been reading about Esalen and some of the other self-help groups and I decided, Well, if you were a werewolf, you would want to cope. This is a kind of behavior you have to control. If you have a drinking or gambling problem, there's a group for you. If you grow hair and rip the throat out of sheep, there probably is a group for you, in California anyway. At the same time there were the Primal Screamers, who said,

It's good to let that stuff out. Shit in your pants—that's a good thing to do, that'll help release great things. Yell at each other. So I figured there would be that faction who just said, "Well, to hell with this sublimating shit, let's go and rip the throat out of some sheep." Once we had defined all those things, it only took a couple of weeks before I gave them something, they had a couple of suggestions, and they were shooting.

I wrote an extremely complicated opening, it's like a 10-minute-long credit sequence. I once did a lecture on openings of movies and to me the opening of the movie has to tell you what world you're entering and give you a warning as to the rules of that world. That opening, besides crosscutting between three different planes of action, was meant to get a lot of exposition, and emotional and informational set-up for the audience. You have the drama of the opening sequence going on, but there's all this exposition that's backstory. You also have to warn the audience that, yes, this is a werewolf movie, but it's a werewolf movie set very much in the here and now, in an urban setting. And that it's going to get into these psychological things. All the psychological

Belinda Balaski in *The Howling* (1980), directed by Joe Dante.

stuff the Patrick Macnee character is saying is what the movie is about.

And Joe manages to make it funny without getting too campy so that it can still be scary when it's got to be scary. The problem is that I can write the stuff, but somebody has got to be able to pull it off. And I was very lucky. Joe pulled off the direction and Rob Bottin pulled off those transformations, which nobody had seen before. Werewolf movies had not been done for a long time.

How did you arrive at the ending where the Dee Wallace character goes on live TV and transforms into a werewolf and then is shot?

Well, once we decided to have her affected, then it really became a thing about, "Well, what is her free will now?" This is a classic Jekyll and Hyde thing. What do people do when they feel like they are destructive people and they can't control themselves—if they have a bad temper, a drinking problem, if they are junkies? Sometimes they keep ripping people off, which is what the other werewolves like the main character's husband are going to do. But very often, what they do is off themselves. And she does it not in a way that's going to make everybody else feel bad, but she's actually doing it in a way that will bring some attention. But it is a very dark thing.

And it's immediately deflated by the cutaways to different TV viewers' reactions—and most of them just shrug it off.

My point about the media all along was: People are walking on the moon, but within a year, nobody is interested in the space program.

Essentially you were writing smart exploitation movies. Were you ambivalent about the form?

Oh, no. They were movies that I had grown up seeing, and all I had to do when I got offered one was ask myself, Can I think of movies like this one that I liked? Could this be a movie that I would have fun going to? And if the answer was yes, and I was available, usually I would say yes to it. I haven't written a slasher movie or a serial killer movie. I have not written many movies that have to do with random violence. So when I got offered those movies, I wasn't very interested in them, whereas giant cock-roaches eating people, like, "Yeah!" Mostly I took what I was offered. For about a day I was signed up to do the rewrite of the remake of *Cat People*, which Roger Vadim was going to make, but it disappeared on me. Roger Corman offered me a couple of writing-directing jobs after *Secaucus Seven* came out. I think one was *The Night the Lights Went Out in Georgia*, which they actually made. Then he wanted to make *Mutiny on the Bounty* in outer space, which I think would be a really cool idea for a science fiction movie.

I've written a lot of stuff that didn't get made. In the beginning I was batting better than .500. Now I'd say it's down around .400 or lower. Basically, the more you get paid, the more you're working with big studios, the less likely it is to get made, because they have the money to develop. If Roger Corman paid you to write a screenplay, he damn well made the movie. He doesn't fuck around: "It's time to shoot. What's on paper—that's your script. If you want it better, work on it at night in between the days of the shooting." Whereas if you're working for MGM or UA, they develop twenty to forty things for every one that they make, so they're used to paying you money and then not making it. I've gone into meetings where I've turned a job down because I could tell, "You guys don't really want to make this."

One of your first produced studio scripts was the 1982 film The Challenge. *How was the experience?*

I was brought in under very strange circumstances. There was a Writers Guild strike and a Directors Guild strike brewing. The Writers Guild strike was to happen in a week. The Directors Guild strike was going to happen right about when John Frankenheimer would be wrapping the movie, but if they didn't get a green light from Scott Glenn before the next week was over, they weren't going to be able to start it, and then they didn't want to start it later because the Directors Guild strike would happen right in the middle of this thing. So I basically had a week before I was on strike.

They brought me in on Thursday. I had read the stuff on the plane. It was set in Hong Kong, all the characters and martial arts were Chinese. In the meeting, Frankenheimer said, "Look, I can get Toshiro Mifune, because I worked with him on *Grand Prix*. He's a great guy, he's still in great shape; he'd be perfect for this lead character." I said, "Well, would he play Chinese?" and he said, "No, we'll make everyone Japanese." I said, "Well, the martial arts and the culture are enormously different." Karate and Japanese martial arts are all straight forward and back; Chinese martial arts are all circular; as are the cultures in their own ways and their ways of thinking. He said, "Yeah, but the audience really isn't going to care as long as we do a good job with either one we pick." I said, "Well, okay. When do you need this?" He said, "Well, here's the thing. Monday or Tuesday we've got to get a green light—is there any chance you can do what you can do?" So by the time we were talking about it at lunch, I was already writing a script as we talked, and I basically stayed awake for the next three days with forty-five minutes or two hours of sleep every once in a while. Monday morning I left it at the desk of whatever cheesy hotel I was staying in, said, "Would you call this number and tell them to come pick up this script," and went home and slept for two days. When I woke up they said, "Guess what? Scott Glenn said 'Yes.' We're going to Japan. The Writers Guild strike has been postponed for a week. We want you to do a second draft in Japan. Here's your ticket."

So there I was in Japan two days later, and I was given five days, and I rewrote the script. Literally, I was on one floor and Frankenheimer was casting on the other, and he would write a note saying, "Well, we just cast Kenta, and he doesn't speak any English, so give all his English lines to Saito, because we cast him and he speaks pretty good English." I was doing that kind of writing, plus they were getting information back from the Japanese about what they would be allowed to do and what they wouldn't—what the Japanese would admit about themselves, and what they would allow them to shoot a scene about, and what they wouldn't. Then the budget was an issue. So it was very practical writing. Frankenheimer would call up every few hours and say, "Here's another idea." Including, "You know, Toshiro's a little shaky with his *R*'s and *L*'s, could we get rid of the *R*'s and *L*'s?" So I had to go through his dialogue and take out as many words beginning with *R*'s and *L*'s as I could—which is an interesting way to write, kind of like iambic pentameter.

The script is ahead of its time in what it was saying about modern Japan, corporate culture versus traditional society, the crisis in values.

Well, I was a huge fan of Kurosawa and had seen his Samurai movies, and very often what they are about is what happens when you no longer have a traditional society. If you were a Ronin Samurai, you lived by certain codes, and you killed who your Shogun told you to kill and there was no moral judgment. It was like being a knight—if you killed, as long as you did it because he told you, that excused everything. The minute that guy disappeared, here you were: you weren't supposed to be a farmer, and you weren't royalty, you were from the Samurai class and you were supposed to keep that code, but the world no longer valued it. I was trying to extrapolate that into modern-day Japan and America. Is there any code worth living for anymore, or is it just about the bucks? And all those martial arts are ways of seeing the world and ways of acting, not just ways of defending yourself, if you do them right. It is a way of living, a way of seeing everything, a way of meditating, a way of organizing life. To place myself in that kind of mindset, I read *Zen and the Art of Archery*, *The Book of Five Rings* by [Miyamoto] Musashi, who was the greatest swordsman of all time, and Lao-Tsu's *The Art of War*. If you take these things, they can be read as Machiavellian, but they can also be read as something spiritual for people who don't believe that God should do all the work. Is that possible in this extremely materialistic world, both in the United States and Japan?

As a rewriter, are you perceived as specializing in anything in particular?

I've been lucky in that I've had this signboard—I can advertise what I can do through the movies I make. You get typecast as a writer just as you get typecast as an actor or a director. I did a couple of creature features for Roger, so people called me up for creature features, and they still do to a certain extent. After *Return of the Secaucus Seven* came out I started getting offered human dramas, a lot of sixties stuff about people. When I did something like *Lianna*, everybody sent me lesbian things. But over the years, be-

Toshiro Mifune and Scott Glenn in *The Challenge* (1982),
directed by John Frankenheimer.

cause I've made movies, it's broadened the kind of things I am
asked to come in on.

Before I take a job, I try to find out what is my mandate. When
I'm brought in, it's usually not about the genre. Sometimes it's just
dialogue. And a lot of times it's just character—they just want the
characters to be a little more three-dimensional, although they
don't want to give up any of the other bullshit that's in the movie.
So the mandate each time is different. I worked for about a weekend, because they were going to start shooting on Monday, on
Love Field, and I just did some work on one character, the black
guy, to give him a little bit more of a backstory. The same thing on
The Quick and the Dead, where I was basically brought in to
punch up and expand Gene Hackman's speeches a little bit, to
give him a little bit more to chew on once they knew that they
were going to get him in the movie. But when I said, "Look, there
are some real structural problems with this thing, could I deal
with them?" they said, "We don't have time; we've already done
the storyboards and built the sets." I actually wrote some stuff for

them, and they said, "Yeah, this is nice, but we can't do it. We're committed to the structure of this movie."

With *Apollo 13* they actually wanted to go back toward the book a little bit, toward the original material. And some of that was Tom Hanks' feeling like, "You know, I think the American public can handle the real characters, and we don't have to push them toward fictional archetypes quite as much, and I think they can handle some of the science, so let's try to get some of the science back into it. That's what these guys were wrestling with. They were wrestling with physics." So I did a lot of work on that. I got the ship-to-shore logs of what they were saying, and I tried to bring back some of that dialogue. Hanks had the idea of putting in the business with the CO_2 gas buildup where they build this device. So I went and I read, and I put that sequence in. Ron Howard works in a way different from a lot of the people I've worked with. He really had me out there. I was sitting in with the actors reading scenes I had written, and then they would all comment, and I might rewrite them or not, which I don't do personally when I direct. I don't ask the actors what they think of the scene. I liked the people who were involved. Tom Hanks is really smart about story. It was interesting to see Ron's process.

It was a lot of work, but you only get credit if you change the story. You're not going to have a woman on board, unless you're working for Roger, or have your astronauts blow up in outer space, or run into some cosmonauts or something like that. I asked for a credit, and Universal submitted me. According to the bylaws, to get onto something that's based on an original book, if you're not the first writer, you have to have changed the story over 40 percent, for better or worse. You could have made it 40 percent worse, you'll get credit; if you made it 39 percent better, you won't get credit. That's a lot of change. And just changing the dialogue, or putting things that were in the book back into the screenplay that weren't in there doesn't do it. So it was kind of a toss-up. I was disappointed because I thought I did some good work on it, but that happens. It's not a big deal.

Wild Thing was an interesting credit situation. That's one where I should really be sharing credit. I just did a rewrite on that. I think what happened is, there was an original writer and then there was a guy who did a major rewrite on it. The producers didn't like his rewrite; they had me come in, I rewrote it pretty heavily, but I didn't come up with the original story. Then they hired the guy who had written the second draft to direct it, but told him, "You can't change anything back to your draft." So it was this weird thing—the director working on a script he thought had been ruined. So when it went into arbitration, I said to the Writers Guild, "Well, obviously I should share it with at least the guy who wrote the original, but I think I should also share it with the guy who wrote the second draft," and I think both of them were pissed-off enough that they just said, "We want our names off it," so I ended up getting sole credit.

What reasons would lead you to turn down a rewrite?

Usually I pass because I don't have the time, because I'm already writing two or three things, or I'm about to go shoot a movie. But sometimes it's that you really just don't have any ideas about how to do it. Sometimes I'll just say, "I don't like the genre," or, "I'm not really interested in the thing," or sometimes, "I think that you could make a good movie out of this, but I don't know how to do it." Sometimes it's because you just get a bad feeling about the project, and you think, "They're not going to make this." When you think there's something you can do, what you do is have a meeting before they hire you, and you come in and say, "This is what I would do with it." Or sometimes you don't have that many ideas, but you feel like, "Well, I could get into this thing," and you ask them, "So what do you like about what's here already? What do you like about the book that you want me to adapt? What is it that you respond to?" Then sometimes at the end of that meeting, you feel like, "Well, I don't think this is going to work out, because this is where I would take it, and this is where you want to take it."

And sometimes you just don't like the people. I had one situation where these producers wanted to make *Breaking In*, which I didn't want to direct, about seven years before it actually got made. And I disliked them so much in the first ten minutes of the meeting that I just decided, "Okay, I'll just start disagreeing with them, and then they'll decide that it's not such a good idea to buy my script." And about a half hour later they said, "Well, we'll call you," and I could tell, "Okay, I finally offended them enough that they're not going to do it."

Casey Siemaszko and Burt Reynolds in *Breaking In* (1989),
directed by Bill Forsyth.

I like writing for other people. I wouldn't do as much of it if I didn't have to make money to put into my own movies. I like it as much as I do because it's not my only gig, because I do get to make movies that are just my own. So I really can come in with the idea that this is their story and I'm helping them to tell it, and I can always keep things on that level. The only movie I've ever had made that was my story was *Breaking In*. I thought Bill Forsyth did a really good job. I haven't had that kind of emotional, "This is my story, and they're going to fuck it up," connection with the things. I've just been, "Well, I gave them a good screenplay, a shootable screenplay; now it's up to them." And if they don't make a good movie out of it, I'm disappointed, but it's not like it's my story that's been thwarted.

Whereas I think if you're just a screenwriter, either you really do get into that mentality of, "Well, I'm just a hired gun, and I could be a copywriter. I could be a bunch of other things, this happens to be what I work in." And then you hand it over and you try not to look at it when it's done. Or you're a very frustrated person. Which is one of the reasons why, when we have Writers Guild strikes, they're so bitter, not just about what they're getting paid—it's questionable whether there's a big problem with that—but they're just pissed off. And one of the great contradictions within the Writers Guild is that the reason there is so much work for writers is because scripts *are* rewritten a half-dozen times by the studios.

CHAPTER 4

The Return of the Secaucus Seven

What finally led you to make your first film?

Union Dues got nominated for both a National Book Award and a National Critics Circle Award. I was the only one nominated in both lists. The people at Atlantic were really hot on me, so I said, "Hey, I've got a bunch of short stories, do you want to make a book?" and they said, "Oh, sure-sure-sure." With the money I was paid on those first three jobs I did for Roger, the money that I knew was coming in because I'd already contracted to do *The Howling* and *Alligator* at that point, and the money I made from that short story collection, I had about $40,000 in one place at one time—and I just figured, I'd make a movie for that much money with Jeffrey Nelson, who ran the summerstock theater. I wrote it in a couple of weeks and we started shooting in '78. *Piranha* came out while we were shooting. I wrote *Lianna*, *Return of the Secaucus Seven*, *Eight Men Out* all in L.A. in 1977 to '78, and I wrote *Matewan* around the time I shot *Secaucus Seven*. *Secaucus Seven* is one movie where the philosophy was, "I want to make a movie myself. Yes, it is an audition piece, but on the other hand, this may be the only time I get to do this. So why make somebody else's movie?" Which is why I didn't make a story about an ax murderer in a haunted house. It's not what I wanted to spend a year of my life doing, even though the ax murderer may have been a quicker ticket to getting a job directing movies, because it took a long time after *Secaucus Seven*. I always say I was catapulted from total obscurity to relative obscurity.

When you wrote it, did you have a model?

The model was basically *Nashville*. And that came out of my not so much saying, "This movie is going to be like *Nashville* in spirit"

John Sayles on the set of *The Return of the
Secaucus Seven* (1979).

or anything, but saying, "If I can't move the camera, how can I
have any movement? Well, it'll have to be a cut. What motivates a
cut?" And in *Nashville*, a million subplots motivated the cuts. I'll
always have a reason to cut if I'm going to another subplot.

Was Cassavetes a model for what you had in mind?

I saw his movies and would see articles about him and the main
influence that had on me was hearing that he took the money he
made as an actor and got some people together and figured out
how to make this movie. That was a great precedent, the possibility of those movies. And they were very influential not in what
they were about, but in that you could have recognizable human
behavior on screen. And they felt that way. They didn't have a
gloss to them and the acting gave the feeling that they were ad-
libbing, although they weren't. So many of the movies were about
people who were inarticulate, so people were repeating things
over and over, trying to get to this kernel of real emotion and real

truth, and it seemed like they were making it up even though it was totally scripted. There were other movies besides his where there was recognizable human behavior, but usually it was still movie behavior. The one thing I always try to achieve is that when people leave the theater, I want them to be talking about human beings, about their own lives and the lives of other people they know or could know, rather than thinking, "Oh, that was like *Citizen Kane*," or, "That was like *Raiders of the Lost Ark*." The references in the movies are references to historical things or personal things, not references to other movies.

Did you write it with the cast in mind?

Some of them. I knew I wanted to work with David Strathairn and Gordon Clapp and a few of the other people I had worked with. Then I had some questions. And we didn't do auditions. We'd ask the other actors who were in it, "Well, who would be good for this part?" and they'd say, "Oh, I know an actor who would be good for that," and I'd go and I'd see him in a play or something like that, and say, "Yeah, that person would be good." There were a couple of people who came in who I didn't meet until the day they came on location—they were just recommended by another actor to me. But because they were playing just regular people of our age, around thirty, I figured, "Okay, well, how big a stretch is it going to be? This is all recognizable human behavior." And an interesting thing happened. I did something I've done on all of my other movies—I wrote a little bio for each of those characters. And several of the actors would come up and say, "How did you know? How did you know that I've always felt like I was everybody's second-best friend?" or whatever the thing was. I said, "Look, this is stuff that happens to a lot of people, and it happened to you. It will make it easier for you to play your part. But you're not playing yourself—you're playing somebody who is familiar."

I didn't know anything technical. I had looked through a camera once in my life. A guy who was an acquaintance of my literary agent was a soundman for a bunch of guys who did commercials in Boston. This guy said, "My boss is a cameraman, and he owns his own camera, and I hold the boom." I said, "Well, hey, they've shot sync sound, and they'll do it for the money." So Bill Aydelott, who was the head of the company, brought in a cinematographer who had shot some of his commercials for him and done the lighting, and his employees were his sound guy and his gaffer-grip, and then a PA (production assistant) who did a lot of the other stuff. So we had a seven-person crew, and that was it. And we shot in 16 mm, which is what they were shooting their commercials in, and what I could afford.

Then we figured we'd build it around this ski lodge that we had up in New Hampshire, which I had lived in when I was working summerstock, because we knew we could get it for the equivalent of $1 per head per night. And we'd shoot a lot of stuff in the woods, and that's free, and then we'd shoot at Crawford's Notch, which is where the diving scene is, and that's free, and we knew this guy who runs a local bar, and he'd let us shoot for a day

Sayles setting up a shot on *The Return of the Secaucus Seven*.

when he was closed down, and we'd shoot in the theater. So we didn't pay anything for locations. We didn't have makeup or a costume department. We just told people, "If you would wear makeup in this situation, bring your own. When we go to the bar, if you think your character would put makeup on, put some on. That's all the makeup we're going to have. And bring the clothes that you would bring to a two-day weekend." We didn't know really what a producer or a line producer or a first AD (assistant director) did. I did many of those jobs, and Maggie ended up doing a lot of them without taking the credit for it. She started kind of being the hostess, which we figured out later was being one of the producers.

Was Maggie part of the summerstock group?

No. She had acted when she was a kid. She's from Williamstown, and there's a good summer theater there. She went to Barnard for a couple of years, then back to Williams. I was in a play with her in my senior year, but we didn't have any scenes together. I actually didn't know her until after college. I met her through mutual friends.

How many days was the shoot?

Twenty-five. But without support services, a good part of our day could get eaten up just with the process of getting up. Because people had lives and stuff they had to deal with, we were shooting five-day weeks instead of six, which is something I started doing later. So it was five five-day weeks. It really was on-the-job training for everybody. On the first day I decided for the first shot, "Okay, we'll try to do a tracking shot, see how long that takes." It took really long to do all the focus with a seven-person crew and kind of a complicated move. I said, "Okay, no more tracking shots." Instead there was going to be a lot of cutting, cutting away to people, and that would keep some sense of movement within the picture. If I'd had a more experienced crew and more time and money, I would have made *Secaucus Seven* look more documentary-like. I wanted *Secaucus Seven* to look like "NYPD Blue." But the technicians just didn't have the confidence that anything would be in focus if we tried that. Basically it looks too good. It's a little too well-lit, and

Jean Passanante and Maggie Renzi in *The Return of the
Secaucus Seven.*

it's a little too in focus. I would have liked to have fucked the frame
up a little bit more. Because the dialogue is overlapping, I would
have liked to have the look of the movie to be overlapping, for the
camera to find the person after they've started talking.

*Did you consciously write in all the games and sports to supply
movement and action within the frame?*

Yes. They can move within the frame—basketball or charades or
volleyball. Also, knowing the kind of limitations I was going to
have, that I wasn't going to have movement or be able to do my
transitions with movement and screen size and a lot of physical
stuff, I wrote many verbal transitions into it. So one scene will end
with somebody saying, "Well, I don't know—it seems like she's
not really thinking about Jeff." Then you cut to the street, and
David Strathairn's character is seeing this boyfriend who's been
dumped—"Jeff!" It's a way of tumbling into the next scene.

Why does everything about the opening of Secaucus Seven, *including its title, suggest a genre film?*

I was doing two things. One was about, "Okay, this is the kind of movie you're going to see," but also this is about the expectations these people had, as opposed to the reality. So it opens with this very dramatic Spanish guitar, and these mug shots. So it could be a movie about terrorists, a thriller. And then the next shot you see, the first shot of their real lives, is a toilet plunger. And so I'm saying, we are not talking about something grand here. We're talking about something fairly mundane. These kids had this inflated expectation of how they were going to change the world. And they had their moment in the sun, and their publicity it turns out happens to be a mug shot. It wasn't the cover of *Time* magazine. It was a mug shot from Secaucus, New Jersey. But here they are now, and they have to deal with the rest of their lives. A lot of the rest of their lives is going to be about cleaning the toilet.

To what extent is Secaucus Seven *autobiographical?*

Actually it's not very autobiographical at all. The movies that probably come closest to my personal experience are *Baby, It's You* and *City of Hope*. *Return of Secaucus Seven* is much more about people that I met after I was out of college who were in some ways more politically involved than I was or more politically aware than I was who were trying to keep their idealism together. They were trying to stay optimistic. But it was a community, even though they didn't live together anymore. Which is why it's called *Return of the Secaucus Seven*, which has some idea of rebirth or comeback. *The Big Chill* was called *The Big Chill* because it's about people who have lost their idealism or never had it in the first place, and that's a cold realization. The people in *The Big Chill* tend to be more upper–middle class rather than middle class or working class, and they're all upwardly mobile—whereas the people in *Secaucus Seven*, the men especially, are consciously downwardly mobile. If the women are upwardly mobile, they're probably having a career that their mothers didn't. Even though the form of the two movies and the plot in some ways are very close, they're really about very different people, which is why I never felt like it was a rip-off. It goes in such a different direction. It's like saying if my movie had an Indian and a horse in it: "Oh, it's a rip-off of *Shane*."

To what extent did you identify with the characters?

Well, I think the way in which I identify is that I've always been interested in the idea of community in the United States. We're such a mobile society. Since the Indians lost the store, there has not been a traditional society here. People are not often doing the same thing that their grandparents were, or being in the same place as their grandparents. How do people then form communities? Well, they seem to find these communities of spirit. It may be stock car racing, it may be the Dallas Cowboys, or it may be Fundamentalist Christianity. Those communities have a real cohesiveness, and people really need them. I was kind of in this very loose community of ideals. The key line for me is at the end of the movie, when Maggie Renzi's character says, "It's nice to be around people you don't have to explain all your jokes to." A community of reference, a community of shared ideals or a way of looking at the world. Even though you don't necessarily live next to each other geographically. And they hadn't had kids yet—they were putting off having kids. Which was kind of the point of the character I played—the people who were already having kids, the people I went to high school with, were already tied down in some way by, "I've got a kid to support, I've got to have a job. I don't like it, but you've got to have one." Whereas there was this community of people who were doing what they wanted to do.

When you made Return of the Secaucus Seven *the sixties backlash was just beginning.*

One of the things that motivated me to do the script is that I was starting to read things in *Time* magazine that were obituaries of the sixties. It was, "Oh, see what's happened to all these people who were activists in the sixties—they're all working for Chase Manhattan Bank, wearing three-piece suits. The minute the Vietnam War wasn't there to scoop them up, they forgot about politics, and they're going with the money now." Well, that may have happened to the people that Lawrence Kasdan knew, and it may

have happened to the people that the people at *Time* knew. It had
not happened to the people I knew and I thought it was bullshit
and wishful thinking on their part, their way of dismissing the
positive things that had happened in the sixties, and the changes
that were not beaten out of people by what happened later. So
yeah, I don't think it was any accident that I was doing it, because
I was starting to feel the rumblings of that pendulum swing. I just
wanted to say, "Yeah, there was some stupid shit about that period, but there's also some valuable stuff that these people are trying to keep alive somehow in a world that's not necessarily
friendly to it." This isn't a movie about the end of the sixties in
terms of, "Oh, they're going to be disillusioned when they leave
this weekend." This is the return of the Secaucus Seven, and this is
when they figure, "Okay, we recharge our batteries, and try to go
out there and live the way we want to live."

Ironically, by the time the film was released, Reagan was in office.

Oh, yeah. I had written this story "At the Anarchists' Convention,"
and Michael Kinsley, who was working at the *New Republic* magazine, which was a very different magazine than it is now, figured
it would be fun to send me to the Republican Convention as the
color man, not the nuts-and-bolts man. So I got to go to the Detroit Republican Convention when Reagan was sworn in the first
time. Which was pretty fascinating, because I could just wander
around and eavesdrop. And I can pretty much eavesdrop and do
about two to three pages of verbatim dialogue without a tape
recorder. So I would just wander in, and I'd sit with the delegates
and hear the shit, and I'd leave as fast as I could so I could remember this dialogue. Anyway, the Republican Convention was a cool
gig. I said, "Yeah, this guy's going to win. He knows what he's
doing." It was such a beautifully orchestrated convention from an
advertising point of view. I had somebody tape it, and when I
watched the tapes of what was going out through the networks, it
was "Happy days are here again," and he never said anything
nasty about people on welfare, and he was kind of a cheerful guy,
and it was a very benign, friendly convention. On the floor, it was
a paranoid Barry Goldwater convention. These were the guys who
kept talking about the Trilateral Commission, and "Jerry Ford,
he's a Trilateralist." They didn't like George Bush because he was

Adam Lefevre and Karen Trott in *The Return of the Secaucus Seven.*

one of them, too, and he was too Left. George Bush as a left-winger was pretty funny to me, but to these paranoid little fucks on the floor. . . .

And I got to talk to these girls who had the STOP ERA (Equal Rights Amendment) buttons on, and I said, "So why do you want to stop the ERA?" and they said, "Well, because they make you go to the same toilets as the boys, and they can force you to have an abortion." I said, "Is that really in the ERA? Have you read it?" They said, "No, we haven't read it." "Well, how you can not have read something that you're against?" They said, "Well, if you read it, that's how they get you." It was really pretty wild-eyed. It was really a Jesse Helms kind of mood on the floor. But they knew that was going to scare people, and they just kept it very bland and pleasant when it got to the podium. And the only people on the podium who got to do their own speeches that had not been rewritten by Reagan's handlers were Jerry Ford and Barry Goldwater. And when Barry Goldwater came on, it was like God was back. And he made a very good speech. So I was pretty aware by that time that the shit was going to turn around.

The script uses a number of devices that give it a certain structure and emphasis—an outsider character who provides a justification for explaining who everybody is, the use of Mike and Katie as the hosts who comment periodically on the proceedings. How did those devices evolve?

I saw the characters first. I started thinking about who are they going to be? It's going to be about a group of people turning thirty. Then I thought, Well, take any weekend with a bunch of people who know each other, and they're going to be in totally different states of mind. So who are the people who are having the most dramatic thing happen to them? Who's breaking up? That happens. So they're having a really emotional weekend. Whereas for somebody else, the arc of the weekend may be about where everybody is going to sleep, and if they have enough towels. That's Katie and Mike, and their relationship is okay for now. They are the bookends, and at the end, the line "What are we going to do with all these eggs?" is about "Okay, are we going to have children?" That's the metaphoric level. But it's also the practical arc of that character, which is, "Well, now we've gotten through the weekend with many more guests than we have rooms and beds." That's their arc. Chip's arc is being accepted. The people who break up, she wants this kind of freedom and the guy doesn't think they've broken up, and doesn't want to—and their arc is that, yes, this is finally over. They have their confrontation. They have the most dramatic arc.

Once I had that worked out, I started thinking about structure. And I said, "Okay, it's a weekend." And there was my structure, in a three-day weekend: there's the people getting ready for them to arrive; people arrive; we introduce people; they do their stuff, and then they go. Those are the three days. That's my structure. Now, what's going to happen with each of those characters? And in the first section we've got to introduce each one, then whatever their drama is, we have to move it along in this middle section, and then we have to resolve it somehow . . . or not resolve it, but that nonresolution *is* the resolution. To me, the epiphanies for each character are spread throughout the last third of the movie. And what I wanted was the feeling that if these people get together in six months, each one of them could be on a different level.

Do you see the group's arrest as a pivotal moment in the film?

No. I wanted to be able to tap into a tiny little bit of the spirit of who they were when they were in college. We have some of the information already when they're playing volleyball about who was who to whom, and some of the fuel that they have is what they got when they were these kids in the sixties and involved in those things, so I needed some catalyst to bring some of that out, and I thought, "Okay, well, they'll get busted." I use the same device in "At the Anarchists' Convention," where all of a sudden, when there's a common enemy, these people, who can't agree on place settings or anything, they galvanize. It's a way for us, the audience, to tap into the energy and the solidarity that they once had—that they still have in some way, even though they're spread out. I've been arrested a bunch of times, and never spent a night in jail for a crime or anything like that, but during the sixties I was pulled over, run in, and let go. It was because they were just fishing. They thought, "Okay, maybe we'll find some dope in their car, and maybe one of them will say something," and we were on our way to a march or something like that. And there was a solidarity you'd get even from that.

Are you still in touch with those friends who inspired this film?

A lot of them. Yeah.

Once the film was completed, how did it get distributed?

I had no idea whether this thing was ever going to get seen or not, and when they said, "Oh, yes, you want to direct this screenplay that you've written—what have you ever directed? Ha-ha-ha!" I'd say, "Well, here is the feature I directed. I know it's very low budget and everything." Orson Welles talks about how his inexperience in movies helped him a little bit. I didn't know what I shouldn't be able to do or wasn't supposed to do and there was some advantage to that. If I'd known how hard it was to make a movie, I might not have started. But it was for my benefit to make a movie. I thought it would be fun and to this day the process is what's mostly interesting to me. When the movie comes out, it's done. It's not very interesting to me. It's nice if a lot of people see it but that's not the reward, the reward is getting to make the movie.

Maggie's mother had a friend who worked for the Museum of Modern Art, which has this New Directors/New Films festival, a woman named Adrienne Mancia, and she said, "Oh, I should look at it." We found a screening room, and we had friends and the people who were in the movie come see it, and Adrienne came, and she said, "Jeez, my associate Larry Kardish should see this, because he and I help pick for the New Directors Festival." I didn't even know there was a New Directors Festival. Larry Kardish said, "Yeah, we'd love this to be in the New Directors Festival. Have you entered it in Filmex?" I said, "What's Filmex?" Sundance didn't exist yet, there weren't really many American film festivals. The Filmex Festival was in L.A., and I sent it out, and I heard later that Paul Bartel was on the selection committee, who I knew from being in *Piranha*. I'd met him on the set. He showed the first twenty minutes of the first reel, and then turned the lights on and said, "We want this, don't we?" And everybody said, "Oh, yeah, we'll go with it." And he didn't know what the fuck this thing was or where it was going, but he knew me and he liked it.

So it played at the New Directors Festival, and almost at the same time it played at Filmex, and the buzz on it was great and they had to put in a couple of other showings. So I got these two writing gigs out of it and a few people gave us their cards and said, "We distribute small pictures." On the East Coast I met Ben Barenholtz, who was running Libra (his big hit was *The Rocky Horror Picture Show*). He had kind of invented the Midnight Movie with

Eraserhead. Then on the West Coast we also met this wacky guy, Randy Finley, who owned a bunch of theaters in Seattle. Randy offered the $20,000 to blow it up to 35 mm, and he just seemed the most enthusiastic of all these guys. We just kind of liked Randy, and so we said, "Do you think you could work with Ben Barenholtz?" "Oh, yeah-yeah-yeah, I've dealt with him." "Well, what if you hired him to run the New York opening, where you don't feel you're very strong?" And they worked out a thing together where Randy's company was the distributor, but they subcontracted Libra to do everything east of the Mississippi. And it took them about a year to get the movie out. I made it in '78. It took about a year to get into the New Directors Festival and Filmex, and then in '80, it finally came out. And Randy basically ran it like a roadshow. City by city, he would do the grass roots work.

It did fine, and during the deals we had made with the cast and crew, we'd said, "Look, it's very unlikely that this thing is going to make a dime. But if it does, here're your choices. You can get first position, what you would have got paid if this was a real movie—in fact, what you would have got paid if you were in a guild or a union. You can take that first position *pari passu* with everybody else, so that if there were fifty participants in it and we get $50, you get $1, until you hit what you would have made if you were in SAG or NABET, which is the technicians union that we were basing it on. Or if you want to roll the dice and just take the same chance I'm taking as the financier of the picture, you can take points in it." And some of them chose to do that, and they actually made more money than the people who said, "Just give me my money up front." And we did it first-position, so before I made any of my $40,000 to $60,000 back, we paid off these deferments. For IRS purposes—because the movie actually did make its profit—it was $120,000.

Right after *Secaucus Seven* played the Filmex Festival, I got two gigs. One was writing a science fiction movie called *Watch the Skies* that Steven Spielberg was producing. It eventually got called *Night Skies* because somebody had the rights to the words "Watch the skies," which is the last line Kevin McCarthy says in *Invasion of the Body Snatchers*. It was about some farm people who were attacked by these little ETs who were mutilating their cattle. I put this autistic boy at the center of the family. My model was *Drums*

Maggie Cousineau-Arndt and David Strathairn in
The Return of the Secaucus Seven.

Along the Mohawk, with aliens instead of Indians attacking the
farm. I think it was Columbia where it was set up. They just said,
"You know, Steven, science fiction is over. This idea of yours
about some boy with a little alien thing. . . . We've got this thing
called *Starman*, go away." In the group of killer aliens who want
to slice and dice this little autistic boy, there's one nice alien who
makes friends with him, who gets left behind by his nasty compa-
triots. And the last shot is a hawk's shadow over him and him
cowering. That's basically the first page of *E.T.* But I was off making *Lianna* so I couldn't work on it. Melissa Mathison did an incredible job. The Writers Guild sent me her script just because
they knew I was somewhere in the chain, but it had nothing to do
with anything I wrote.

Then I had a meeting with a woman who gave me a development deal to write *Blood of the Lamb*, an idea I had had for a long
time. It was about two guys, one who worked at a kind of Pacifica
radio station and the other who was a yellow journalist for alternative papers. The sixties were definitely over, and they weren't

doing very well. The Pacifica guy's station is taken over by Fundamentalist Christians. He's kind of a hyper guy, I wanted Jeff Goldblum to play him. He gets his friend and says, "Let's infiltrate this group, and then we'll write a book on it." And they start infiltrating, they go to this boot camp for the soul, and they start moving up because the group is into media. And the radio guy becomes the designated successor to the charismatic leader of the group, and the writer ends up falling in love with a woman who basically is like a Janis Joplin, recovered from an overdose to become a Christian, and he just wants to get her out of the cult in one piece. It's like two guys who decide, "We'll change the corporation from within," and one of them gets seduced and the other one wants to get out, and then all of a sudden one of them has power over the other. And the final thing that they were fighting over was abortion. The guy was going to go and do a major radio thing to get abortion made illegal in their state, and his friend said, "Well, this is it. You can't do this. Our actions are now affecting people other than ourselves; we have to leave." And the guy says, "I'm not leaving." He's starting to believe in the stuff. They were like *The Big Chill* people, people who thought that they were more radical than they were, but it was basically about the action and not about the principles that the action was supposed to be based on. It was a deal for me to write it and eventually direct it. And we finally parted ways because it just wasn't generic enough.

CHAPTER 5

Lianna and *Baby, It's You*

Before making Lianna, *you wrote and directed two interlinked plays set in the world of professional wrestling,* Turnbuckle *and* New Hope for the Dead. *How did they come about?*

We moved back east just before *Secaucus Seven* came out, to Hoboken, New Jersey. Jean Passanante, who was involved in theater in New York, said, "You know, you've always talked about writing a play." "Yeah, that would be fun." So I wrote this play, and she helped me get it produced. She knew the people at the Manhattan Theater Club when it was right across the street from the Port Authority. They said, "Oh, yeah, this is a funny play, we'll put you up."

Wrestling is an unlikely, not very practical, choice for theater. That immediately limits who you can cast.

I'd grown up watching professional wrestling on TV, and I felt, what a nice format for something that's really about a guy who is disintegrating and his marriage is disintegrating, but we can tap this very theatrical format basically about kitchen sink things, and it will make it more theatrical. It relates to that kind of carnival theater life where big things are really dealt with, and people's fears and people's prejudices are brought out. Having been a jock, and knowing a lot of jocks who were starting to act, I knew some of the people already who I wanted to use. David Strathairn was in it, and Adam Lefevre, and John Greisemer, who has been in a bunch of my movies. My concept was: wrestling is theater. I had been in this production of *One Flew Over the Cuckoo's Nest*, and I had this epiphany one night when the audience was cheering: "This is a professional wrestling match." The guy who wrote it, Dale Wasserman, had done this beautiful job of taking the novel and making it a play with very, very broad characters. He made it a professional wrestling match in which there were all these reversals of fortune. The good guys won by being honorable and good, and the bad guys won by cheating. So Nurse Ratchet was like the nasty wrestler who won by cheating. And I realized, that's what theater is.

One of the interesting things that I did before I did the play is, one weekend I went to Madison Square Garden with David. I talked to promoters later, and they said: "Oh yeah, whenever we play the Garden, there are certain rules. The good guys can't lose more than two fights in a row, so if you were betting, and the good guys have lost two fights, they're going to win the third fight. You don't want to get people in a bad mood. In the Garden they ask us to always have the good guys win the last fight so people go out happy, so there aren't problems in the parking lot. And always, the next-to-last fight is really boring, so we have two scientific wrestlers, who are both good guys, do a lot of tumbling and grappling and stuff, because we're about to close the snack bar, and we want people to get bored and go and get that last Coke or beer or popcorn."

What about New Hope for the Dead?

Well, the original night that we presented it, it was with a play that Adam Lefevre had written called *The Window Washers,* directed by Jeffrey Nelson. Then when I redid it, I wrote *New Hope for the Dead.* Adam had actually written a poem called "New Hope for the Dead," and he got the title from a *Reader's Digest* article about cryogenics. I just wanted something that was about ten or twelve minutes long, and it was a curtain-opener. A lot of the actors I know had worked at the O'Neill. For a while there was a janitor up there who was an idiot savant. Basically, his regular dialogue was, "Oh, another day, another dollar," you know. But you could ask him anything about Egypt, and he would tell you pretty complicated stuff. When you asked, "Have you read this?" or "Where do you know this?" he answered, "I was there." And I got fascinated with the idea of that character. One of the guys who had told me that story was Gordon Clapp, who played Pharaoh in the play.

What was the trajectory from that to making Lianna?

I already had the script. It would get sent out sometimes by my agent as "Here's an example of his writing," and people would say, "Well, it's nice writing, but unless Jane Fonda wants to do it. . . ." People were really not interested in Hollywood, so whenever we did an interview for *Return of the Secaucus Seven*, we said, "And we're also looking for the money for our next feature." After I paid off some back taxes, and we paid all the actors and the technicians their deferments, I probably made about $50,000 on it—which was pretty good! So I could invest that $50,000 in *Lianna*. And we were going to try to make it in 35 mm for $800,000. And a year and a half later, it wasn't happening, and I was doing this play thing and treading water. I was getting writing offers, but I wasn't getting any directing offers. Finally we just said, "Let's do it in 16 mm, and try to make it for $300,000." So I put in my money, and Jeffrey and Maggie found these two kids who put in $50,000 each. The rest we pieced together. Today, if you had a thing that was a hit at Sundance the way that *Secaucus Seven* was a hit, you'd have a six-picture deal or something like that. Which is too bad in some ways, because it's a lot of pressure that I don't think kids who are starting out necessarily need.

What inspired you to write the script?

It was not originally necessarily about gay women or that world, and that wasn't what brought me to it. It was the women's movement and seeing an awful lot of marriages and relationships break up. Some of it was the pressure of women realizing, "I don't have to put up with this shit where I'm not happy, and I can drift out of this thing." And then there's this generation of people whose marriages are breaking up who are five to ten years older than me who internalized those values of you're supposed to get married and have kids and stuff, and they did that right out of high school or college. Here are these women, and they're thirty, thirty-five years old, and they're out on the job market and relationship market—and they haven't ever been there. They were in high school when they met this guy. And they're lost.

I started thinking about that, and about the people who break

Linda Griffiths in the title role in *Lianna* (1982).

up who don't have kids—"Sayonara, have a nice life, we'll run into each other"—some of them are double-dating within a year. The people who have kids, BANG, they're in court. It was when joint custody started being given out by judges. There were a lot of heavy-duty court battles over kids that I was seeing third-hand or whatever. And I was trying to think, "Well, what's a situation where the woman would be the one left on the outside looking in?" I had known some gay women who had gone through these heavy-duty situations, who told me about how weird it was for their kids. Every three years they had to kind of renegotiate, because when the kids were little it wasn't a big deal, but when they got to be adolescents and their own sexuality was coming out, it really affected them in different ways.

I said, well, there's a situation where the woman is going to be on the outside looking in, plus it's going to be an even more interesting moral decision that she has to make—it's not just, "I'm getting out of this marriage," but, "Who am I going to sacrifice? Who do I want my kids to have as a role model, especially my daughter? Somebody who eats shit for the rest of her life to keep this marriage together that's no good, but normal? Or somebody who makes the tough decision and says, 'I'm going to live outside of accepted society, and I may even lose custody of you kids, but the role model that I am is the person who stood up for herself'?"

Also, knowing the gay people that I knew at the time, coming out or realizing they were gay did not solve their other problems, and they brought all those problems into their relationships. One of Lianna's problems was that she was a student and married to her teacher. Who does she fall in love with? Another teacher.

One of the interesting things that was happening at that time, the early eighties, was that in the gay male world, there was a lot of role-playing. It was before AIDS, and it was exuberant in a way, but also destructive in another way, and that role-playing could get into the personal relationship. Gay women were coming out more, but there were also a lot of women who were on the fence, and the women's movement was very much against role-playing, and it influenced this gay women's subculture, who began saying, "Well, maybe we don't have to get into this butch and femme thing anymore—maybe we should rethink our relationships and not have them be patterned after male-female and patriarchal relationships, but maybe we can invent something new that's a little more equitable." So I was interested in getting into that with Lianna—here she is wanting this student-teacher relationship, when what her lover wants is something a little more equitable; she isn't comfortable with the fact that she's dating a student and wants somebody a little bit more on her own level.

Certainly I didn't know enough about the subculture to feel comfortable making a movie about a woman who had been gay for a year or more. So I said, "Okay, I'm going to get as far as I can go in. Here's this woman, and it's her first experience, and it's all very strange to her."

To what extent does the film equate Lianna's husband Dick with Ruth? They're both teachers and both of them manipulate her and are emotionally dominant.

And Ruth kind of catches herself doing it, and doesn't like herself for it, unlike Dick. She's a little bit more aware of it, and saying,

Jane Hallaren and Linda Griffiths in *Lianna*.

"Is this really what I want to get into with this person, and is she ever going to be able to come up and be a little more interesting to me even though I've really got the hots for her at this point?" Whereas Dick is really just unthinkingly using that position. I had to make him pretty negative so it was clear that Lianna was eating a lot of shit staying in that relationship, that it was just conformity that was keeping her in it.

The drawback in making him so negative is you can't believe she's with him at this point. It also sets up an antagonism or expectation of conflict that isn't actually worked out in the film.

Yeah. To a certain extent, the film is about somebody who is growing up at the age of thirty, and the relationship that she has with Dick is still this infantile one, the student-teacher, and they've never gotten out of that, and there is a way in which traditional marriage accepted that women were infantilized in some way—and I wanted that to be very, very clear and stark. Coming out is one thing, but really what she's doing is growing up, and she's starting to have to not just fall into things—fall into marriage and then everything will be taken care of, fall into motherhood and everything will be taken care of. She's having to invent herself. And growing up, for her, is taking those risks, along with going into that bar alone, getting a job, and all this shit that she's never done for herself.

What were you trying to say in the scene introducing Dick, where he's talking about the inherent falsehood of film? Or is it just documentaries?

Documentaries, which are always considered pure and honest, because you're not making things up allegedly. He was basically saying you can re-edit it and say the opposite of what that footage said in the first place. That was a very simple thing in that he is a cynic, so that was about his point of view. He's the guy saying there is no reality, it's all about how you manipulate it. It's like a politician who says it's all the spin you put on it—it's not what you do, it's what you have the audience, which to a politician is his constituents, believe.

Jon De Vries and Linda Griffiths in *Lianna*.

Lianna is trying to get beyond that surface. She's trying to say, "Well, wait a minute. Can I be honest with my kids and my friends? I'm going to stop living this manufactured lie. I'm not going to have an affair with a woman and continue to pretend to be married and have kids and not be a lesbian." And what she learns is, yes, you can be honest, but there's a huge price for it. Yes, you can put in that unedited footage—for instance, Fred Wiseman does. He still edits it, but he edits it less. Well, the problem is his movies are less and less accessible. The audience has to do more and more work to get anything out of them. They're just not as much fun as something that is very edited like *Hoop Dreams*. I think they're pretty honest guys, but they definitely made it into a drama, one that's more accessible to people. Wiseman's willing to pay that price of "I'm a prisoner of PBS. That's the only place where people are going to see my movie."

Lianna is very dependent on her relationships for her sense of self. One of the things that's hard about the film is how isolated she quickly becomes, and it's not satisfying dramatically. Yet at the same time, it's about the price of independence.

Yeah. It's something I dealt with later on in *Lone Star*, with the idea of individual accommodation, and that it's possible to make an individual accommodation, to do something that goes against society—but it's going to isolate you. Some part of her has to know, "I'm burning bridges here. Before I was a mother, I had status in that mother thing—as long as I kept showing up as a wife and a mother, I had status." And she has to be isolated at some point—she doesn't realize just how much at first, until she doesn't even have her best friend. I needed her to go out on that limb to grow up.

Then there's this series of renegotiations with everybody.

With everybody. So that's the last third of the movie, those renegotiations with her children, with her best friend. And one of the renegotiations is with that subculture of gay women. She goes out on her own, and she says, "Okay, it doesn't have to be me with Ruth—there's something here for me."

Lianna is the only film of yours that is strictly a character study. But as such, it doesn't have much time for psychology or the human condition, it's much more grounded in social dynamics.

Once again, it's a way of seeing the world. I was a psych major, and I read Freud and all that stuff, and I always felt, "Well, Freud is just great literature. These are wonderful metaphors for things that don't have any scientific basis, that are nice ideas, but they don't necessarily live their way out." I was much more of a believer in behaviorism, in B. F. Skinner and that crowd, than I was in Freud, even though Freud was more attractive because his theories were wonderful stories. I don't believe that any social animal, including human beings, evolve/live/grow/change/exist outside of their connections with other things. They do things in reaction to each other.

So to be reductive, character is context.

Scott Fitzgerald said, "Character is action," in terms of drama. Well, to me, it's interaction. That's why my fiction doesn't have much internal monologue. It has people seeing things and reacting to each other. One of the reasons Lianna is a frustrating character is she is not a very well-formed person. She is not complete. She is a very weak character. And the same thing with Jill in *Baby, It's You*. That's one of the big problems the studio had with her. They wanted us to root for her all the time. She does terrible things in that. She denies her former boyfriend and makes fun of him, makes fun of her former self, sells out, and finally has some kind of little redemption at the end. Lianna is not a kid, but she's still acting like one, and that's what's frustrating about her.

That spills over into Linda Griffiths's performance, which perhaps doesn't overcome that frustration.

What I try to do with the actors is say, "Let's talk about who you are, and then let's have you play the moment." And for Linda, the moment is often absolute confusion and despair, but she's in this very quotidian context; she's not Anna Karenina. I didn't give her Greek drama things to do. She runs into her kids outside a movie theater. She's at the checkout counter. She's got to make ends meet. She's in that world, even though she's having these major, major

Jo Henderson and Linda Griffiths in *Lianna*.

problems. And she just doesn't know what the fuck to do next, or where she stands in the world, or where she stands with this other woman. So I really just say, "Play the moment," and very often in that moment she doesn't know what the fuck she's going to do next—she just knows she's very upset.

The film begins and ends with Lianna and Sandy in the play-ground, a setting that expresses something about them. By the end, their relationship seems like the key one.

Yes, it is. And it's not a sexual one. But that's the person who she needs to connect her to the world. She's going to have a running battle with her kids, and she's still going to be their mother, and she's going to have to do it from a greater distance than she should have to. But the one thing that does come full circle is she gets this friend back. She has to take a stand to be who she is at the end, and grow up that much, and her friend has to grow through this gut-feeling prejudice that she has and realize, "Well, wait a minute. There's a person there who I knew. What is different about her? Not enough for me not to be her friend anymore."

Is it important that the film's set in this academic community, a closed world?

Yeah. I wanted a certain amount of claustrophobia. In the academic world, there's a lot of talk about tenure, and whether somebody got it. When you give somebody tenure, you're not only hiring that person—you're hiring their wife or husband. They're going to be your neighbors, they're going to be at your cocktail parties, their kids are going to go to school with your kids, they're going to be on the school board of the local school. That's community. Because it's so hard to move in academia, and not be moving down, people stay at those colleges ten to fifteen years, sometimes until they retire, and then they stay in that community. And when they judge you as to whether you are going to be a tenured professor, they say, "Well, he's a great guy, but his wife's an alcoholic. Do we really want to be around this embarrassing situation?"

One thing your films always insist on is the reality of economic necessity and of work—it's the bedrock of every film.

Yeah. The preface to Studs Terkel's book *Working* says, "You don't make love for eight hours a day, you don't eat for eight hours a day—the only thing that you do for eight hours a day is sleep and work." That's a huge part of your life, and of how people, in this society anyway, identify themselves, and are identified by other people. That's why so many of Hitchcock's guys are architects. In the ecology of certain movies, you need the person to be able to be missing for a long time and off having an adventure—and nobody knows what the fuck an architect does. They have little plans that are rolled up, and they go visit a building site every once in a while, but they kick off for a week and a half and have an adventure—nobody misses them. And it's kind of a classy thing; they obviously went to college, and da-da-da. Otherwise you've got to go and work.

What did you have in mind in terms of a visual style for the film?

It was actually a harder movie to do than *Secaucus Seven*. I got less done each day because of the logistics. We were in Hoboken, New Jersey, and it was hard to park things, it was hard to get equipment

in, it was hard to get things quiet. So basically, I just wanted it to
look as normal as possible. I said to the cinematographers, "Try to
have it look good and get us through the day." We were working
six-day weeks, and we had about thirty days to shoot it. We were
shooting on location, not on sets, and that makes things difficult. I
could touch both walls in Lianna's apartment. So you're shooting
it up and down, and by the time you've lit it you've got this maze of
flags and lights and stuff. So it would take me five minutes to crawl
through these things, trying not to knock them over, just to go talk
to an actor and not shout across the room.

*You bring a specific stylistic idea to the three sex scenes—they
evolve visually from one to the next.*

Well, basically, the emotion is different. Instead of "Here is the sex
scene," you try for mood and emotion and expression of the characters through their movement. You think of it as dance, the way
you're going to move the camera and the people. So the first scene
was very awkward and sudden and came from a lot of dancing
around each other verbally. Then the last scene was not really
about sex—it was about saying goodbye, about this emotional
feeling, all this kind of desperation. It wasn't like the sex scene in
Baby, It's You, when Jill and Sheik first get it on, where it's cold
blue light and she's banging her head against the headboard, and
at the end of it you see her sitting alone and he's asleep—where
there's no connection. This was about connection—a very sad
connection, but it was very warm at the same time.

What's the significance of the dance production?

Well, it's just a little time thing, which means you're cutting between two periods of time. You're cutting from that last lovemaking scene to days after, and she's reflecting on it. I didn't want all
the emotion to be in the lovemaking scene and then pick up the
movie again. I wanted to have an afterglow. I wanted the emotion
to extend, so we know she continues to carry that all the way to
the scene where she's talking with her friend. That goodbye and
that physical contact and the emotion of it is still in her. And she's
crying as the dance happens. She's connecting the emotion of the
song and the dance with that experience.

Jane Hallaren and Linda Griffiths in *Lianna*.

What happened in terms of distributing the film?

UA Classics finally took *Lianna*, and about a week after it opened, all the guys at UA, Tom Bernard and Michael Barker, walked and formed Orion Classics. So we were at a company that didn't have anybody running it, and the guy who took over the parent company didn't want a Classics division any more. So we were just kind of left high and dry with *Lianna*, which got great reviews. It just was not well taken care of. We never got another statement on it, because the big computer raped the little computer, and they were basically phasing UA Classics out when our movie was out there in the world. Nobody was minding the store when it was time to sell it to video. Also we couldn't sell it to cable, because, you know, HBO and Showtime would just say, "This doesn't have stars in it. This is about lesbians. If it had stars in it and it was about lesbians, we could run it." So it's unprogrammable. So we didn't get a dime for any of those ancillaries. *Lianna* took so long to get a distributor and then get put out in theaters that in some towns it came out the same week as *Baby, It's You*. In some towns *Baby, It's You* came out first and *Lianna* second.

How did Baby, It's You *come about?*

Amy Robinson and Griffin Dunne, who were actors who had started producing, had a company called Triple Play. They had produced Ann Beattie's *Chilly Scenes of Winter*, which in its wisdom the studio retitled *Head Over Heels*. They had seen *Secaucus Seven*, and they came to see *Turnbuckle*, and Amy just pitched this idea to me, which was based on her high school experiences in Trenton. It turned out that she was about two years older than me, and we had gone to very similar high schools, and I knew what was going on in the boys' locker room and she knew what was going on in the girls' locker room. Amy really had a lot to do with the form of the story. She didn't sit down at a typewriter and write, but she was really the co-writer in that way. Then every once in a while, I'd just say, "Okay, this is a girls' locker room kind of thing. Talk to me about Sarah Lawrence." And a lot of her input into the writing of the script was about an all-girls' school. I may have met and known girls from that school, but I was never there to know what was the conversation, what was going on.

Although this is essentially Amy Robinson's story, the film feels more emotional and personal than your other films.

Baby, It's You and *City of Hope* are the movies I've made that are closest to my own experience of growing up. It is this kind of melting-pot high school. There was this feeling of this is the last time that democracy is really going to be put into action in our lives, and in senior year already some people are going away to college and some are going to Vietnam, and what's that about? But in gym class and earth science, you're in the same class. In fact, somebody who is not going to go on to college may have more status in the high school. At my high school anyway, it wasn't that cool to be smart. And Amy's school had the same thing going for it. So it was very familiar territory to me. Then the class thing I was always very interested in. America doesn't like to think it has class, and it does. There were such things even in high schools, there were Romeo and Juliet stories. And you just wonder how long can that last? Can it last through the whole junior year, or just one semester? When are the differences between their friends going to break up these two people?

Do you think there is a sense of nostalgia about the film?

I think so, for people who were from that particular era or had a similar kind of thing happen for them. So at almost every show-ing of *Baby, It's You* that I ever went to, there are one or two women weeping in the audience at the end of it, and you talk to them. We pitched this around for quite a while and at that point some younger executives were women, and at almost every pitch one woman would come out with us and say, "Look, I really hope they make this—I had this boyfriend in high school"—and then you'd get the whole story. So I think there was that kind of nostalgia in it. I don't think that was particularly my reason for making it. Amy always said, "The problem with this movie is I think that it's a romance, you think it's a class-conflict movie, and Paramount thinks it's a teenage sex comedy—so something's got to give somewhere."

Paramount was a little tentative about it, but they said, "Okay, sure, we'll take a whack at it, can you make it for three as a negative pickup?" Meaning that it wouldn't be an official studio movie, so we didn't have to use IA (International Alliance of The-atrical State Employees)—we could use NABET, the other techni-cal union. Paramount's signatory agreements wouldn't be broken, because we were making it with basically a piece of paper from them to a bank saying, "When these people finish this movie, we're going to buy it, so give them a loan." And the politics as far as us making the movie were great in that the studio wasn't around. We didn't know if we were making the movie until about two days be-fore we started shooting, because they hadn't okayed the casting, and they weren't crazy about Vincent and Rosanna. They said, "Is there anybody more glamorous than Rosanna Arquette?" And they wanted us to cast Maxwell Caulfield, who had just been in *Grease 2*, which hadn't come out yet but they thought was going to be a big hit. And we said, "No, these are the guys we want to go with, and we're willing to walk away and put it into turnaround if you don't okay them, because we haven't found anybody else re-motely right for these parts." And they said okay. But because it was negative pickup, that's the last we heard of them until the first cut. So we really just got to make the movie the way we wanted to. Michael Ballhaus, the cinematographer, had just started working in this country, and I knew his stuff from Fassbinder, and he is very fast and a good guy to work with. It was a pretty long shoot, maybe forty-three days altogether, and we actually got to go down to Miami to shoot the stuff of Sheik in Miami for those last three days. We had 35 mm, which was pretty exciting for me. We had Teamsters. We were almost legitimate.

Is the acting style here different from the previous and subsequent films? It seems more "cinematic" and "professional," less naturalistic. There's a certain facility and sex appeal or glamour in the two leads, too.

Paramount didn't think so. They don't look like models, but they are more glamorous than most of the people in the first two movies. I actually don't think the acting style is that different. I think you just have more kids, for one thing, and that brings a different kind of energy to things. And the style of writing is differ-

Rosanna Arquette and Sayles on the set of
Baby, It's You (1983).

ent. The writing in both *Secaucus Seven* and *Lianna* is generally very oblique. There's a lot of kitchen sink quotidian detail. And many times what people are saying is not that important—it's how they're saying it, and the fact that they're saying it. In *Baby, It's You*, they're late adolescents when we meet them, and they get a little bit older. They care so much about their image and what other people think of them that everything is a performance. There is very little quotidian detail. Everything is done for effect. Even with her friends in high school, Jill is acting in front of them. When she gets out of the car with Sheik, they ask, "So what happened?" and she's a little enigmatic. What Sheik does in front of Jill is for effect. He's playing Frank Sinatra, he's playing this hot guy, and until we get to Miami, he has barely had a straight moment with her that wasn't in anger. So the writing is very different, just because these kids are trying so hard to make an impression.

When you get to the big scene between them at the end, it seems like it's the only time they're really talking to each other.

It's very raw. Jill is actually breaking through to feelings in her acting class, and she's sneaking around them in the two other times she talks about Sheik, when she's in the dope scene and when she's getting drunk with Matthew Modine's character. She's trying things out. But she's trying a character on for size. In that scene with Sheik, Sheik's not playing a character anymore and she's not playing a character, and to a certain extent what I liked was that they were both hiding out from this party. And what they finally do is a performance—a performance with each other so other people will see them. They could spend the night talking. Instead, what they don't do, because she understands him and how important display is to him, and she understands to a certain extent she has to make a statement in front of these other people, is sit in the room and talk all night—they go out and do a performance. "We were the hottest couple in high school—we're going to pretend we're that again, and these people are going to have to deal with it. This is going to be an affront to them, but we're going to go out there with some confidence."

So before the performance, there had to be the real stuff. It's almost like the work an actor does before the performance, when you get real. And in that acting scene she's using as a sense mem-

Vincent Spano and Rosanna Arquette in *Baby, It's You*.

ory the time Sheik kidnaps her. The acting is really important in it. That's why I made her an actress, in a way. It's not just because Amy had been one. Amy once said that she went right from this good diction kind of acting in high school where if you just spoke clearly and held your head up, you were considered a good actor, to I forget the guy's name who was a famous New York City director who went up to Sarah Lawrence, and had them crawling around on the floor and pretending to masturbate, what I used to call flying fish acting because you spend a lot of time on the floor writhing. *Marat-Sade* was a big play in those milieu. So she's actually getting towards something, but it's for a purpose—it's to manufacture an emotion. In this one, she's not manufacturing an emotion—she just can't help it. To me that is them growing up together, facing some things in the romanticism of the songs. Very few songs recognize that romanticism is doomed. Even Springsteen is trying to say there's some hope, and they're just saying, "Okay, guess what. There's a ceiling, there's a wall, and you're on one side of it and I'm on the other, and there's no way we can keep crossing it—we can't kid ourselves anymore. There is some real emotion between us, but I'm not going any further. I can't deal with it. But don't think that I'm doing it because I'm in great shape and you're not. I'm fucked up, but that doesn't mean I need you. All I need you for now is just one night to help me do something— I need you now."

Aside from the obvious opportunities of a full-scale production, were there any specific things you hoped to learn or try?

Well, one was to write and direct it in a more physical style. We were going to have the time, with over eight weeks, to do tracking shots and car shots. In the car shot on *Secaucus Seven*, our car mount was me in the back seat holding on to the ankles of the camera operator as he lay across the roof and suspended the camera and shot through at Chip and Irene. It was kind of a human Steadycam, but you still couldn't drive very fast. It got him very nervous when we'd go fast—and I was just holding on to his ankles. So I knew there were technical things that I would be able to use in the telling of the story. I got to work with the New York stunt guys, and I had very strong ideas about what I wanted them to do.

I got to have music playback on the set, which I hadn't done before. Also, knowing that I was going to be able to buy some music, I was going to be able to have montage scenes with dissolves. On *Secaucus Seven*, in 16 mm, dissolves come in equal lengths: you could have 8, 16, 32, 48—in increments of eight-frame dissolves. And we had the money to guess once. So during the few dissolves in *Secaucus Seven* I guessed and I just said, "Well, I'm going to make some marks here and run it through the machine a couple of times—I think I want a 48-frame lap dissolve here." And if it didn't look good, you were stuck with it, because we didn't have any money to redo it. On *Baby, It's You* I knew that I was going to be able to play around with the montage scenes a little bit.

In both *Lianna* and *Secaucus Seven*, because I was trying to shoot a very low ratio, I would overlap two lines on anything. So if I had a scene, I would cut it before I shot it. If I had a scene that started out as three or four people talking, I would shoot the master shot for four lines, and then I would cut. Because I would say, "Well, I'm not going to go back to the master shot after I cut away from it, and about on this line here, line five or line four, I'm going to want to go to a closeup. Therefore, I'm not going to do a master all the way through, because it's a three-minute scene."

Do you still work that way?

Sometimes I do, if I really know what I want. It just doesn't make sense to wear the actors out. So I would overlap by two lines, and then I would go back and say, "Okay, we're going to be into the singles, and we're going to be into the two-shot part now." On *Baby, It's You* I could sometimes say to Michael, "Let's just try a master shot, and I don't know, maybe I'll leave it in the master shot—but we'll play the whole scene. Then we'll see where it took us." We didn't have video assist, but he's the only DP where I've never felt like I needed to look through the camera or video assist. When I said, "Low and wide," what I saw on the screen was exactly the low and wide that I imagined. It's not a big deal, because you can always adjust: "Well, what do you mean by 'low and wide'?" But it just hit, BOOM, that was what I wanted. So by the second day I wasn't even looking through the camera anymore, and I would just talk to him about, well, what did we have there. "Well, when did Vincent wander off screen?" "Oh, about this line." He's an excellent operator, and he listens to what the actors are saying. Most operators don't. They're just looking at composition. He actually would adjust. He'd never lock the camera off, even on a tripod. Then I'd say, "So we don't have him on screen for that." Then the script supervisor and I would talk, and we'd just say, "Okay, let's start him here—this will cut." So I was able to do a little bit more of the editing, not in the writing but in the shooting, and then even just give myself ammunition to do it later on in the editing room with Sonya Polonsky. So that really did affect how I covered things. It wasn't so much that I did more takes. It's just that I could be a little looser with the coverage, and I didn't have to know exactly where I was going to cut anymore. And it gave the actors a little bit more of a sense of just playing with each other instead of, "I'm going to do this piece, and then I'm going to do that piece, and then I'm going to do that piece."

In the final fight between Sheik and Jill, I said to Michael Ballhaus, "Can you give me a more general lighting, because I want the people to move anywhere in the room?" And Michael is a great camera operator, and at that time he wasn't in IA yet, so he could operate, and his focus-puller, Hans Buching, was a great focus-puller. They would just whisper to each other in German, you know, and Michael would say, "I'm going with the girl." I'd

say, "We'll just go with the heat of the scene, and we'll do a couple, and if you say you've been on Rosanna most of the time when
you break out of a two-shot, then we'll do a couple where you go
with Vincent. But I don't want to do this more than three times,
because they're both blowing it out, and you don't want them to
pace themselves." We did three takes, and Michael knew that he
had mostly been on Rosanna so he made sure that on the last take
he went with Sheik for the parts where they broke away and they
couldn't keep a two-shot. But he lit it very natural, but not specific, not Gordon Willis pinpoints of light where you've got to sta-
ple the actors in place and the light is doing half the work. It was
general enough, it was still good for the room, but they could
move around, and he could pull focus on them, and they could go
anywhere they wanted.

*At the same time, the film still has a very economic use of shots—
you don't have any scenes that have multiple angles.*

Yeah, it is economic. But the other thing is that because they were
very good when I did have motion, I very often said, "Geez, that
played really well—let's not do anything more." So the one thing I
will do is that if I have a master shot with some tricky movement
in it, I'll commit to it. But if we're going to take extra time to light
something that's difficult, and the acting seems to be working, and
I'm close enough to people when I want to be close and the motion is efficient enough so that it doesn't take too much screen
time, so that I can cut off at the ends and I don't feel like I have to
cut the middle of it out—I won't cover it.

*Has that ever backfired on you? Have you ever looked at some-
thing in the cutting room and said, "I should have covered it
more"?*

Usually not in terms of performance, because I'm really into the
rhythm of a performance. Even before I had video assist, I would
listen to the tape of the scene and to the rhythm of it. If I felt I
couldn't cut something tighter, I wouldn't want to cut it tighter.
The only time stuff backfired was with technical things. In *Lianna*
we had a scene where she comes home after sleeping with Ruth for
the first time, and we follow her from the living room, where her

son had been watching TV, into another room. We follow parallel to her, and so we lose her for a second, and then through the next doorway we see her again. It was very dark, and we were shooting dark—we weren't going to darken it later. The operator was so worried about whether he was going to hit Lianna and have a little nose room on her and have her in focus that he didn't notice until a month after we were done shooting, and I didn't notice when I whizzed through our dailies fast forward on the little Steenbeck that I had, that as she entered that second room, you could not only see the soundman, but the soundman wearing a Hawaiian shirt, and he had his headset on, and he was looking at the camera and Lianna—I had to do an invisible cut to get rid of the image.

But no, I've been pretty happy when I've made those commitments. And if there is a lead-up, if there is an intro to the shot, I'll often say to the cinematographer, "I may cut into this at any point. So do whatever you want, but be aware that I may even cut the whole thing out. I may cut the first two lines out." Sometimes that affects the "Okay, don't keep creeping in, because I may want to cut after the second line, and if there's just a little bit of a creep it's going to look weird. So get to them, and by the end of the first line I want you to be stopped." So you just plan ahead so you don't paint yourself into a corner as an editor. Usually, when I'm committed to a camera movement, it's because it really is a storytelling thing. So we try to hide it most of the time. Very often if you want to readjust, you have a character move. One way to go from a wider shot to a tighter shot is by racking focus—the classic example of an obvious rack is in a detective movie where let's say the detective is on a car phone, calling his wife and saying, "I think somebody is following me—I'll be home in ten minutes," and then he puts the phone down and you go PHEW and rack focus, and you see the people across the street who are following him. Well, that's an editorial focus rack. If you need to do that but don't want that to happen, you have an extra or one of your characters walk away, and you pull focus with them, and then when they peel off the screen, lo and behold, those people who used to be out of focus are in focus. The same thing if you're on a zoom, and you're going to go from wider to narrower, or vice versa. If you have a character to do it, the audience doesn't even know that you've readjusted slightly.

One more thing I had on *Baby, It's You* that I didn't have on the others was that I had the music beforehand. I wrote the lyrics into the screenplay, or a suggestion of the lyrics. I knew then that it was not always so easy to get the exact song you wanted, so I would have two fall-back songs. But usually we got the first choice, and very often I would have it playing. In the opening sequence we got "Wooly Bully" and we just cranked it up, and we said to the kids, "Just jump around to this inside your rooms, and then the minute we turn it off . . ." In fact, we didn't even turn it off until two lines in from Rosanna, because we didn't see her mouth yet. So the kids were energized by this really loud, blasting music as they poured out into the school hallway, and they had some of the rhythm of it. Since there was no dialogue in the montage sequence where Sheik is about to get kicked out of school, and you see him walking in and hanging here and there, and then you cut to the teacher who he's about to have a fight with, originally I was going to have them doing "Don't Mess With Bill," and I cut it to that. When I got the first cut done it just seemed too on the nose, so I took the song out. But the rhythm of "Don't Mess With Bill" was in their movement; they were swaggering in rhythm with it, and I cut to it.

It's surprising how much you used pop music in the film—it's not something you've done since.

Well, at the time music rights were a lot cheaper, so it was about $300,000—which is what we made *Lianna* for, basically. But to me, so much of that time and so much of how people identified themselves had to do with music—even in 1966. Class was not necessarily the thing that separated you in high school. It was: these guys listen to the Beach Boys, and these guys over at this table listen to the Yardbirds, and these guys listen to Motown. That was a real identification, and almost more important than what your parents did for a living and how much money you made. Music to me just had an incredible energy. The movie is set in 1966. There was this incredible flux. It was about to go fifteen different directions. Bob Dylan was around, the very beginning of psychedelic music happened that year, there was still Motown and still girl groups, and then there was Frank Sinatra cranking it out. All that stuff was there. And part of the metaphor that I wanted is that here was this girl, she was about to jump from this high

Vincent Spano and Rosanna Arquette in *Baby, It's You*.

school world to this college world, but it was a bigger jump than ever because she was going from the fifties to the late sixties. Where she was from, everything that made her popular and cool and accepted in high school was something that probably made her a social liability in college—in one year. And her boyfriend is this guy who's still doing Frank Sinatra. How is there any way that those people can go? And how do you keep any kind of sense of your self together when the world is changing that fast? How do you not lose any self that you ever had, when there's that pressure to be this, to be that? And she loses herself for quite a while.

When you were in high school, what music were you listening to?

I mostly listened to Motown, Ray Charles a little bit, but kind of everything that was there. I remember when I was a kid being in bed with a little transistor radio and getting everything from early Bob Dylan to really raw Country-Western stuff. I tended not to like the Beatles because they seemed too clean-cut. The early "I Want to Hold Your Hand" stuff seemed a little lame to me. They got interesting later when they got more psychedelic. And I liked their covers of rhythm and blues stuff okay, but that wasn't their popular stuff at first. I liked the Stones, the Yardbirds, and the Animals.

Given that the film originated in Amy Robinson's experiences, did you work with her on the songs you wanted?

Yes, quite a bit. We really talked about Sinatra, but also the Jersey scene. There was something called "The Philadelphia Sound," basically what everybody was listening to, a combination of rhythm and blues from the blacks, but also from these Italian guys, like Jay Black and the Americans. "Cara Mia" was one of those songs, sung by guys who a generation earlier had been Fabian, and a generation earlier than that had been trying to be the next Sinatra. Many of their songs were based on Italian *canzoni* or opera stuff. For instance, the Dusty Springfield song "You Don't Have to Say You Love Me" was written by Pino Donaggio and was a pop hit in Italy. And if you hear the opening of it, it's Italian, romantic, thick, pounding stuff. I guess Pino was an Italian pop singer before he started working for the movies. I saw his name and I said, "That's the guy who wrote the music for *Piranha*!"

What was the nature of your collaboration with Robinson and Dunne?

One of the main things I work with when I work with producers, whether it's Amy and Griffin, or Sarah Pillsbury and Midge Sanford on *Eight Men Out*, or Maggie with the various partners she's had, is the casting. I really use the producers as tie-breakers. Because sometimes I'll act with the actors as we're auditioning a scene, and I have my own feelings, but sometimes they are subjective about how this person would be to work with. And when I narrow it down to, "Okay, here are my possibilities—does anybody have any strong feelings?" very often they do have a strong feeling, and it is an almost objective feeling of, "Well, just as a moviegoer, this is the quality that I saw in this person." And Amy and Griffin, because they were actors, really had very strong, very good taste in actors, and they actually brought me a lot of people. Margie Simpkin, who was the casting person, had cast *Fame*, so she had worked with kids before—and she was very young. I said, "I want kids who are pretty close to the ages they're playing." The first day or so, people were a little too old, and I said, "Margie, I really want kids." She said, "Do you really want them? They always say that." I said, "I really want them." So we had kids that were actually younger than what they were playing, in some cases most of them within a couple of years. So it wasn't Dustin Hoffman at thirty playing a college graduate. Which you can do as long as everybody else around them is also older—and I just didn't want a whole bunch of twenty-five-year-olds.

One of the things I really relied on Amy for was the look of the clothes. Clothes and production design are not something I'm great at. I always have somebody else—Maggie Renzi on the movies that she's worked on—watch out for me for the sociology of what people are wearing. Women are always saying to me, "Oh, she would never own that." "She's an assistant district attorney, but she couldn't have that kind of apartment—that's just movies." I'm not that sensitive to that kind of stuff unless it's very, very broad. Or they'll say, "I can't understand it. They paid all that money for that film, and the clothes didn't fit." They looked fine to me. So I basically asked Amy, along with the costume person, to be my eye there. I said, "When the costume person brings me stuff, I may say 'okay,' but I want you to second me. I want you to either be there with me or kind of talk to me about it if you have problems with it."

Why didn't you edit this one?

Well, it was partly to make the studio feel better about it, but also I thought it would be interesting to work with an editor and to have somebody assembling stuff as we went along. I was working with Sonya Polonsky, who also cut *Matewan*, and she had been an assistant to both Thelma Schoonmaker and Susan Morse, who does Woody Allen's movies. I got along with her really well. Basically, during the cutting I was there every day, on my own machine. Sometimes I would say, "Okay, trade scenes for a while—I'm going to play with this montage scene, and you do this." Then if I'd get stuck I'd have her come over, and if she'd get stuck or I didn't see where she was going I'd say, "Well, I'll try it for a while."

We had this hurry-up scare because Paramount said, "Look, we have a big opening in our schedule. Can you have the movie done in six weeks?" In those days you had to do a blind bidders print, which meant that even if it wasn't the exact final cut, you had to slap something together and show it to exhibitors so they wouldn't be buying a pig in the poke. I think after *A Bridge Too Far*, where a bunch of people bought it thinking it was a Robert Redford movie and then he was only in it five minutes, they complained, and then they made this law. Anyway, all of a sudden a little bell went off in my head. "Only six weeks to cut. They'll put it out. That means we're not going to have any arguments about the cut. They're just going to be so happy to have a director who can actually deliver a decent-looking picture—yeah, we can do it in six weeks." And then as I understand it *An Officer and a Gentleman* had not been testing well. They didn't have much confidence in it, and they thought it was going to last a week and be dead in the water. Then it started testing better, and then it opened and did great—and they just called us up and said, "Never mind. Go back to your own schedule."

How bad was the fight you had with Paramount over the cutting?

Paramount saw the first cut of *Baby, It's You*. They disagreed pretty much 180 degrees from me. This was Jeff Katzenberg and Michael Eisner. My distanced opinion on it is that they had seen *Valley Girl* and *Porkys* and *Fast Times at Ridgemont High* and felt, "Jeez, we could have a big hit high school comedy." And *Baby, It's You* just was never going to turn into a high school comedy. So they said to me, "Look, the high school section is really great, and we really want to cut down on the college parts, because it's kind of long and it's kind of a downer." I just said, "Look, as far as I'm concerned, I want to tighten the high school part a little bit, and the college part is exactly where I want it, and I don't see anything that I want to cut." So we worked on that level with them, kind of grumbling for another week or so, and then they started doing previews. They did one in Paramus and one in Chicago, and after Chicago they got to the point where they said, "This is what we want you to do with it—the numbers aren't good." And I said, "Look, it's your movie. If you want to re-cut it yourself, it's contractually your right, but I'm not going to have my name on it as writer and director." They said, "Well, we're sorry you feel that way," and they hired another editor. It was bad because I was fired off the movie and out of the editing room for a month, and I had no idea if they were going to put me back in or not. I worried that I'd spent all this time doing this thing, and I wasn't going to have my name on it. I was pissed off in that I felt like if you sign off on a script and you've delivered that script, you don't rewrite it. I didn't pull any tricks on them. It was a serious movie when I wrote it, and they read it and said, "Yes, let's make it." You shouldn't then blame the director and try to turn it into something else.

So Jerry Greenberg came in, and he cut for quite a while, a month or more. I went to one of their screentests, and I thought that he had done some very nice physical cuts in certain places, but I felt that the emphasis was totally wrong, and it made Sheik look like a boob—I thought it was a real mess. And it tested one point lower than ours had! So they said, "What do you think?" and I said, "Look, there's a couple of good physical cuts, but I would really go back to my own cut." And they said, "Okay, go ahead—you go back in." I think by that point they realized I wasn't playing poker, and I really was going to take my name off it, and they just gave up on the picture, figuring, "Well, we're not going to do too much with this picture anyway—why get the bad publicity, have it be ugly, and have a guy actually take his name off the picture?"

And what was happening was Simpson and Bruckheimer were working with them, and they were just about to have an incredible winning streak. And right when we were coming out, *Trading Places* and *An Officer and a Gentleman* were making so much money that it was crazy for them to try to make their money back on this $3 million picture, when the same people who were doing the marketing could be maximizing their profit on these other movies. So they opened in very few cities, and in a couple of places they told the guy who ran the theater in that city, "Well, we don't care if you want it—we're not opening Atlanta," so he was forced to bang on their door until they'd run another print. So it escaped rather than was released. They had it in New York, and they didn't even have an ad in the paper. Amy and Griffin came to me and said, "Well, would you put up some money, and we'll buy an ad ourselves?" And when they smelled that, I think they got a little afraid that there was going to be a story about these plucky producers putting their own money into an ad, so they put an ad in. And then they yanked it out of the theater after a week.

I don't think anybody tries not to make money . . . but, for instance, they told Griffin that they would take care of the video. You buy the rights to songs in two pieces. You buy the theatrical rights, and then the video. And they didn't take care of it. So there was no video available of *Baby, It's You* for almost six or seven years. Anybody who wanted to see it on tape had to know somebody who had taped it off of Showtime. And by the time it came back, certain songs had gotten much more expensive. Originally, of course, they wanted to do it bargain basement and get the K-Tel version of *Baby, It's You*, and get rid of the Springsteen and Paul Simon songs we had gotten a good deal on, and I just said, "Well, yeah, you can do that, but anybody who asks me, I'll just say, 'Well, that's not *Baby, It's You* because all the songs have been changed.'" They would have had to cut some scenes, too, because if somebody is lip-synching "Stop! in the Name of Love," you can't change the song.

The visual style of the film is very lyrical and as close to glossy and glamorized as you've gotten. Its look is grounded in the actors' physical beauty and appeal and a certain visual elegance that your other films steer away from. What was your attitude toward this?

Much of it is about kids who are twenty years old, who are all about the future. It's all about their dreams. It's all about Jill saying, "That's not who I want to be." Those Springsteen songs in the film are about dreams; even though you have these funky surroundings, you've got this dream to get out of them. I wanted to play with that in the externals, in that the way they see the world is somewhat idealized, and every once in a while there's a comedown. So there's Sheik, and he's got the Sinatra playing when he walks into the cafeteria, and that's his own little soundtrack that he carries around in his head. Then we see him finally, the night of the prom, and there's his father in his t-shirt in front the TV in this tiny little apartment. And when we go to the nightclub, there he is, and he's lip-synching to Sinatra, and he thinks he's one of the Rat Pack, and he's playing Vegas. Whereas I don't think in *City of Hope* those guys carry those things around in their head, because they're older, and they know they're fighting over scraps.

Yet while it's become clear that Jill and Sheik have no future as a couple, the last shot with the crane up is a classic happy ending release shot. So there's something reassuring about the film's grammar.

It's also that they have given each other something. She has said, "Well, you're the best-looking guy in the place." She's going to give him a little of his dignity back but not in a condescending

Rosanna Arquette and Vincent Spano in *Baby, It's You.*

way. And he is giving her a little of herself back, in that she has the nerve to go out there in front of her friends. What I wanted to do was segue into the way that they're going to remember that night. So there's this really funky band that doesn't really want to play "Strangers in the Night," and halfway through the song it segues into Sinatra. When they remember that night, it's not going to be that band—it's going to be Frank. That's what's going on between them. At the same time, as you go out, it's just these two people who aren't going to stay together, who are going to become strangers in some way. It wasn't just a down ending. . . . They're still young. There's still some of that romance. You don't think that he's going to have a great career as a singer or anything like that, but there's still some hope for them because they're young.

What motivated certain moments of visual lyricism—for instance, in the scene after they've made love and she's looking out the window?

I wanted a little release for the audience. As depressing as the scene was between them it's trying to play the grimness off with something that was still kind of beautiful and promising and lyrical. So it's a very beautiful shot, but it's also a shot of two people very separate—it's a still. And the still is, what is she thinking as she looks out at that neon, and you hear the waves, and there's this kind of promise, but what we know is she's not feeling very good. It's just playing those two things off against each other, which is: there they are in Sheik's dream world with Paradise all around them. But finally, Miami Beach is in some ways one of the tackiest places in the world. He's looking around and saying, "Isn't this great? You ever been to a place like this?" And she says, "My parents used to take me here when I was a kid." So constantly here is the beautiful thing and here they are deflated—side by side. To me, that's some of what youth is, doing these things you heard were so great, and then you do them, and there's that kind of "Is that all there is?" or "It was supposed to be better than this."

What about the shot in the brief goodbye scene at Miami Airport? He's reflected in the window.

Well, we couldn't go to the real airport. We had to go over to Newark Airport and just shoot it. He's reflected, he's already starting to fade. That was all I really was playing with there—it is a goodbye, but there is something hard in between them, a layer of something. He is already, in her mind, starting to fade. He becomes historic. He becomes somebody she does bits about in acting class and tells stories about.

The way she keeps reusing that anecdote about Sheik suggests that deep down it's very important to her.

It is her past, and she's trying to deal with it. Eventually she's making it into a joke. I think that's what people do very often with things that are powerful over them, or hurt them a lot—one of the ways you deal with it is you make a joke about it. And Jill says, "I don't want to feel like I'm a snob, but I don't want to be the girl who walks into a party with Sheik anymore, because all the people I want to be my friends will laugh at me. How do I deal with that? Who am I that I now am embarrassed about who I used to be?" And she doesn't make up some other bullshit. She used to be one of the classiest kids in school, and now she's the girl from

Trenton. And that's one of the things that going to a place like Sarah Lawrence is about, it's about once being the valedictorian, and looking around and seeing how many other valedictorians are in the class. If you're from Trenton, you're saying, "Oh, shit. These guys were the valedictorian of some hotshot Chicago or New York school—I was just the smartest kid in Trenton."

And that's a lot of what she's trying to deal with, trying to find an identity that's acceptable—but there's some person there who's not just a sellout, she wants to keep something of it. And that's finally why she walks in with Sheik. It's her announcement to these other girls, "I'm not just going to bend myself out of shape anymore for whatever you want me to be. I'm not going to kiss your asses anymore. Here's part of who I am, a girl who goes out with a guy like this. That's part of who I am. I'm fuckin' Trenton, New Jersey. Deal with it."

The shot immediately following the airport farewell is another one-shot scene of Jill and a group of friends smoking dope while the camera does a 360-degree pan—a very conspicuous effect, again not typical of your filmmaking. When you wrote that scene, did you visualize it being shot that way?

Yeah, pretty much. There's something very circular to me about your thinking when you're smoking dope. I wanted the feeling of emotional time having passed. She's still in these very straight clothes when she comes to college. She's got this little red-white-and-blue outfit on. Even when she goes down to Miami, she's still dressing pretty straight. When we see her there, she's in these hippie clothes. She has gone whole hog. They're smoking dope. The music is about as far as you get from Frank Sinatra. You go around this room and these girls are overlapping, and it's this kind of word association that they're doing with each other, and they're getting their little digs in, but it's influenced by who they're trying to be behind this dope. And she's trying to be as cool as she can, and she's trying to make a story out of Sheik, and they're making jokes. So she's trying to get this identity that's kind of cool. And I just wanted something that had that kind of dreamy, floaty quality of smoking dope, but also had this undercurrent of she's still getting needled, but she's holding her own. She's trying really hard to fit in.

In general when you're writing, do you visualize it very specifically?

After the first couple of movies I realized, "It doesn't matter how I visualized it—I'm going to have to do it the simplest way possible." I get together with the cinematographer, and the location may dictate something different. Usually, the general sense of what I want to do is left in. So if I want it to be staccato, it will be staccato, if I want it to be wide and distant, it will be wide and distant. But the exact storyboard that I did or the way that I wrote it in will probably change. The first several films we didn't have the time or money for me to do anything but the simplest thing, so it was pointless for me to storyboard anything. You'd get to the place and ask, "What is the simplest, quickest way to shoot this?" Sometimes literally the direction was, "Put 'em up against a wall and shoot 'em." On *Baby, It's You* I did a little with Michael Ballhaus. We'd trade little pictures drawn on the backs of things, but that was on the spot. The first film I storyboarded was probably *Matewan*, and even then it was only certain sequences. Before that I kept track of eyelines and that was about it. We'd just ask, "Is there any way we can possibly do this just in a master?" After the first take I'd know—if it's too slow, I'd realize there's no way I can speed the actors up as much as I want to without a cut, so we'd do coverage. You shoot something like *Brother from Another Planet* in four weeks. It was all catch-up ball. We were getting to locations that we didn't own—like a Korean market that was still serving customers, and the owners were getting mad at us because they felt customers couldn't get in past the equipment, so we were trying to get that done as fast as possible. Let's figure out the quickest way to get out of here and have the sequence with the emotion that we want—not the nicest way to shoot.

The montage sequence of Sheik driving north to find Jill suggests a very different approach to filmmaking and editing than in your first films—he changes a flat tire in about three seconds.

The only thing that's close to it would be the wood-chopping scene in *Secaucus*, where time is elided even in a short, physical sequence, so it's not taking out hours, it's taking out seconds. I do it when Sheik is trashing Jill's room's too. Often montage sequences slow things down, and they tend to be lyrical and a little winding, and I wanted this thing to actually build, to just push the thing forward so I used the Springsteen song "Adam Raised a Cain" and it's very driving, percussive music. I just needed to keep his anger going through this whole sequence and have that feeling of "I'm going to get there." When he changes the tire, well, he does it angrily—he runs into the bathroom and wipes his face off, and then blasts back in the room. In the song there's this long crescendo where everybody is just hitting the same note, and that's when he asks the girl, "Do you know Jill?" and when she says, "Yeah"— BOOM, you get back into the percussive and he's in her room. Once again, having the music beforehand, I could play it out with Michael Ballhaus. We talked about the shots, we played it for Vincent Spano, so he was listening and moving to that. So the music really informed the cutting and the shooting.

And perhaps as with Dred in Pride of the Bimbos, *Sheik is gradually stripped of his identity during this sequence. By the time he finds Jill, he's become a real person for the first time, he's no longer playing a character.*

Yes. He doesn't believe that he is going to be the next Frank Sinatra anymore. As he says in the argument with her, "I'm going to be a garbageman like my father." He's gotten to that point. He comes to that on his own, but there's no humor in it for him, whereas with Dred there's a little bit of black humor.

Is the motivation for him to trash her room really there?

He's pissed off. She's not there. Everything that he sees around him is a reproach. This school, these girls, this world that he is not going to be accepted in. He opens up her drawer—the Pill. She's on the Pill. What are these posters? What are these clothes? What the fuck is she doing in this world that won't let me in? And that just increases his anger.

That would be what you'd say to the actor if he said what I just said.

Yes. So the physical objects in her room were important. It's not that she became one of those classy ladies in Miami that he was talking about, which he could almost understand. She's gone totally in this other direction. It's a value thing. It's almost like, "Are you mocking me with your values?" It's like in the sixties when leftist groups would dress down to go into the neighborhood and try to organize people, and people said, "Wait a minute. This is a formal occasion. What are you wearing shitty clothes for? Are you making fun of us? Your version of the way we dress offends me." So in a way this world that she's in is a ceiling, and he's banging his head against it, asking, "What's she doing on the other side of that ceiling? Why can't I get to her?"

The film is very much about cultural codes and how they are interpreted—music, dress.

And class. Classes have their codes. That whole argument they have is about values, and she says, "That's not who I want to be." She doesn't know who she wants to be, but she doesn't want to be Sheik's wife. She doesn't want to be somebody from that class. And his values are: to be a success, you're Frank Sinatra; not just the voice, it's the clothes, it's the look, it's the surface. She's right at the place where everything that he thinks is valuable, her friends think is tacky—and she kind of thinks they're tacky, too.

Also, he's aspiring to be a copy of something, an artificial construct, where she's trying to find something authentic in herself.

Yeah. But in a way she's doing it totally wrong, because she's pretending to be something when she's with those other girls. But she's looking for a person to be. And all she knows are the ones that went down before, and she doesn't want to be them. She knows too much to be that.

As a filmmaker, your sensibility is relatively conservative. You're not particularly a stylist. There's nothing unruly about your films, there's a certain civility to them.

I'm not sure if *conservative* is the word I would use. I'm totally uninterested in form for its own sake. But I am interested in storytelling technique. In a movie where there's a lot of fast cutting and a lot of music, and a point is being made, sometimes I get the feeling that the technique is blowing something by people, that if you just turned off the music, the scene wouldn't work. Because there's something false about what's going on. If you slowed the cutting down, people wouldn't believe it. You need that stuff. It's like a fast-talking salesman who sticks his foot in your door and says, "Here's your vacuum cleaner," and he's already got the dirt on your floor, and he's scooping it up, and at the end of it you've bought the vacuum cleaner. Whereas, if he just came in and asked, "Do you need a vacuum cleaner? Here's what a vacuum cleaner does. Here's what mine can do," and he told the truth about everything, people wouldn't buy it. I want them to have the time to consider it, and buy it or not buy it. I won't go into a movie saying, "I've always wanted to do a wide-screen movie. What can I do that needs that technique?" It's always, "What's this story? What do I want to get across? What do I want people to deal with as they are watching this story?" Then, "What are the techniques that I can afford, that can bring it across best?"

There was a period of journalism starting in the late sixties and going through the seventies, the period of Tom Wolfe and Gay Talese and a bunch of these guys, where the subject didn't matter that much. Or the subject was a pretext for some creative writing. And so it was more about a chance for a good writer to throw down their style and make people wonder, "Who's the next victim?" And although I liked reading that journalism, I was never interested in it, because I felt that the article wasn't about this actor or this singer or this politician. The article was about Tom Wolfe, about Gay Talese. And after reading three of their articles, I'd start to see how *they* see the world, but not how the character sees the world. So I guess the kind of journalist I'm interested in is the one where you read the by-line after reading the article, and the name might not make much difference to you. You feel that you've met the people that the story is about. You haven't necessarily met the writer.

Is using music as extensively as you do in this film a way of blowing things by the audience? Isn't the music helping you convey things that aren't there unless you have the music?

What I try to do is use the music to inflate something that is then deflated. Sometimes it's deflated musically, but usually it's deflated by what's going on around you. So the music should underline things. Sometimes you're just riding on it like a surface, and it's what is moving you along. Because these kids are inarticulate, the music is articulate for them, because it's about emotion. The music is so powerful in these kids' lives, and it expresses their emotions so much. The lyrics can be simple, like "Baby, It's You." The lyrics are purposely inarticulate, which is why they are so good. I needed that music, but I also wanted to use it every once in a while as a romantic thing. And sometimes I just wanted it to be exciting, because that's the other part of it, which is there is this incredible energy about these kids, and sometimes it's positive, and sometimes it's destructive.

Why did you use Springsteen's music, given that it's from a later period?

I really just took a chance on that. Almost all of the music is source music as opposed to track music, except for the Springsteen. Everything else is a jukebox, a car radio, whatever, and we made changes in the mix so it flows from the compressed tinny sound of the jukebox and gets wider. Whereas the Springsteen is used editorially and thematically. That's one of the reasons I wanted to use it, so it wasn't just a nostalgic soundtrack. I wrote the songs in, and we cut for them. Then we got in touch with Springsteen through his manager, Jon Landau, and we just said, "Okay, here's a rough cut of the movie. If you hate it, we'll take them out—we've got alternates. If you like it, can you give us a deal?" You have to buy the publishing from one person, which Springsteen owns, and the performance from the record company, CBS in his case. Both Springsteen and Paul Simon gave us a nice deal on their end of it, and CBS charged us what they charged everybody.

You were a fan of Springsteen?

Yeah. I had liked the music musically, but I also liked the writing. I really feel like a good song is like a good short story—it's just more concise and can grab a feeling. If you wanted to know if *City of Hope* reminds me of a short story, it wouldn't be a short story—it would be the Springsteen song, "Meeting Across the River."

Did you consider using Springsteen songs in City of Hope?

In a way, because the film was so much like the songs, it would have been redundant. It would have been a little too on-the-nose for *City of Hope*. In *City Of Hope* I tried to use much more generic music most of the time.

CHAPTER 6

The Brother from Another Planet and *Matewan*

How did you come to receive a MacArthur "Genius" grant?

We were doing the sound mix for *Baby, It's You* and I was really tired and I got a call and I wasn't supposed to get calls into the mixing studio. Somebody said, "Hi, I'm calling from the MacArthur Foundation," which I had never heard of. "You've won a MacArthur Award." I made this free association to *The Front Page* and thought, Oh, it's a newspaper award; Oh God, I have to go make a speech and get a plaque. I said, "Oh, that's great, yeah." And he sounded kind of disappointed at my reaction, and said, "There's a sum of money involved and we were wondering if we could give the *New York Times* your phone number because somebody wants to interview you about this." I said, "Well, I hate to do interviews," and he said, "Well, it would really help us." So I said, "Okay." Then he said, "It's $32,000 a year for five years, tax free." Now I started to pay attention—Whoa! It's based on your age—if you're sixty-five or older you get $65,000 per year for the rest of your life.

Peter Sellars, the opera director, probably got $28,000—he should have waited a couple of years to become a genius, he would have made out better. Bill Irwin did better than I did; he was much older. They had been going for three or four years and it was pretty early in the thing. They hire people to be on the recommendations board in different fields for a year, and they also hire people to be investigators, to go and talk to people that you've worked with and say, "Don't tell this person what this is about but . . ." So they'd talked to a professor I knew in college and then a woman who was a producer of something I wrote and they'd say, Do you think this guy's going to do interesting work in the future? How were they to work with? And do you think this is somewhat innovative stuff? I think the only filmmaker who'd gotten it before was the documentary filmmaker Fred Wiseman. And it turns out that Charles MacArthur, the guy who wrote *The Front Page*, was in fact the brother of John T. MacArthur. He made a fortune in insurance through the mail to poor people during the depression and invested in real estate in Chicago. He was one of these guys who could not stand the idea of paying taxes even after he was dead, so he formed a tax-exempt foundation. Most of the Foundation money goes out every year to mainstream charitable organizations, many in the Chicago area, and a very small percentage is this grant. MacArthur's son challenged the board to do something more interesting and dynamic with it and the so-called Genius grant is the one which gets the most publicity. They give it to twenty people a year, and it only runs for five years.

What did it mean to you at this point?

For me, it meant that for *The Brother from Another Planet* I could spend all my money down to almost nothing and still pay my rent and make the movie because a check came every two months. I was the only investor and I could keep making the movie and not take another writing job because in May I'm going to get another $5,000 or whatever.

This was the period when I was just not having an easy time raising money for movies. The next movie we were going to make after *Baby, It's You*, which tanked, was *Matewan*. In the spring of '83 we had started casting and we were running around trying to get financing for a million and a half. We found a location and had cast a couple of parts, and we were one day from going down to West Virginia and starting the pre-production. We had this one company that put some money into movies and, like most investors, they were doing it through a bank loan. They had to get the bank to sign off on this loan. And the bank said, "We're not giving you more money. You lost money on the last movies you invested in, and you don't have enough collateral to borrow anymore. No." So these guys called up and said, "Oh, by the way, we're not investing in your movie."

I was sitting commiserating with Maggie and Peggy Rajski, who was our partner on that. We had all this momentum and I said, "You know, I have this other idea for a movie, and I've got like $300,000 in the bank. We could make a movie with that." They

Joe Morton in the title role in *The Brother from Another Planet* (1985).

said, "Yeah, what can you make for $300,000?" I said, "Well, I've got this idea about a black extraterrestrial who crash-lands in Harlem." They said, "Right." I said, "No, really!" They said, "Well, if you don't want to shoot in the winter, we'd have to get going pretty quickly." I said, "Look, you start producing it and I'll start writing it, and we can shoot it and get it done before winter." This was probably about August. And I'd say in about six weeks we were shooting.

About the same time I did a play at Williamstown. I played the brother in their first production of *The Glass Menagerie*, with Joanne Woodward, Karen Allen, and James Naughton. They did it again at the Long Wharf with Treat Williams, and then they made a movie with John Malkovich in the part. I think Richard Thomas was going to play it, or Richard Dreyfuss, or one of those Richards, and they fell out at the last minute. Maggie's father had been on the board of this theater, and Nikos Psacharopoulos, who ran that theater, had been a family friend of theirs, and he called Maggie's parents to see if he could track me down—and I was visiting with Maggie. I talked to him on the phone. Two days later I was in the play. It was one of those great last-minute things. It was really hard for me, because I hadn't done stage in a long time, but it was fun, a really good production, nine days, full houses—and then it's over. I don't know if I have the kind of theater chops to do a long run of something, but it was nine good performances. All this was happening about the same time that *Matewan* had fallen apart.

I wrote *The Brother from Another Planet* in a week. I was writing *The Clan of the Cave Bear* at the time, so I had a reading period week in between drafts. I was also adapting *Valley of the Horses*, the book that was the sequel to *The Clan of the Cave Bear*, because originally they were going to shoot both movies at the same time. Then they ran out of money on the first one, they went over budget, and the first movie didn't do well, so they decided, "Never mind." Anyway, I wrote the thing, we started casting it, and I would say, "Whatever money I have in the bank, that's what we have to make it." I wanted to get as many black people as heads of departments as possible, because we were going to shoot in Harlem. I didn't want this to be a totally white movie with some black actors in it. So we started looking for black cinematographers, which are to this day very rare, and Ernest Dickerson's reel came in. And not only was he a black cinematographer, it was the best reel we had seen from anybody for a long time. He had done Spike Lee's *Joe's Bed-Stuy Barbershop* and a couple of other short movies. He was obviously a talented guy. It was a crew where almost everybody was doing a job one job above what they'd ever done before, and that was how we got them for that cheap. But also it was only a four-week commitment. And we just threw ourselves into it, and it was just helter-skelter filmmaking and running around town.

What inspired the story?

I'd had these three dreams. This is the only time I've gotten a movie out of one. The short story "Fission" in *The Anarchists' Convention* came out of dreams. I had a dream when I was in the sound mix of *Baby, It's You*. Sound mixes are really expensive. It's hundreds of dollars an hour and it's a lot of pressure, and I'd been through the whole cutting fight with Paramount, and I started having these dreams, because I wasn't getting much sleep. The first dream was that I was writing a movie for Joe Dante, and it was about these bureaucrats, mostly at the Motor Vehicle Department, with little antennae. They looked like human beings. I just remember seeing the title of it, coming out in 3-D—"Assholes from Outer Space." Then there were these guys saying, "You'll need another form." I woke up from that, and I said, "Well, boy, that's weird— that's like a skit. This is funny. Joe could do a good job with something like that." But I couldn't think of any other ideas except the title. Then I had another dream that I was directing this movie about a Bigfoot, and it was called *Bigfoot in the City*, and I realized this is a remake of *Odd Man Out*, except this is not James Mason, it's a wounded Bigfoot in Seattle, and there was a scene where he's wounded in the back of an alley, and this detective in a trenchcoat comes up and looks down, and there're all the cops around him, and he just goes, "Book him." I woke up. Then I had a third dream. It was a silent dream, and it was just this black guy, and he was wandering around 125th Street, and he just seemed really lost and alienated. Everybody else was talking, and he was just looking. And in the way you realize things in dreams even though they're not spoken, I just said, "Oh, I know. No wonder he's so alienated. He's not from this planet. How alienated can you get?" I woke up and I said, "Well, there's an idea that's kind of interesting. There's a way into Harlem." Who would be a more interesting guide into Harlem than somebody who looked like he belonged but didn't even know what planet this was? When you see somebody walking a dog down the street, he's wondering, "Well, what a strange-looking creature. How does it get that humanoid-looking thing to do all these things for him, like pick up his shit? I just got intrigued with science fiction as a way to get into basically a fairly realistic story.

Is the film an attempt to invoke the Corman/pulp imagination, but translate it into a nonexploitation format?

Absolutely. In the first five minutes of the movie we have some purposely very tacky special effects, to say, "Folks, this isn't *Star Wars*. This is a $1.98 universe you've walked into. This is about the character and not about the special effects." That thing of letting people know what world they've entered is something that I try to do in every film.

The writing style and the dialogue is very different from the films up until then—in particular in the bar scenes there's this idiosyncratic, oblique quality.

Yeah. It's like my short stories. Each character asks for a different style. In this one, because we have a hero who does not speak, and who at first doesn't really even understand what he's hearing, he is privy to a lot of conversations. In fact, many of them are one-way conversations where the people talking think that he understands. Like the white guys say, after he meets them in the bar, "It's really great to talk like this," and he hasn't said a word. So there is that strange rhythm, which is that there are two things happening. There is his story, which is almost a silent movie story. In the first ten or fifteen minutes of the movie, there is hardly any dialogue that's directed at him. You hear voices, but they're on the sound effects track, that's how undirected they are. They're not on the dialogue track. And then, every once in a while, he accesses into somebody's story, somebody's world. So it's like the old "Route 66" TV show or "The Fugitive," who finds his way into somebody else's story, and that would be the story of the week, and then he goes. That's kind of the format of this thing. Eventually some things

Darryl Edwards and Leonard Jackson in *The Brother
from Another Planet.*

tie. They don't tie as tightly as they do in *City of Hope* or *Lone
Star*, but occasionally there will be some kind of connection. But it
is his journey, and it's a journey of assimilation, but he accesses us.
So he works in the video place for a while, and we come back to the
bar and the type of world that a bar can be, which is its own little
unreal world of guys with their dreams and their dialogue.

It's the first of your cross-section movies.

Yeah. It's almost like he's in a short story collection, and he's wandering into these dark short stories. But there is that throughline
of this guy trying to find out about the planet, and he's our eyes.
And what I wanted from those eyes was for us, the audience, to
see things that we usually take for granted in a slightly different
way. So at first it's just by being purely blunt about what is going
on with closeups of things we usually wouldn't do a closeup of,
because they wouldn't have a meaning. Why is this green paper
going into somebody's hands, and somebody taking food? So he
goes over thinking, "Well, if I give her some money, she'll give me
some food. So I go and open the cash register, I hand her the

money, and now can I take the food?" Then he sees a cop, with a guy spread-eagled up against a car, and then he sees another cop, and like there's this guy with different skin than him and he's got this badge and this club, and he's got this guy—I think it was Giancarlo Esposito—spread-eagled. And then he's running away, and he looks, and there's a crucifix—"Oh my God, this is a tough planet. Get out of line here, and they nail you to wood."

So once again it's about shifting to a new point of view that gives a different perspective.

Right. And then he starts to identify Harlem and this subculture of black America as a neighborhood—and what's going on there? What is this stuff that they're putting in their arms? What does that do to you? That's very much inspired by the Rinehart episode in Ralph Ellison's *Invisible Man* where he puts these sunglasses on. And with the sunglasses everybody thinks he's this guy Rinehart, and guys start coming up to him, "Hey, Rinehart, man, what's going on?" And he realizes that this guy Rinehart is a Pentecostal preacher, a pimp, six different things. It's almost like X-ray specs. The minute he puts them on, they show him a whole different Harlem than he, as an outsider, ever saw before. He's walking the same streets, but he has an in. So the brother smokes some dope and all of a sudden he's got this guy named Virgil who takes him through nighttime Harlem, and it's kind of weird and fucked-up.

I also wanted to talk about waste. Here's a guy with incredible talents that he's going to have to hide, that he's not going to be able to develop. He's going to be able to do it in tiny little ways. He'll be able to fix the video machine. But once he learns the way the world works, and that that's going to get him a kind of attention he doesn't want, he's going to have to cover it up. So much of it is about assimilation, just as in *Baby, It's You*. The second half of *Baby, It's You* questions what you gain and what you lose when you join that new world. Joe Morton's character in *City of Hope* questions the same thing: "What do I have to give up of the old neighborhood guy to be this new guy?" Most of the kids I grew up with were sons and daughters of immigrants or immigrants themselves. At what point do you stop being Italian and start being Italian American? At the beginning of the film when he's at Ellis Is-

Joe Morton in *The Brother from Another Planet.*

land, he walks through this crowd of other people, and he hears the vibes of all these languages. One of the first people he meets is a Korean woman. She's not yelling at him in English—she's yelling in Korean.

So in effect the film compresses into two hours an entire experience of acculturation and assimilation.

Oh yeah. Each time we see him, he moves and looks a little more like one of us. He stops wearing those weird clothes by the end. I said to Joe, "As you start to understand things, you're less lost. You're watching people move, and you learn how to move like them. But what do you lose?" At the end there is what I call the E.T. Stays Here scene, where the guy says, "Here. We're not going home. We're stuck here." All the aliens who he meets are assimilated, but they are not doing the things that they're capable of doing, they're keeping them quiet. And there's this theme of there being things that are offered in the culture that are looked down on, but they're never made unavailable—in fact, they are very often very available—that narcotize people and keep them from getting to the point where they are ready to physically revolt. While he's playing this video game, he's hooked on that. Other guys are drinking. The two kids are starting to shoot up. The little boy is hooked into the TV. There is a sense about this stuff that it may not be a conspiracy, but the dominant culture wants that stuff out there and it does its job—it chills people out. The same thing in *City of Hope*. A lot of what David Strathairn's character in *City* is spouting is about that. It's about mass culture. He's hooked into something. You know, a couple of hundred years ago, or even fifty years ago, it would have been somebody saying "The end is near" and "Jehovah" and all that kind of religious stuff. Well, the new gods that look over us all are mass media—and they are tranquilizers to a certain extent. So when the brother gets interested in women, what he sees are not necessarily live women. They're all those big sex posters for sneakers or for Colt-45, and he tunes into that.

To what extent is the Dante's Inferno sequence a structural turning point in the film? It seems to me that after that tour, he becomes much more of a protagonist.

It gives him a focus, which is not just to survive, but to understand what's going on. And eventually he actually does something about it. He is trying to assimilate up to that point, but then he sees something is seriously wrong with this place. And he cuts deeper and deeper until he comes to this dope, and then he says, "I'm going to follow this dope and see where it leads." When dope is prosecuted, it's like in *Alligator*—social problems are prosecuted when they finally get out of the poorest neighborhoods. When Richard Price was doing research for *Clockers* over in Jersey City, the cops there called the ghetto a self-cleaning oven—"we just take the bodies out every once in a while." And it's the point where you realize the brother really has some character. He's going to risk his butt a little bit, that's when he puts himself the most at risk, from these men in black who are basically intergalactic slave-catchers, based on UFO lore. I liked this idea that there was somebody following him, to keep that runaway slave thing going.

What did you have in mind for the inferno sequence stylistically?

What I wanted was the idea that, if he is the guide for us, he would have a guide to something he would ordinarily not see, and that literally his consciousness was going to be altered. So he actually takes this dope. The Rasta lifestyle was based on the idea that herb was a religious sacrament, and that these guys who stay stoned all day long, twenty-four hours a day, were living in this parallel reality, which that will do for you. Time is very different, things have a different edge on them. I was interested in that being one of the levels he would go to. And also getting him to something even more concrete and real and gritty, and to some kind of slave reality. Virgil says something like, "Take the ship back." Get on board this thing, and you're going to see and connect with things that you wouldn't normally connect with. We started talking about the colors you see at night, and Caribbean colors, and those sodium vapor lights, which give a lot of yellow backlight. Without necessarily going fuzzy with the focus, we wanted to change the color scheme and get those real hard, stark things that you see at night when you're out at three in the morning in New York City where somebody is banging themselves against a wall underneath a streetlight, and then it falls off to nothing. We came up with my favorite shot just because of what was going on at the moment. We were shooting in Harlem all night long, and people just stayed up and followed us around. We were guests there—I didn't want cops moving them around. We told the cops, "Stay two blocks away—if we have any trouble with anybody, we'll call you," because we didn't want to draw the negative energy that cops draw in a situation like that. So we had about a hundred people, and it was about three in the morning, in the shot where he's just taken the dope, and I wanted to do a 360 pan, and when we came back to him he was stoned. And it was just clear that there was nowhere for us to put these hundred onlookers. Ernest said, "Well, what if I go away from them, and I go up over them and into the streetlights, and when we come down he's stoned?" I said, "Yeah, and while we're up there, he can come real close, so we can change the focus, and he'll be right in our face." That just came out of me wanting to do something woozy with the camera and the fact that those people were there. It's just a reeling shot.

How did having an almost silent film narrative affect the acting?

Most of what you see in the film is a first take. We mostly did about three of anything. Joe did a really good thing, which is he stayed away from the other actors. I did rehearsals where it was just about blocking, no acting. So once the actors got in a situation with him, because very often he was meeting people for the first time, they would do what people usually do when there's somebody who doesn't speak their language or who is deaf—they talked a little louder and a little slower. So we really got better performances out of them on the first take. Joe came up with the idea that he had to see their eyes to understand what they were saying. So if they would be talking to him and look away, he'd get over in their eyes—there was something a little weird about his body motions. We didn't really have a title for the film—it was *The Harlem Project* or whatever. We were thinking about plays on *The Man Who Fell to Earth* but didn't like anything. Joe had been on *Another World* and one day Ernest Dickerson heard someone say, "Hey, there's the brother from *Another World*—I know that guy." Then we made some joke about "the brother from another planet" and it just clicked.

Most of the stuff that David Strathairn and I did, unless we were talking, which is usually static, we did backwards. We would start in the seats, and back out of the bar. It gives a weird feeling to the motion. And when we walked out on the street, we had cars backing up for the shot, so that we actually were backing into the bar, and cars were backing up. It's fun on such a cheap movie to play around with that stuff. What superpowers does he have that we can do very cheaply? Most of our effects were $1.98 things like the eyeball point of view. Ernest Dickerson came up with the idea of step-printing, where you print the first frame three times, and then the other two are in sequence, and then the next one is three times, so you get this strange, almost pixillated quality.

What was it like making a film for the first time out on the streets, in a community where you were an outsider?

It was actually pretty good. It was hectic, because we had so much to shoot in four weeks. So we were really as mobile as possible. One good thing about Harlem is you can find parking. And we shot there before crack. There were junkies and street people and

Joe Morton and Dee Dee Bridgewater in *The Brother
from Another Planet.*

all that, but there wasn't crack. We decided very early not to de-
populate the blocks and then repopulate them with extras. I said,
"New York City has done all our art direction and our extras for
us—why not take advantage of it?" People in Harlem have things
to do. They've got to go to work, so people didn't hang and watch
us forever. So the first scene we shot was the scene where he's
walking on 125th Street, and you see all those people there. We
had some of our extras and people who had certain lines in certain
languages and we just put them in the flow. I wrote dialogue for
each of the people that we planted there. There was a West Indian
woman behind him, who was having a conversation with her
friend, or there was a Haitian guy talking—because I wanted the
alien to go through these waves of languages. Then there's this
Puerto Rican actor who's having an argument with his wife who is
up in a window. Well, there wasn't an actual window. On one of
our takes, you can see somebody stops behind this guy, and looks
up—"Who the fuck is he arguing with?"—and finally just shrugs
and walks away. And every take was different because different
people would be criss-crossing with them. We never said, "No-

body can come through this frame," unless it was supposed to be deserted, and then we'd go at an hour when nobody was there. So we basically said, "There's going to be a documentary. Whenever we're out on the street, we're talking documentary here. And there's a guy in weird clothes. Some people are going to look at him, and guess what? Because it's New York City and it's 125th Street, some people are going to walk right by him and they're not going to look"—which is exactly what happened.

Did you encounter any hostility in the community?

Every once in a while you'd get a street character who didn't like white people, who would scream. My first AD, Craig, was great at this—he was this black guy almost my size who dresses much better than I do, so everybody thought he was the director and I was only the PA—he would basically engage whoever was crazy and just start talking with them, but drift away from the set. So by the time we were ready to shoot, the argument would be a block away. He'd just keep going until he felt like we'd had enough time to shoot. But usually people were just interested and would say, "Well, that's cool. Don't tell me any more—I want to see this." So it was really nice.

How did the film come to be picked up by independent distributor Cinecom?

Lianna had been in Cannes during critics' week, Semaine des Critiques. And we just figured, "Well, we'll try to get invited to Cannes, but if we don't, we'll put the money up ourselves. I have some money left. We'll go there, spend some, and just show it." Well, we didn't get invited. Maggie and the other producers and the foreign sales agents cooked up a plan. We did a radio contest on the local rock-and-roll station where we gave away round-trip tickets to Harlem, because we wanted to get teenagers in to prove that the moviegoing audience and even white people would like it. And the radio people did a good job, and we had a theater full of French kids for a subtitled movie—and we made sure there were enough seats and told the half-dozen players in the world of independent film distributing then, "This is where you're going to see this movie. We're not going to have any other screenings. Send somebody to see it." It got a good reaction, and it actually worked—there was a tiny feeding frenzy, not a huge frenzy like there would be now. We got three or four offers. Cinecom basically made the best offer—not the highest, but the best as far as commitment to the film, and they seemed to understand it. They did a very good job with the film. They had just started business, but they had some good people working for them, like Ira Deutchman. Until *Lone Star* it was probably our most successful film in terms of the money that we made back that we made back over its budget, and our production company actually made money.

Next, you did three music videos for Bruce Springsteen. How did that come about?

Bruce and Jon Landau had seen *Baby, It's You* and liked it, and this was right when he decided he wanted to actually be in one of his videos. He'd already done one with Brian De Palma, "Dancing in the Dark." He called up and said, "I want this one to be a little

John Sayles and David Strathairn in *The Brother from Another Planet*.

more gritty." I said, "I can do gritty." The first was "Born in the U.S.A." We shot that in 16 mm, and Bruce didn't want to lip-sync, so we had to rough-sync it. We shot three concerts in L.A. to get the performance part, and then we went around Jersey and shot a lot of documentary—and Ernest Dickerson shot most of that. Michael Ballhaus came in and ran one of the cameras at the concerts. I liked the documentary stuff. I had a good time cutting it. There's a lot of hard cutting, and then some nice dissolves. That went well, and then we did the other two in fairly short order.

The video for "I'm on Fire" is particularly distinctive. It has some of the dreamy lyrical style of Baby, It's You *and it pushes the boundaries of what you could do in the music video form in terms of a narrative framework.*

We went slicker with it; Michael Ballhaus shot it in 35 mm. The idea was to have something with that slow burn. Springsteen came up with the story. He said, "I've got an idea about a guy who's on the outside looking in, and we may or may not see the woman. There's something in between them, and he's not going to get her." And we talked a little, and then he had this idea, "What if he's a guy who works on her car?" And I really liked that. It also was the first time he was going to be playing a character, and I wanted to give him an entrance—you know, like they did in old-fashioned movies. I thought, "Well, where should Bruce Springsteen come in? What's his image?" And I thought he should slide out from under a car, with some grease on him. I mean, what a beautiful entrance for this guy. The other element is the woman and her world, and something dreamy about that, with long dissolves. And also the music has more of that, it's not a percussive thing, it's really a mood song. It's a simple song that repeats itself quite a bit, but we wanted a story that didn't repeat, that had a through-line. It starts in this garage, and then he gets his nerve up to go to her house, and he goes there, there's the lights—and because it's not *Body Heat* he doesn't break the door down. Because the song doesn't resolve in that way. It's still heat and longing. And the same thing happened in "Glory Days." Bruce had this idea about a guy who used to be a pitcher, but now he's got a family. And he wanted an intro and an "outro" to it, a bookend for the thing, and he wanted the band in it—so it inter-

weaves a story and Bruce Springsteen and the E-Street Band. So
he's telling a story as Bruce Springsteen, but in the story he's playing a character.

*Did you view these three commissions as a chance to work on
technique?*

You have a little more time and a little more money to do those
three minutes than I usually spend on three minutes of a film. It's
like directors I know who work on commercials. They say, "God!
They give you cranes and smoke. . . ." You're shooting a lot of
MOS, meaning without sound, so you could spend a little more
time on the lighting and the movement. I was going to cut them
and play with them, but I already had the music I was going to cut
them to. So it was a very, very focused kind of thing. And they're
narrative. They're not expressionistic like a lot of rock videos,
where it's just something interesting while the boys are singing the
song. I'm not that interested in non-narrative stuff. I'm interested
in looking at it, but not necessarily making it.

Have you considered doing any since?

I haven't been that interested, mostly because in the music business, the bullshit aspect of it is more intense than in the movie
business. Bruce Springsteen's people we knew, and in the music
business, they're a miracle: They're reasonable. They know what
they want. He's not called "the Boss" for nothing. He controls his
life. So we were able to duck into that world and get all the coop-
eration we needed. But it's a couple of weeks out of your life. It
just didn't seem like the way I wanted to make a living.

How did you relaunch Matewan?

Brother did very well, not well enough for people to be banging
down our door, offering us money, but Cinecom did so well with it
they felt, "Well, what do you want to do next?" and I said, "What
we've been trying to do is *Matewan*." It was eight years since I
wrote it. And everything cost more. Insurance had gone way up.
There was a silver crisis and the Hunt brothers in Texas took advantage of it, and because film stock is based on silver, Kodak was

able to jack their prices up. So all of a sudden, this million-and-a-half-dollar movie is a $3.6 million movie, which is a little hard to put together. Cinecom couldn't afford or didn't want to put in $3.6 million, so they ended up piecing a deal together where I put in a bunch of money, we found some independent money, they got a couple of partners to put in a little, and they put in a little. So it was this pastiche of money.

Can you describe the writing process for the film, given that it derives from material in your novel Union Dues?

Well, a lot of it was the research into the coal wars and the labor history of the twenties and thirties in America, and the rise of the unions that I did for *Union Dues*, and then I extrapolated it. I put in more about the coal-mining industry, right down to getting Bureau of Statistics reports on which mines still had mules in them, and who was still picking and shoveling, how mechanized was this mine, what was the racial makeup. And they had statistics on that stuff; not complete ones, but enough around so I really was able to get a good picture of it. Reading old copies of the leftist publications at the time, reading the *UMW Journal* when it first started. And then reading the national news media, which were all very anti-union, and then the local West Virginia papers, which were rabidly anti-union because they were owned by the coal operators. Then saying, "Okay, what do they all agree on? Is there anything they all agree on? Then I can pretty much say that probably did happen, and then let's see the biases of each of these groups."

Is Matewan *a true story, or is it a composite?*

The characters whose personal lives you don't get into are almost all based on real guys: the Sheriff Sid Hatfield and the Mayor, Cabell Testerman, even the agent provocateur, are all based on real guys. The people whose personal lives we get into, like Joe Kenehan and Elma Radnor, are all composites of people I had read about in autobiographies or diaries. Joe Kenehan is a composite of a bunch of organizers, Wobblies, Socialists, and nonaffiliated guys who just got involved in things. Danny's character is a composite of guys' accounts of their life as young miners. There really was a big black guy named Few Clothes, the character played by James Earl Jones.

We accept
company scrip
50¢ to the $1.00

Sayles on the set of *Matewan* (1987).

And the actual scenario with the state of siege and the company bringing in black workers and then Italians?

That's based on places other than Matewan. But there were scabs brought in. The racial mix was different, but in West Virginia in general there was this policy that was called the "judicious mixture," and they really got down to percentages. You had to have a certain percentage of blacks, because the coal mines in Alabama had just tapped out, so you were able to get blacks from Alabama who were experienced. You were able to get people out of Ellis Island who had no experience at all, but they were so hungry they would go down and risk their lives—Italians, Yugoslavs, and Greeks mostly. And then a certain amount of mountain people. And the mountain people, you didn't want too many of them, because they would form unions if you left them to their own—but if you had these three different groups who didn't like each other and you kept them apart, they figured their natural antagonism will keep them from making a union. But the common enemy was so bad, they actually did sneak around and form unions. And there really was a shootout on Main Street.

The baseball game in Matewan *offers a brief interlude of utopian community. Were you in some sense anticipating* Eight Men Out, *and do you really buy the idea of baseball as some kind of idealistic expression of coexistence?*

I was getting at something that I've touched on in some of the other films—that in the alleged melting pot of America, music and sports are the first places that people start to melt. In *Matewan* there's what we called "The Birth of the Blues" scene, where one guy is playing the mandolin, and the hillbillies start listening to him, and then all of a sudden the black guy in the next camp over starts playing his harmonica. Well, that's American music—these guys, even before they would sit on the same stage, would cop stuff from each other. And in sports, though black guys didn't get in professionally, certainly on a town level black teams and white teams were always playing each other, and in fact there were quite a few integrated teams. Even the Italians were yelling and everything, and within a generation there was Joe DiMaggio. I also wanted that feeling of the lull before the storm. It was also somewhat based on the Ludlow Massacre in Colorado in 1913, this other incident that the Baldwin-Felts Agency was involved in. The week before the massacre, the National Guard played baseball with the striking miners, and then a week later they were killing them. There is this kind of neutrality to sports. It's a great thing for men to have. And I think in times of contention, even in the late sixties, you could go to a baseball game, and there would be hippie baseball fans right next to hardhats. In this country you very rarely fight with each other physically over sports things, even if you're for the Mets and the other guy is for the Phillies and you have an argument. But if you get into politics, people get serious.

To what extent do you regard your body of work as political? Certainly Matewan *was your most political subject to date and was made at the height of Reaganism. Did that place you in an oppositional position?*

Yeah. I think that it was important for people to remember why there were unions. One of the first things Reagan did when he got in was bust the Air Traffic Controllers Union, and he picked exactly the right one to bust because they make a lot of money. Now, most of what they were complaining about was not their salaries—it was their hours and safety. And almost everything they complained about the next five years they got. It's just that those guys all got busted out of the union. They were just replaced. So what was the original situation in which unions were formed? That situation doesn't exist necessarily in that many places today in the United States, but it certainly exists all throughout the Third World.

I was also interested, when doing my research, in finding out just how polyglot the miners were in those days, which made me pick that incident, rather than just having something where it was just all white guys who were on strike. I wanted to get into the way in which democracy and the melting pot work when there is a common enemy, and how you could already, even at Matewan, see the strains of racism and ethnicity pulling at it, and the minute that that common enemy either goes away or becomes a little less oppressive, you feel like it's likely to pull itself apart—which is pretty much what happened in most of those unions, including the UMW. Every once in a while one of the characters will say, "I don't see why we should listen to a bunch of hunkies out in Pittsburgh about what we do here," and Joe Kenehan is constantly saying, "No, the minute you join this, you have to give something up." Which to me is not just the story of unions, but the story of organized society. What are you willing to give up to be a member of the United States or a member of a team, or married? It can be boiled down to just two people.

This is a recurring motif in your work—the realities of trade off and compromise. And Kenehan is a relatively moderate figure—he's not preaching revolution, only social justice and collective interdependence.

It's why he's a Wobbly and not a Socialist. The Wobblies tended to be the least skilled workers, like lumberjacks and farmworkers, rather than skilled workers who had come from Europe. So Kenehan is this guy who has certain ideals, but they are very American ones. So he can talk to these hillbillies and get them across. I thought the true crux of the whole thing is the conversation he has with the character Cephus, who says, "Look, you're going to leave here and you're going to go organize somewhere else, and what is good for the union movement as a whole may just get us fucked up. We've got to stay in this hollow."

Do you feel any affinity with what he stands for?

Well, I feel an affinity for it. But I think that it is this dream that has remained alive in the United States. Doctrinaire Marxism never really made much of a dent here. It was something that was brought in from Europe. Emma Goldman and people like that influenced the labor movement very much in this country. But really, on a personal basis, it was not a strong American thing. There was this more Wobbly kind of individual-within-the-group kind of thing that was around, even before the Wobblies existed. Rather than seeing a huge picture of an eventual one-world worker class, they were much more specific. "This is what we want here." It didn't have the analysis that the Marxists did. It did not posit, for instance, "We need a New Man," and that's what Marxism always says when it starts running into the wall of the people who are supposed to be embracing it, resisting it. They say, "Well, besides a new system, we need a new man, a new consciousness." Whereas the American strain, that home-bred strain of the Wobblies, said, "You're just fine. You don't have to change. Here's what we want you to get together and do." There was just a populism to it. At its worst it's a bunch of survivalists who worry about black helicopters. And at best, it's a way of thinking of the government skeptically, which I think is healthy.

You seem less interested in Kenehan as a character than as an activist.

He's an itinerant preacher, and he's not a phony. He's preaching union, and that's what he came to do, and he's trying not to get more involved personally. So he's somebody with a mission. And it is really hard for people to deal with somebody like that, because he is going to go somewhere else. That was one of the beauties when I started doing the research and having it be set in Hatfield-and-McCoy territory—the Hatfields and McCoys are the epitome

Chris Cooper as Kenehan in *Matewan.*

of personal business turning into violence and vendetta. All the stuff that as a good labor guy makes you say, "You've got to forget that. I don't care if you're a Hatfield and he's a McCoy—we have a common enemy, and we have to join ranks and fight against it." So yeah, he is a tough character for them all to deal with. And the person who looks up to him the most, of course, is this young kid who wants to be a preacher, who has a messianic streak in him and feels like he can change the world the way that Jesus did.

But Kenehan is perhaps the only idealized character you've ever created—is there a gray area in him?

The gray area for me is that he's making this up as he goes. The Wobblies were not a very old organization when they were broken apart. He's a guy who had just come to this new religion, who is trying to figure it out and apply it. So he is very likely to get his people killed. Both my novel *Los Gusanos* and the film *City of Hope* are interesting in this regard. They both posit that believers can cause as much trouble as cynics. You might like the believers a little bit more, but whether they're Shi'ites, union men, or pro-lifers, they cause trouble because they absolutely believe.

In contrast, his opponents in the film, the Baldwin-Felts agents Hickey and Griggs and the company spy, are too exaggerated and cartoonish—they're too moustache twirling.

Well, according to William Goldman: What is true and what people will believe in a movie are two different things. I had to tone those guys down. When there would be relief efforts for those tent camps, and the Red Cross or some organization would bring milk in, the Baldwin-Felts guys would intercept them and put kerosene in the milk for the kids who were starving. They were basically hired killers. But a lot of people have said the same thing, and my only reaction is that from what I was reading, these guys were basically hired to break heads and, if needed, kill people. It really was, "This guy is giving us trouble—he's got to go," and they'd disappear in the woods somewhere. Basically they were the same as the regulators in the West that Cimino tried to get into a little in *Heaven's Gate*.

But there are characters in some of your other films, for instance the cop in City of Hope, *who function as bad guys, but who you nonetheless represent with some dimensionality. We see that they are carrying their own kind of emotional baggage.*

Well, the cops in *City of Hope* also live in that city. They are from there. They go out there every day. They are connected to it in a way that, if they were soldiers in Vietnam, they wouldn't be. So to a certain extent, all we know about Hickey is that he's had this heavy-duty experience in World War I, and that he hasn't come back from that—he's stayed in battle in his own way. That's what I talked to the actor about.

What is Danny's function in the narrative? On one level he's telling the story but on another he's the subject.

He's the narrator, you hear from him three times. It's his voice bringing you in, and bringing you out. But he is the guy who, to me, can go either way. You know the famous mining song, "Which Side Are You On?" There are a couple of points in the movie where people go one way or the other. One is when the scab miners, the blacks and the Italians, decide to throw their shovels down and walk out. They know that they are going to get creamed, but they make the decision: "Okay, we're going to at least feel good about ourselves while we're getting creamed." Then there's a really important scene at the very end when Danny can just kill this unarmed Baldwin-Phelps guy, who is really just along for the ride, but he's one of the enemy, and he waves him across the river instead of blowing him away. So there is this struggle for Danny's soul, and the struggle is not whether he's going to be a union man or a company man—the struggle is whether he's going to hook into this idea of nonviolence that Joe Kenehan brings; basically, whether he's going to go with the New Testament or the Old Testament. There are the hard-shell Baptists and the soft-shell Baptists, and there is enormous justification for violence in most mountain people's version of religion, because it is the Old Testament, "an eye for an eye."

Will Oldham as Danny in *Matewan*.

Why do you end the film with Danny as an old man coming down the mine corridor?

Well, there is a contrapuntal thing going on there, between what he's saying—which is, "From then on I preached Union"—and the fact that he's a coal miner again, went back into the mine, and took what the company offered. And what he's saying is, "We lost. We won the battle and lost the war, and it was another fifteen years before we got the union in there." And that was pretty much the story of the labor movement: there were these incredible outbreaks of violence but usually what happened is the workers went back with very little to show for it.

One of the film's original insights is its connection between the labor movement and grassroots religion.

I think if you look into the real hard-core Marxists and Anarchists in Britain, there is something religious about their quest. Not the massive labor movement, but the purists. There is a Puritanism that often came with it. And you had to take an awful lot on faith, you had to have faith in humanity, in Marx. The established Baptist churches in West Virginia really fought against the union, because very often the coal companies built the churches. On purpose. They built the school, they built the church, they built the newspaper, and they controlled all the social organs. The hard-shell preacher I played really believes that his reading of the Scripture tells him that union people are in league with the anti-Christ—he's an absolute believer. But that's one of the things that is tough about it all—there can be wonderful stuff in religion, but it can be used to chop people's heads off. And the same thing with any political belief; you can pervert it, just in the way you read it and interpret it.

As an independent filmmaker, what's your relationship to the film industry unions?

Well, it's been different on every film. On *Matewan* we said, "Well, we're making a movie about a union." *Matewan* was our first all-union film. We had both NABET and IA on it. Haskell Wexler and his camera department came from the IA and all the other crew people were NABET. It would not have been possible for us to have had as many heads of department as we had be black on *Brother from Another Planet* and also be a union picture. It may be possible now because of Spike Lee and other people who have gotten a lot more black people into the technical end of the business. You can film nonunion in New York City if you can justify how low your budget is. On *Lianna*, we basically ended up paying the Teamsters not to show up, because we were right under their noses and it was just an understood thing that, you know, here's what we would pay. But they didn't expect to work for that much, and it was fine. The thing is, even within the movie business, because of the Taft-Hartley Act, each of the separate crafts has its own union. So by the time of *Baby, It's You*, we were a Screen Actors Guild signatory. I think we may even have been a signatory to SAG on *Lianna*, but nobody was in SAG. So that's one guild. I was in the Writers Guild through all of them, so I got paid at least minimum Writers Guild for those things, which is usually what I took.

The one thing that I don't like to do is just accept the roster. That's sometimes what you're expected to do with IA and the Teamsters, which is, "Well, you can't pick which people you're going to hire—you're just going to have to accept the people we send over." We've never agreed to do that. Not even in Ireland, when the union guys came to us and said, "Well, you're going to need five people for this job, and then we'll tell you which five." We said, "No, we've already asked enough Irish directors to give us a list of people, and we've already made offers to them. So if you don't want those people to work on the picture, you, the union, is going to have to go and fire them—we're not firing them." And they backed off then. The movies we make have a different rhythm and a different hierarchy than regular movies. We really need to get a crew who know what that is and can accept it. There is a bit more of a spirit of everybody helps with everything. You know, there's none of this, "My job description is to pull the plug out of the wall, not to put it back in, so even if I'm the one next to the plug, and everybody's waiting for the plug to be put back in, it's not my job." We just don't do that. It's basically, "Look, we're trying to get this thing done. We shoot very fast. We try not to waste your time." So if stuff needs to be carried everybody, including the actors, grabs something and carries it away. It's harder and harder, but we try to break down this kind of separation between the crew and the talent.

Above the line, below the line.

Yeah. People are pretty much always staying in the same hotel, you stand in line to get your food. There are a lot of union rules that force us to be more hierarchical than we want to be. For instance, lunch doesn't officially start until the last union guy has gone through the line. So if you have fifty extras on that day, unless you want to add another half-hour to lunch and lose that half-hour for shooting, you have to take those fifty extras aside and sit them down and put the crew through the food line, then let the extras go. Which I really don't like, but it's going to cost us too much money.

To a certain extent, film producers view the unions as an obstacle. You're on that side of the fence.

Yeah, absolutely. It's not that they're an obstacle. It's that their rules, especially IA, were formed when things were made in the studio. They weren't formed for little fly-by-night, independent productions out shooting on location. So their hours and this, that, and the other thing are all set up for, "Okay, you go to the studio; you punch in; you do this much work; then it's lunchtime; then you come back; you punch back in; you do this much work; and then if you go overtime you get paid this much." Most of those rules still make sense if you're working on a TV show mostly on sets, whether it's in the Valley in L.A., or someplace in New York. But for independent features, they just don't make sense anymore. And most of the guilds have been pretty slow in dealing with it. I just rejoined the Directors Guild so that Maggie and her producing partner Paul Miller could get into the health plan. I joined for *Baby, It's You*, because our producers felt that with three million dollars and a very ambitious movie, we really needed an experienced production manager. Since Bobby Colesberry, our production manager, was in the union, he couldn't work on the picture unless the director was in. So I joined. But I said to the guy who was the head of it at that time, "What happens when I go back and try to make a movie for a half-million dollars or less, and you have these rules that the first AD and the second AD, or the director, have to have thirteen weeks guaranteed? I'm making movies in four and five weeks here. One AD would be a third of my budget." And he basically said, "You can't make a movie for a half-million dollars." I said, "Well, what if I can and I want to?" He answered, "Well, maybe we're not the organization for you." They were that inflexible. So the minute I went back and made *Brother from Another Planet*, it was clear I couldn't stay in. So I quit. In the Writers Guild, you're just a writer—you don't need a first assistant writer or a second assistant writer or a production manager writer. The DGA is a very good union and gets good minimums for its people and good guarantees of time, and that meant I couldn't afford to be in it—we were so far below their radar.

How did you feel about making Baby, It's You *as a negative pickup, which studios use to circumvent unions?*

I don't have any problem with it, because basically they only dare to do it on movies that really should have been made independently. The minute they got over say three million dollars, they went with the studio. They knew they were going to ruffle feathers too much. And everybody knew it was happening, and the IA's attitude was, "If you want to make some kind of semi-experimental student movie for three million, more power to you. Just make sure you call us when you make *Tootsie*."

On Matewan *a key decision was bringing in Haskell Wexler. How did that come about?*

I had actually never met Haskell, but I had talked to him for an hour or so on the phone once, when he had finished directing *Latino* and was looking for a distributor and needed some advice on independent distributors. So I gave him some advice about the players at that time. Then Maggie and I were driving, some long, cross-country drive, and I was reading to her from this book, *Masters of Light*, about a bunch of cinematographers, and we read the Haskell Wexler section, and Maggie said, "This sounds like the perfect guy to shoot *Matewan*." Anyway, we tried to get in touch with Haskell. We were already down in West Virginia, and we got a message from the woman at the desk at the hotel. She said, "Well, somebody named Haxall Wicksler called, and he said he was calling from his car. And he said, 'Whatever they're askin', the answer is yes.'"

What was his impact on the film's look?

Having seen *Bound for Glory* and how he handled period in that, I felt "Well, here's a guy who's hasn't always had the hugest budget in the world. He's done color, he's done black and white, he's done many different styles, so he's not married to one, and all of them have worked. Plus, he understands what the movie's about." When we shot the scene where the Italian miners turn back at the head of the mine singing "Avanti Popolo," he turned to me and said, "I think I'm the only cinematographer in Hollywood who knows the words to that song." The difficulty was that we didn't have the money to build anything, and most of the coal camp stuff that you see in the beginning of the movie isn't there. You know, there will be five houses in a row way over in this part of the state, and there will be a piece of a coal tipple way over in this other part. The town where we shot most of it didn't have a main street, it just had a railroad track. But it's all spread out. The opening sequence when they're walking out of the mine and down the hill to the town was shot in twelve different parts of the state, maybe eight different weeks. We were going halfway across the state to shoot an eighth of a page, and Haskell had to figure out what time of day to shoot so we had the most possibility of getting light that's going to match the shots on either side.

We really thought a lot about light in the prep. In *Thinking in Pictures: The Making of Matewan*, I talk about thinking about the philosophy of how to shoot a color film when the pictures that people have from the era are black and white. What do you do with the palette of colors? What do you do to give that feeling of being warm? I find that sometimes when you go with gauzy effects, when you prefog the film—*McCabe and Mrs. Miller* is a good example—there's a point at which it gets a little daguerreotype, and it loses some of its weight. One of the movies I talked to Haskell about was *The Wild Child*, and just how everything was very solid. You just feel like you hear that wood knock and it has weight to it. We wanted to take the edge off things so it didn't look like a Disney movie, but we didn't want to lose the weight of everything, because it's about coal-mining and people who have to work all the time. Even Mary McDonnell's character, you never see her when she's not doing some kind of physical work. And so we talked about using neutral density filters rather than sepia or something like that, which will change the color, and doing it not so much in post-production but by controlling everything that went in front of the camera and knocking it down—knocking the signage down, knocking down the clothes, putting coal shmutz on them and washing them a zillion times. They had lye soap back then. That's how you got stuff out, which weathered the clothes really quickly. So it's a functioning town, but everything looks really worn, and that gives you the feeling of some weight and some age and the place having been lived in. We had to be careful with the color red—you'll notice you see very, very little red. And we did that with the production designer Nora Chavooshian.

Wexler's use of artificial light is very natural and almost painterly.

Yeah. One of the advantages that we had is that people were still using kerosene lanterns, so your sources can be very beautiful. We were shooting at eight candlepower at one point—it's really tough to shoot at eight candlepower (that's eight candles' worth, you know) down in the mine, so there's not that much to see, but you let everything else fall out. He's really good with exterior light coming into a day interior and letting that light fix. One thing that I like to do, once we've seen who the characters are, is to not show every detail of their face every time we see them again. I tend not to play them totally in darkness—the actors don't like it and it's hard on the audience. But I'm willing to have them go through darkness for a line or two, or to just have one little Gordon Willis-y piece of light on their face. Also, Haskell's speed-to-quality ratio is very high, and when you're making a low-budget movie that's very ambitious and you don't have much time to do it, that's what you need. There are guys who can do beautiful stuff, but they just can't do it that fast.

This is the first film where you seem to achieve a freedom in terms of complex staging.

Harlem is a character in *Brother from Another Planet*, but *Matewan* is the first movie where I really felt like the physical place itself was part of what I could use to create mood. Even though you're outside, you're not on the Great Plains. It's not a Western.

The shootout at the climax of *Matewan*.

The claustrophobia of those hills on both sides, of being penned in by those things. Oh, guess what: You're in this hollow—there is no escape. We really talked about that quite a bit. Originally we wanted this huge coal tipple, a big tower with a chute coming down to the railroad track that went through town, that would dominate the sky. As it was, there was a big water tower, which helped give a feeling of domination.

To stage the shootout at the end, I got a bunch of toy soldiers from the A&P. . . . We had only two days to shoot a lot of footage and I had to storyboard it. I wanted to start very architectural, like *Shane* or one of those gunfight pictures, where you keep the integrity of the directionality when people are shooting at each other, the architecture of the continuity. My model for after the gunfight, was a massacre. It wasn't a fair gunfight or anything like that. It was a mess. People on the miners' side were killed by crossfire or just were in the wrong place at the wrong time. I had seen *La Notte di San Lorenzo/Night of the Shooting Stars*, and there's this fight in the cornfield at the end between the Fascists and the Partisans where they're just banging into each other, and you can't see and you're very likely to shoot one of your own people. I wanted that kind of chaos once the lead started flying. There were one or two shots I didn't use, and one or two things that we were able to combine, so instead of doing three angles, we found a way with a camera move to really make it flow, which was nice.

And the aftermath matters more than the event itself.

And to a certain extent, the awfulness, close up. It was important for me that the first blow, somebody just pulling out his guns and shooting two guys in the head at point-blank range, be really nasty and close. And there's something important in it that you have to think about with the movie in the late sixties, when the first of the big race riots happened. People basically burned down their own neighborhoods. Maybe it was important to go out and burn everything, even though twenty years later it won't be rebuilt, just so you don't eat shit anymore and you feel a little better about yourself and get that rage out. In the movie Kenehan is saying, "Violence in this situation is going to be self-destructive."

And on the other side were those miners who were saying, "Look what they've done to us. How can we hold our heads up?" It is the dry, tactical point of view versus the angry, "We've been treated like slaves, and our women have been raped and killed" outpouring, which is much more human in some ways.

Having edited most of your other films, why didn't you edit Matewan?

Well, I had a good experience with Sonya Polonsky on *Baby, It's You*, and I liked cutting with her. It just seemed like this was a big thing, it would be good to have somebody dealing with the dailies, maybe cutting some sequences together while we were on location if there was time to, and then to just work with it.

Was that partly so that if she spotted a coverage problem during shooting, you still would have time to get a pickup shot?

Yes, very much. Probably where that was most a factor was in *Eight Men Out* when we were shooting the baseball, because we had to change the whole stadium over. My editor slapped together all the baseball sequences, and then the last day that we were going to be in that park he had five shots he needed before we gave it a hiatus and changed it over to the Cincinnati ballpark. The way I work with an editor is the way I work with an actor—I'm very specific. I talk about it, they do it, and then it's Take 2: "Okay, let's make some adjustments here." So with an editor, I usually will go through and pick takes or lines, and I'll say, "This is what I want you to cut together. This actor is really good in the first half of this angle on Take 3. Then after this line, go to Take 5 for that one line if you get into a close-up with him, and then try to work with Take 7 for the rest of the scene with that actor. Then with this actor, Take 2 is fine all the way through." When I edit myself, I don't do an assembly. I just go straight to a first cut. We shoot so much so fast. A regular two-hour movie is shot in twelve to twenty weeks. We're shooting a two-or-more-hour movie in eight weeks, so the amount of stuff that's coming in is much greater. So the assistant editor is trying to keep up with the dailies.

You don't regard editing as another chance to rewrite, as some filmmakers do—on the contrary, most of the editing is done during the writing.

When I'm writing it and when I'm directing it. When I'm editing, I'll take something out if it's not needed anymore. What you usually find is, even if it doesn't seem totally overwritten in the script, sometimes you just don't need a scene when that scene is about character, not about plot, and the actors are so much that character in the preceding scene that you don't need it anymore to establish the point.

So is editing just a straightforward process of putting together the best takes? You never explore or try something different?

As I've gone on, just because I've gotten more efficient at using those five-to-whatever weeks I've got, I have more footage, so that I have a few more choices within the scene. And now and then, I'll actually flip the order or something. I compress things all the time. And that's about rhythm. I'll even write a little bit more than I know I need if I know I'm going to have time to cover it back and forth, just so the actors have a little bit more body to something.

So you're giving the scene a head and a tail that you'll lose later.

Yeah, exactly. One of the things you try to do as a screenwriter if you want a rhythm where things are moving forward, is you try to enter the scene as late as possible. Now, I actually enter it pretty late in the screenplay, but sometimes I say, "Well, we shot it pretty late in the scene—guess what, we still don't need the first three lines." People will understand where they are. We can come into it halfway through this line, and people will still be oriented enough because they're into the story by this point, and the flow and the context will tell them where they are. So you can do that kind of editing. Sometimes it's just a matter of overlapping. You get actors who are taking big pauses, and God, it's almost lunchtime and you want to be done with this scene. Well, I'm not going to spend another hour after lunch getting these actors to speed up. We're covering it. I can speed them up in post-production.

As a result, transitions between scenes aren't a big deal until Lone Star, *where complex transitions lock things in more.*

Transitions are actually toughest, because sometimes when you cut a whole scene you often end up with two scenes with a nasty transition between them. When you wrote it the transitions were great. You end one scene in a kitchen, and then you have a scene in City Hall, and then the next scene starts in the kitchen. Well, now you have two scenes in the kitchen back to back with very similar lighting—what are you going to do for that transition? If you're lucky, you've got a cutaway to something like a pan full of scrambled eggs, and time can elide. But sometimes you have to put back that scene in the middle just because it's too nasty, and it just kills the rhythm of the section.

CHAPTER 7

Eight Men Out and "Shannon's Deal"

How did you approach adapting Eliot Asinof's book?

Eight Men Out was the first screenplay I ever wrote that I showed to an agent. It took eleven years to get made. I had been drawn to the book by a long prose poem by Nelson Algren called "Ballad for Opening Day," which was about the Black Sox, and quoted Eliot. So then I got Eliot's book. And I felt that I could go back to the *Chicago Tribune* and this and that and the other thing and piece together the story, but Eliot had done the leg-work, he'd talked to these guys, many of them just before they died. And they had not talked to each other since the scandal. So he was able to put together a story that most of the participants didn't even know. He was giving them information: "You mean he got $20,000?" or, "You mean Arnold Rothstein was betting on us too?" All that was news to the guys. Plus, Eliot had been a minor-league ballplayer, he actually did a *Playhouse 90* episode for David Susskind about the trial of the Black Sox, but I'm not sure if they made it or not. And he started into it the way a lot of people do, "What bums! What kind of ballplayers could throw the World Series?" But then as he got into more detail, he realized there were a lot of mitigating factors. So Eliot brought to it a point of view that I found interesting, that I wanted in the movie. So always in my head was, "I'm not gonna do this unless I can get Eliot's book." Some of the information is unique but we could find a way not to use that information and go to other sources, but to me it was his point of view that was unique—he had that upstairs-downstairs perspective and he'd get into the heads of a lot of people instead of just staying with the ballplayers' point of view.

D. B. Sweeney (as Shoeless Joe Jackson) and Charlie Sheen
in *Eight Men Out.*

At what point did Midge Sanford and Sarah Pilsbury come in?

I had written *Perfect Match* and was sitting around talking to the
director, Mel Damski, about great historical stories. I told him
about *Matewan* and he said he was interested in doing a movie
about the Ludlow massacre and that there was a very good book
co-written by George McGovern when he was a young man. And I
said I wanted to do the Black Sox scandal. He said, "Well, my
friend Sarah Pillsbury just bought the rights to it." So I called
Sarah. I didn't know her from Adam, she had just become partners
with Midge Sanford and produced a short film about Down's syndrome kids that won an Academy Award. She had seen *Return of
the Secaucus Seven*, liked it and thought, "Oh God, somebody
from the movie business is calling me!" And she'd gotten the rights
very cheap: she was at some festival talking about how hard it was
to get distribution for her short film, and some Texas guy came up
and said, "Can you give me some advice? We've bought the rights
to this book, and we can't do anything with the screenplay we have
written about it." Sarah was not a big baseball fan but she read the

book and really loved Eliot's take on it. And she said, "Well, we'll buy the option from you." So for something like $25,000, she bought an option of a couple years. And when I called they figured, "Oh, we'll get it made right away. John Sayles—he's made a movie." They asked, "So you're interested?" and I said, "Well, I have written a draft," and I sent it out to them and they liked it but they said, "We don't really have any money to pay you and keep you on retainer." I said, "That's not important, let's just make an agreement that we're gonna do this together." And eventually what happened is there was maybe six months left on their option and I had made some money on, I think, *Brother from Another Planet*, and I was able to take $75,000 and buy the rights out. So they kept their twenty-five in and I bought the other seventy-five and we just got the rights from the Texans.

So then we were able to go around to the studios and start pitching it. Which we did for another eight years or so. Every couple of years I'd come out and most of the studios would have played musical chairs, so there'd be new people in new seats and we could run it by them. We'd run it by Orion again and Mike Medavoy, the guy there at that time, would just say, "Well, before you start, let me tell you, to me baseball is like watching paint dry. Go ahead, tell me the story." Orion had already turned down this project two or three times over the years, and finally they said they would do it because I had more of a track record and so did Sarah and Midge as producers—they had produced a couple of movies that came in on budget and on time, including *Desperately Seeking Susan*, which Orion had released and made money on. So when we said we could make this for six million, they believed us. But then they just started saying, "Well, what about the casting?" And what we agreed is that they would write down a list of people who they thought it would be cool to have in the movie, who would give them an element of pizzazz, and we would write down our list, and we'd see if anybody was on both lists—and it ended up there were like seven or eight young actors on both lists. Orion said, "Okay, if you get three of these guys who are on both of our lists, we'll do it."

Did your feelings about the material shift during the eleven years between writing and shooting it?

I reread it a couple times; I barely rewrote it; I added very little to it. Sarah and Midge had some ideas that were good and I added those. The main thing that changed was who I thought I was going to cast in which part. I still have a three-by-five card with my dream cast on it—I've got Martin Sheen at third base and I ended up with Charlie Sheen in center field. I think George C. Scott was Comisky; Stacy Keach was on the team. If you look at the cast of *Catch-22*, I think some of those guys would have been in it. I was thinking of Sam Waterston for Ring Lardner. I originally had myself penciled in for one of the smaller ballplayer parts, because I was still of the age when I would have been right to play it. And by the time we started shooting I was like thirty-eight, I was just about Ring Lardner's age. He was over six feet, I'm six-feet-four. He was a writer, I was a writer. And looking at pictures, I actually looked a bit like him.

In Eight Men Out, *the idea that the Black Sox scandal caused baseball to fall from grace implies the existence of a pure baseball to begin with.*

Yes. Or a pure country.

Yet at the same time you're saying it was already corrupt.

Yeah. The moment it becomes professional, it's automatically corrupted. The moment you get into something that's a labor situation, it's automatically not just plain fun anymore, and that is just too much to ask of something. I was also getting into the idea of baseball as being metaphoric for the country. You can think of a nation as a person, and America was going through this idealized adolescence. The Fatty Arbuckle case happened right around the same time, and the idyllic days of Hollywood were starting to get looked at. World War I happened. America was becoming worldly and corrupt and cynical. And the 1919 World Series, right on the eve of Prohibition, is the last gasp of what happened before the Roaring Twenties, which was one of the most cynical, corrupt periods.

Nevertheless, at some level, the moral struggle for the soul of base-ball going on in the film is one that you're caught up in.

John Cusack in *Eight Men Out*.

Baseball is the sport of my youth. It was the sport that you could play when you were a kid. The ball wasn't too big for your hand, like a football or a basketball is. When you're a little kid, you can play a version of baseball. But it's also the sport of America's youth, and writers and poets often evoke it as the American sport—they don't play it anywhere else, and there's something pastoral about it, and to understand America you have to understand baseball.

Do you think that?

Well, no. To a certain extent, it's useful as a metaphor. I think it was deeply ingrained in a lot of Americans' heads and hearts, including guys who played it. And the game itself isn't about politics—if you're on the field, and you can play, you can stay. This isn't about where you're from or who your parents are. You could be a rich kid or a poor kid, and if you could hit the curve-ball you could stay. And that's the part those little paperboys play—the guys that we have sympathy with on the Black Sox still have a part of them that is like that. Joe Jackson is a child. He's illiterate. He's not even smart enough to do what he's paid for. He goes out on the field and he forgets. He just gets excited, and he plays one of the best series anybody had.

The opening fifteen minutes of the film sets up many characters and situations—what were you aiming for?

I realized with all these characters, and especially all these players—maybe fifteen white guys with short haircuts in the days before they even had numbers on their backs or names across them—there was going to be a certain amount of confusion. So I realized I was going to have to introduce people twice, maybe three times. So I gave everybody an introduction that's in character, that is a seed of what we're going to see them do later. So Eddie Cicotte is pitching: we see this famous incident when a guy asked Joe Jackson if he could spell "cat," but he's this great player, you see the factions on the team. And throughout there are also two motifs, baseball and money. You see the little boys, and they're right on the level. You see dollar bills being plunked down to get in. They're standing in the stands cheering, and all around them people are making bets. There's a lot of exposition in it, and I tried to make it dramatic at the same time. So we're cross-cutting between these kids out there in the stands and the guys who were doing exposition, giving us information and backstory about who's who—Burns and Maharg, the two guys who were going to originally start the fix, and the sportswriters who are talking about Comiskey. So there is this idea of True Belief surrounded by gambling and money.

And then you add another layer by intercutting it with Comiskey talking about the team.

Right, which is the upstairs-downstairs theme, and to a certain extent you start to see the tensions here. Because there's the juxtaposition of him saying, "My guys are a family," and every time you cut to the field, they're a pretty dysfunctional family. So you already realize that there's a facade, and then there's a reality behind it.

Michael Rooker, Perry Lang, Don Harvey, and Charlie Sheen as
the conspiracy ringleaders in *Eight Men Out* (1988).

*Baseball is richly suggestive as a microcosm for talking about all
kinds of social tensions.*

The fact is that baseball lends itself to movies because the rhythm
of the sport is about a drum-roll. It's about situations where
somebody is facing somebody else. It stops. You can talk on the
mound, you can step out of the batter's box. Basketball and football are all much more fluid. In baseball it's all about, "Oh my
God, it's a 3-2 situation, the bases are loaded, and the World Series is all on this pitch." And the pitcher can just take a walk
around the mound, you can cut away from twenty people. That's
what the TV coverage in big games does now—they'll have fifteen
or twenty cameras, and they have a whole scenario when they get
to those situations. They're cutting away to Ted Turner and Jane
Fonda and the audience, very much like I did, but they're doing it
live. It's a game that lends itself to that.

*A recurrent device, in the games but then in other scenes too, is the
dramatization of the action through wordless looks between characters facing hard choices.*

Yeah. It's a conspiracy, but it's a complicated conspiracy. One of the things I was thinking about when I wrote it was the Watergate conspiracy. As that conspiracy became public, it always reminded me of the Black Sox. Just like those guys, they get into trouble in different depths for different reasons—sometimes because they're weak; sometimes because they're greedy, evil motherfuckers; sometimes because they really don't know it's wrong, it just seems like everybody else is doing it: "I guess it's fine—we work for the President." But what was unique about this conspiracy is that everybody was selling everybody else out. So Abe Attell got these guys involved and said, "I'll give you the bankroll to bet a lot of money and make a lot of money on it," and then he didn't because he knew the players were going to do it anyway. What were they going to do? Call the cops? So then he could just watch them, and bet his money on it, and not come across with the money to the players. Once the players are involved, you can always go to them saying, "We're going to tell the cops that you threw the first game if you say you're not going to throw the third." So all the gamblers were selling each other out, a couple of the players were not admitting to the other players how much they had gotten, because they were the point men. So it just lent itself to everybody looking at everybody. Sometimes it's like, "What's he doing? Who is he betting on?" At other times it's, "Well, wait a minute—are we winning?" It was unclear to some of the conspirators whether they were going to just lose a couple of games or the whole series. That hadn't been explained to some of them, in order to get them in—because if it had been, some of them would have said, "Well, I'm not going for that."

Plus after they started it, the players themselves were too ashamed to have another meeting. They had a couple of little hushed conferences in twos and threes, but they never got together and said, "Okay, in the third inning you're going to start doing this and you're going to start doing that." So it all came back on the pitchers. It was, "Wait a minute, one of us had better start throwing this game, or we're going to win, and we're in big trouble here." Then people started doing this stuff that was so embarrassingly bad the sportswriters started circling. They watched the players because they heard this rumor. The players watched each other. The gamblers watched each other, plus they watched the players. And because they were supposed to lose two of the games that they won because the pitcher Dickie Kerr was not in on it, it seemed like they were crossing the gamblers up. So it became a really paranoid, who's-watching-who? situation. And the architecture of the ballpark is very good for that, because you have people facing in the same direction, so you can just rack-focus and see a lot of people watching people.

The social hierarchy, from street kids, players, and gamblers up through the sportswriters to management anticipates City of Hope, *in microcosm.*

Yes, that's true to a certain extent. There're hints of it in other things. Certainly in the novels I'd done that already. You start to get a little feeling of it in the end of *Brother from Another Planet*, when he starts tracing the drugs, and you feel like, "Oh, this leads to this, and this leads to that." But he's a very distant observer. He's not a player. Physically, what presages *City of Hope* is the scene we called the Marx Brothers Scene in the hotel. We built a set and we did a master shot, where one guy goes to one room, and somebody's peeking out and then just closing the door, and there's all this coming and going, and we're trading people sometimes, the way I later did in *City of Hope*, and I didn't want to cut it. Now that we have Steadycams and we can move a little bit more, we can do it better; we don't have to sit back in a wide shot and shoot at a big set. It was this comedy of errors type of thing.

Given that this was your biggest project in scale and scope, what were the major logistic challenges during shooting?

All the baseball comes pretty close to my storyboards. I didn't bother to storyboard the rest of it, but I storyboarded the baseball, because I knew how hard it is to shoot action, and I wanted to find an easy way to get a lot of footage very quickly. It's always 90 feet from home plate to first base, and if you're shooting from third base you know the blocking. And I had a play-by-play, strike-by-strike description of the World Series, so I knew where all the actors were going to go. I also knew from Elliot Asinof's description what part of the stands the various people who were watching were standing in. So when Bob Richardson came on the job, we

Cinematographer Robert Richardson and Sayles on the set
of *Eight Men Out*.

went to the ballpark in Indianapolis and walked to the various
places where I wanted to have camera positions for various action. We had 12 games to cover. We had a couple of PAs and we
put a 75 mm lens on and had them move to the edge of the frame;
then we'd put a 50 on, and we'd have them move out. We'd block
those, and get the overview of the stadium with a seat chart, and
say, "Okay, if you use a 50 mm lens from third base shooting to
first base, we need 550 extras to fill the stands." So every day, the
first thing that I got was a report on how many extras showed up.
Then I'd go to Bob and say, "Well, we're shooting with a 75
today," or if it was really bad, "We're shooting with a 100 today—
we can't pan," or "Let's bump these three shots, which I really
want to have, until a day when we get more people." We were
shooting in the same ballpark, so we shot all of the stuff that was
in the Chicago Stadium first, then broke for a week and did other
locations while the art department changed the stadium to the
Cincinnati Stadium—put new contact paper on the seats, changed
the wall, changed the dirt, changed the scoreboard, all that stuff—
and then we covered the rest of the games. Then we also had home

and away uniforms, so we shot all the stuff when they were in their home uniforms in Comiskey Park first.

Then what I did is decide, "Okay, this is blue-sky baseball, and these are the games that I want to have a blue-sky feeling, these are overcast baseball, and these are really kind of dangerous, dark baseball games." Almost every day at lunch, it would go from being a beautiful blue day to being overcast, so we'd say, "Okay, it's not game three anymore—it's game seven." If you're going to start shooting in the morning and end up shooting just before the sun goes down, the sun moves around all day, yet you're trying to shoot things that take place within five minutes of each other in the game. So Bob's idea for getting some consistency was everything would always be back-lit—but if we were shooting toward the stands, they would always be back-lit. You don't watch a movie rationally, but it just seems right, an even light all around.

So we would always start shooting toward home plate, because the sun was coming toward us then, and then we'd move around eventually through the outfield toward third base at the end of the day—it would always be back-lit. So I would say, "Okay, our first camera position is just over the shoulder of the pitcher. How many shots in all of these games that I've storyboarded do I have over the shoulder of the pitcher in home uniforms?" So then first we'd get one pitcher out, and we'd have him throw in a bunch of different situations and strike guys out. I tailored it so that I could get all the coverage I wanted. We didn't have that much time or money really to shoot a very complex movie. We got some nice moving shots, but those would be our big deals. Luckily, it was a part where we didn't have people in the stands as well, so when we shot out toward the outfield, all we had to do was avoid the light-poles, because there weren't lights back then. If we were shooting from the dugout toward the outfield, we used to have a coach standing there—if he moved, you would see a big pole. We also had a factory stack that moved around a little bit on a scissors lift, so if we moved it on a parallel axis it would block the pole. John Tintori, who I had worked with before as an assistant editor, and who had been a grip on *Lianna*, was editing as I was going along, and he really knew baseball, and we had been working with the storyboards together, and I was able to get enough ammunition to let us condense those games. I had a big story, and I really couldn't let it go on, so I needed a lot of shots to be able to punch and punch and punch.

I feel Eight Men Out *never quite gets beyond its own exposition to really explore its themes.*

I'd say in some ways it is more like my novels than anything else. And the thing with the novels, certainly *Los Gusanos* and *Union Dues*, is that they are mosaics. And this is not only a mosaic, but it's a mosaic about a very specific event. Our deal with Orion was that, besides agreeing on the cast, it was going to have to be two hours or under, because they really didn't want it to be an epic, and it was very ambitious. And what that meant was that I had to really cut to the quick with everything. Not that I cut much out of the movie, but in the writing I really wasn't able to expand some things. I did what I wanted to with it. To me the movie is about male confrontation and competition, and the things that men do to each other, and the question, Is there anything left that's pure, that can survive that world? And it can't. There're all these confrontations. And only a few of them are the confrontation of the pitcher against the batter. Most of those confrontations are about the way that men work on each other. It could be the scene between Joe Jackson and Swede Risberg, who comes to him and says, "Joe, all the guys are going in on this conspiracy, and they're going to think you're an asshole if you don't," and he turns him. All of those recruitment scenes are important to me.

The straitjacketing of the script is at the expense of character development in particular.

Yeah. What we were trying to do was drop the needle on three guys, so you got a look at the home life and a little bit under-the-skin. One of the things about baseball is that the world that you live in at home is so different from the world you live in at the stadium. It's like people who work on movies. They're on the movie set and that's their world, they're totally involved in it. Their home lives are totally separate worlds. So there's really not a way to integrate those two worlds very well. I didn't want to be cutting away to the wives in the stands all the time, so when I had those wives involved, they were people we met at home. So you drop the needle on Buck Weaver, John Cusack's character, and on Eddie Cicotte, David Strathairn's character. And in a very minor way you drop the needle on Joe Jackson and on Lefty Williams, who is the pitcher who throws the last game when his wife is threatened. And

John Cusack in *Eight Men Out*.

that person who they were when they were young ballplayers is not who they are now. It's like making a movie about the D-Day invasion—having flashbacks to the guys at home really just gets in the way. So only when I felt like there was a way I could integrate these home scenes with the drama of what's going on with these guys, did I feel like it was germane enough to the drama, which is: How is this guy going to suffer or be accepted in his own wife's eyes when he comes home with this problem? Other than that, it really was like a war movie, where the only way to place these guys is in their interrelationships on the field, in the locker room, and in the barrooms. That was really the dynamic that interested me most—this absolute man's world, about men and the ways they compete and win and this pure idea of baseball just can't survive once it's out in the real world.

Isn't that what you're getting at in the film's coda when we find Joe Jackson playing in the minor leagues?

He's backed away from the monster. Certainly you could take it as a metaphor for doing anything artistic, like *Big Night*, which seemed to me to be about some guys who want to make a nice film and they've been out in Hollywood for too long and the restauranteur across the street is the studio guy and he's going to manipulate you and he's going to win in the end. And there's no way he's not going to win. Maybe you'll have a nice meal, you'll make one nice party, but you can't expect to stay in that business and stay open. So there's Joe Jackson and this crowd over in New Jersey is applauding him but in his head he's hearing that World Series crowd and you know it's a step down, but he still has that moment of exhilaration. It's like *Baby, It's You*'s cross-fade from the tacky band doing "Strangers in the Night" to the actual Frank Sinatra. Joe's able to survive for moments at a time. And the rest of the time he's a guy who goes home and drinks and grouses a lot. But he played baseball until he was sixty, so he still had those moments of purity and grace that are possible.

In an odd way, the only other character who has such an absoluteness and purity is Landis, the baseball commissioner—like Joe Jackson he seems to be on a completely different wavelength, where he's immune to reality or in a state of denial.

There is a purity to what he does, but it's the purity of a king. He's not corrupted. I read a good book once about a guy who was the public defender for Chicago for years and years, and he outlines the nine types of judges. There's the workhorse judge, the cranky judge, the meek judge, and the lazy judge who just postpones everything so somebody else has to actually sit through the trial. And one of the types was the showboat judge—he talked about Judge Hoffman in the Chicago Seven trial being the showboat judge. The showboat judge likes his own voice, but he very often is reversible because he'll just take a dislike to a lawyer and he'll do all kinds of stuff that is not really legal, that should be grounds for a mistrial. And Landis was a showboat judge. He had gotten a certain amount of public favor for standing up to Standard Oil in some big antitrust case. But also, some guy would be going up for sentencing for burglary, and he'd say, "Tomorrow I want you to show up here with your wife and children," and he'd do a one-hour lecture about what a loser this guy is in front of them. It was not enough to give the guy twenty years, he had to give him a lecture too.

One of the ironies for me, of course, is that Landis was the guy who sent the Wobblies either into jail or exile. Whatever the level of judge just below Supreme Court is, he was the Chicago guy. Because of the Haymarket Riot and various organizational things, the Wobblies had a lot of their big guys, like Big Bill Haywood, in his district when the Wobblies not only said, "Don't report to the draft, don't enlist for World War I," but also, "We should commit sabotage against it because this is an antiworker war." Which it pretty much was—they weren't too far off-base there. The big Red Scare was in 1920, but they pretty much broke the back of the Wobblies by sending all their leaders to jail, or the ones who didn't want to go to jail went into exile. And Landis was the guy who read the sentences on these guys.

What is it that motivates you to appear in your own films?

In the smaller parts it's usually kind of practical—this is somebody I can play, I don't have to cast him, I take scale, it's one less question mark. I'm on the set so it gives us an enormous advantage in that those scenes can get moved around. Whereas if you're flying an actor into Eagle Pass, Texas, you've got one day to shoot.

Sayles as Ring Lardner, with Studs Terkel as Hugh Fullerton in
Eight Men Out.

When I look at a part, can I, number one, do justice to this part?
because I'm going to be busy with directing, and number two, can
I do justice to the other actors? I expect the other actors to do a lot
of work when I'm not there, to get together with each other, to
talk about their relationship from scene to scene, so when they get
into a scene together they've had a little grounding. I don't have
that time to spend as an actor. So I just play these guys who can
drop in from left field, do their stuff, and then allow me to go back
on the other side of the camera. I actually feel I learn more about
acting in other peoples' movies than acting in my own, which is
one of the reasons I haven't been in my own that much lately.
Every once in a while there'll be a part and I say, I'm perfect for
this, maybe I should do it—like in *City of Hope* or *Lianna* where I
really understood the part. The accounts of the time would be of
big tall Ring Lardner, who looks like a funeral director, with little,
portly Huey Fullerton. They were this strange pair and I liked that
as a cutaway option, these guys who looked so different from the
ballplayers. And in *City of Hope*, because of the fight that Nick,
Vincent Spano's character, gets into, I needed Carl to be bigger
than he was so that there would be some threat of retaliation, even

though Carl's got a limp. I needed somebody who looked like he could take a guy's head off if he wanted to, somebody of a certain size and that started me thinking about me playing it. What's interesting is that I go on these sets, and people say, "Jesus, you're so tall." Stallone looks tall, but is not tall. Because they put the camera down. If you put the camera about eye-level, it makes me look smaller than I am.

What almost all the characters I've played in my own films tend to be—and this is what I know about myself as an actor and about acting in movies—are guys who don't change. So they're able to stay outside of the action emotionally. The hardest thing about acting in a movie is that you don't get to do it in sequence. If you have a relationship with another person in the movie and that relationship changes throughout, if you're shooting out of sequence you really have to be on top of "Where are we with each other right now?" Whether it's Mary McDonnell and Alfre Woodard in *Passion Fish* or the ballplayers who are in these conspiracies together in *Eight Men Out* or Nick and the various people he runs into in *City of Hope*, there's some kind of progression in those relationships. The preacher in *Matewan*, I didn't even have to learn lines the way you usually do with a response. It's a perfect director's part. I just yelled at people and they said, "Yes! Amen!" So I got to ad-lib with them.

Carl's a guy for whom the title *City of Hope* is ironic because there is no hope for him. He's the same guy at the beginning as he is at the end; he doesn't change and he is not changeable. He has hit that point of cynicism where he doesn't want things to get better, because if it gets better it's going to threaten his world view and his actions. Any scene in that movie, Carl could have wandered in and I could have played him because I could play the same attitude in any situation. I didn't have to be different with anybody. Ring Lardner's the same. He's an observer, he's not caught up in this thing. He was a very removed person.

What was the first role you were cast in that wasn't from one of your own films?

Hard Choices, I think. I played a gentleman dope farmer. I did one day on it up in Catskill where they were shooting. Then they liked

Margaret Klenck and Sayles in *Hard Choices* (1984),
directed by Rick King.

the part, and they rewrote the plot so they wanted me to do another day on the movie.

*Which performances in other peoples' films did you particularly
learn from?*

As far as the acting itself being interesting, I really haven't played
characters who have much depth to mine, so usually they're a
function in other peoples' films. You can give them a little character, but you understand that your job is to hit these notes for the
flow of the film. When I've been offered bigger parts now and
then, I don't have time to do them. Studio things that would be a
week of work on our picture turn out to be a month of work on
theirs, because they want you around all the time. I don't have a
month to hang around a set, I don't need to act that badly. Most
of the parts I've played aren't very instructive about an actor except that this is the life of a day player. And the life of a day player
is very concentrated. You know they're trying to make their days,
they really don't have time for you to fuck up. So there's that kind

Sayles as Carl in *City of Hope*.

of pressure on you. You've got to figure out the rhythm very quickly not only of the set but of the actors who are in the scene with you. Sometimes the rhythm of where they are in the shoot affects things and you get a hit on where they are.

On *My Life's in Turnaround*, I was in the first shot of the first day of shooting. In fact the guys who made it were at the table with me when I helped them figure out that they had totally figured out the shooting ratio wrong and that they were going to shoot about 16:1 instead of 4:1. And I started to give them shit—which was also my character—about which one of you is going to go find this extra $50,000 you're going to have to pay? Whereas with *Malcolm X* it was the twentieth week of a twenty-one-week shoot, and everyone was like the walking wounded. It was a really long tiring schedule for them, a very ambitious movie, so you get a very different hit on that world that you're popping into for one second. Plus, if they're bothering to bring you in as a day player, to a certain extent the scene is about you. And you're the newcomer. So you actually get a little more time sometimes than the leads do. The leads are in their rhythm, they're a known quantity.

That is what we did with the *Lone Star* day players, they got three-quarters of the day and then Chris Cooper would get one-quarter of the day for his angle. In the case of Wesley Birdsong's long scene, we were able to give the actor three-quarters of the day for his angles and then turn around and say, "Chris, guess what? Once again there're two hours before the sun goes down and we've got to get all your stuff in three pieces. So there's gonna be no flow to what you do. We're going to shoot this, then you move, we switch eyelines on this line, and we're going to do three different pieces and you're going to do your seven lines in three different pieces as quickly as you possibly can." But the minute you're done with your bit and you're shot out, you're furniture. You go to the trailer and you may wave goodbye to somebody, and you're gone but they keep making the movie.

So a lot of what I'm looking at is not necessarily the way the director works, because I'm not going to hire the director. I'm looking at the other actors; I'm looking at the crew; I'm looking at the DP; I'm looking at the production—how it greets a new actor, how they make you either feel like they know you're there or you just hang around the office for an hour and then they realize, "Oh, we should do something with this guy." The office is either humanistic or you're just hooking into a big machine.

Have you ever had a scene with an actor and then cast them?

Sure. I had seen Tony Denison, one of the main cops in *City of Hope*, in "Crime Story" and liked him and the series quite a bit. Then I got to work with him in *Little Vegas*, where he plays a very different character, and I just liked the guy and enjoyed working with him. At lunch he said, "I'd like to be in one of your movies sometime, if there's anything that would be good for me." Then when I was writing *City of Hope* I thought, "This would be a good thing for him." And there're actors I haven't gotten to direct yet who I've met on sets and would love to work with.

What was your involvement in Mountain View, *the thirty-minute film for PBS written and directed by Marta Renzi?*

In 1985 Maggie and I had both worked on Marta's previous dance video, *You Little Wildheart*, as PAs basically. It was really not that ambitious camera-wise; she was really staging things in front of a camera that wasn't moving that much. It was mostly to Bruce

Sayles' motorcycle cop cameo, with Melanie Griffith, in Jonathan Demme's *Something Wild* (1986).

Sayles with Dick Miller and John Goodman in Joe Dante's *Matinee* (1992).

Springsteen songs and it was on PBS a couple of times and you don't have to pay for the song rights on PBS. She had this idea for another one and she needed to get grants for it, but she's not a writer. She'd written this treatment to explain what she was going to do and I could understand what she was getting at but I felt like in order to get the grant, I could rewrite it in a way that was a little more linear and plotlike.

The themes of the piece certainly relate to your own films.

A lot of what Marta was getting at was community and the connectedness and disconnectedness of various characters, who, through their dance, or through where they come to be, are going to stay connected or seem like they're spinning out of the orbit of the other people. In some ways it has some parallels to *Return of the Secaucus Seven*, where you realize at the end that the Jeff character may not stay part of that group, and amongst the dancers there was partnering and repartnering to a certain extent, so the group may stay the same but the partners may change—and the same-sex friendships are sometimes more enduring than the opposite-sex relationships.

Does the title come from the location you shot in?

Yeah, that was the name of the bar. It was an old resort and the idea was that it had been run by the old guy as a roadhouse hotel and it had kind of been discovered by the younger people.

How did you take part in the production?

Maggie basically helped produce it and I'd seen the dances on the floor. I helped by talking to Marta: "You don't want to do them as a theatrical performance, you want to make a movie out of them, so let's talk and think about rechoreographing them." When you bring a camera in, you're moving within the space with the camera. The dancers are creating space around or to and from the camera, and dance is all about space unless you just sit there and do a proscenium notation of what the dance looks like to an audience. So it was about, "Here's the many things you can do with a camera, here's what lenses do, here's what camera movement will do, and if this person is moving towards the camera and the camera is moving towards them, this person is moving twice as fast as they were before, so you have to think about that in your choreography." And then the rest of what I did was just to help her during the shooting—it was on-set consulting. And I sat with her and the camera operator after she would do a phrase of the dance and talk about the coverage. In terms of content, none of it's mine. If they gave a facilitator credit, that's what I would have taken.

Why the sidestep into episodic TV with "Shannon's Deal"?

Stan Rogow, the guy who brought me into *Clan of the Cave Bear* as a writer, had a conversation with Brandon Tartikoff, who had seen *Baby, It's You* and really liked it because he was from someplace like Trenton. Stan said, "This guy's a great writer and we should have a TV series." I think his idea at the time was to do *My Life As a Dog* as a TV series, which could have become Andy of Mayberry in a dying factory town. He felt I understood Jersey and those kinds of towns and he wanted something centered around a small boy in a similar town, combining a couple of movies he'd seen. And I came in, I talked with him, I liked Brandon, and I said, "Look, I'm about to go and direct a movie and I'm editing it as well, so I'm going to be out of it in about a year. Good luck with this idea. If you're still making TV I'll come talk to you again." He said okay, and I did that, and about a year later I came in and talked again with Stan. I had three different ideas for TV series. Two of them were something vaguely like what somebody else was making. And the most amorphous of the ideas, the one with the least hook, was "Shannon's Deal," which was about failure and a guy who had become the object of his former contempt and had crashed out and now was trying to rehabilitate himself—and about a lawyer who never went to court. Almost everybody fails at some point, and it's what you do with it.

So they financed it to write a pilot. And they liked what I wrote and we got Lewis Teague to direct the pilot movie and they gave us a green light to do a first season." And I said, "Look, I don't have the time to write every episode, but I'd like to write the pilot and the first two episodes to get the thing started, to really give the writers an idea of where it would go." And they said, "Great, we like a lot of these characters, we like the guy, and we think a series

Jamey Sheridan as Jack Shannon in "Shannon's Deal."

could be made out of this. It's very risky. It's dramatic. It's definitely a 10 to 11 P.M. series. Can we have more jeopardy? Can he
carry a gun? . . . It may just be a little too—" they didn't use the
word *smart*, but that was the intimation of it, that it may just be a
little too cerebral for a TV audience, but it was worth a try 'cause
they liked it.

Was there a model for Shannon?

I knew a lot of guys who had to work their way through school.
And who, in the eighties, ended up being around people they had
never really been around except at college. And that gave them a
kind of divided loyalty. I was interested in black guys I knew who
did well enough in high school to go to college. There was a certain amount of, "Oh, you're selling out if you go to a mostly white
college and you get a job in a mostly white corporation and you
get out of the neighborhood." Where do your loyalties stand as a
black man? And they were graduating from high school in 1968
and going to college from '68 to '72, right at the height of the
Black Panther movement, so it was heaviest for black people then.

But it was still a struggle for children of immigrants or people
who were the first one in their family to get through college and
their parents couldn't pay for it so they were on scholarship and
had a job. Well, they got through and there was an opportunity to
work for these corporations where you were mostly with guys
who went to Ivy League schools, whose parents and grandparents
had gone to those Ivy League schools, and what they were doing
during those years was selling out the working class. I remember
hearing a lot of grousing from the mid-seventies onwards about—
"Jesus Christ, this guy dropped out of high school and he's driving
a forklift in Florida and he's making eighty grand a year." And the
person grousing would be somebody who had gone to liberal arts
college and then law school and was struggling to pay off their
student loan. Or a guy who had done that ten years ago and had a
job that was only paying him $60,000 a year. The laws that were
being passed and modified and what business was doing in those
years was basically, to me, whether it was articulated or not, a
huge backlash of the educated classes against the working classes.
They busted those unions, and there aren't too many union guys
getting $80,000 a year anymore, in fact there aren't too many

Jamey Sheridan and Elizabeth Peña in "Shannon's Deal."

union guys anymore. Their pension funds were robbed from them as well, by smart guys who went to law school and corporations that did greenmail and wiped their businesses right out. And the unions were pretty blind to that and didn't make concessions when they needed to and in some cases they made the concessions and they were ripped off anyway. They were promised, "Oh, if you take a rollback," when the owners knew they'd already bought the factory in Hong Kong and it was only a matter of, "Let's save some money, let's put a scare in these union fucks till we can get rid of them anyway."

Shannon had come from a background where he had to work his butt off to get through school. And he partly financed law school by being a good poker player. And there's a certain cynicism that comes from being a good poker player. And he bought into that cynicism and became a hired gun for the corporations, in his own way not much different from Hickey and Griggs in *Matewan*. And he helped the corporations, absolutely legally, play with the law and pollute New Jersey, or the eastern urban place he was from, for another fifteen years and pay off the minimum amount required and only when they had to and to keep throwing the mercury into the water for another five years while they held this thing up in court. So he'd been a part of that whole era—up to his neck in it, but over his head in other ways. And now he's come to this point where he realizes, "Geez, I really fucked my life up with this gambling." How are you a lawyer with morals? It's not about your moral code, you're supposed to be representing the client.

Is Shannon more The Big Chill *than* Secaucus Seven?

Yeah, he is, but he didn't go to the same school as those guys either. He's really somebody who kind of fought his way in. He's more like the guy who would work for one of the people in *The Big Chill* more than being one of them. You don't feel like *The Big Chill* characters were upwardly mobile, you feel like they were upper-middle-class kids who just stayed there and are trying to make bucks. At least that's the feeling I was left with. It's not articulated in the movie, but from those actors that's what I got: "We were always here and we're going to stay here. And now it's just unfashionable to be politically active and we're going to reveal our true selves, who we were all along."

What was the function of the poker-playing element?

A really important thing about the series is that it is based on poker logic. And that's how he prevails—not by taking people to court, but by bluffs and strong arm stuff and poker logic. I had played poker but not in a serious way. Talking to guys who are serious players, what's interesting is that it's about personality. It's very much like what I was talking about with *Eight Men Out*, of these confrontations between guys and their wills and bluffs. David Mamet wrote an essay about it and I read a very good book by Frank Wallace called *Poker: A Guaranteed Income For Life* and none of it is about cards, it's all about personality. Basically there are certain rules if you're even going to think about being a successful poker player. You learn those and they are second nature to you. You play certain things in certain situations, not that difficult. "This guy I can bluff, and this guy I can threaten, and this guy I basically do whatever he says because he's holding all the cards." So he says, I'm a professional card player, or I was, and he goes to these private games. What he wants is to win money.

How do you win money? Well, you're the best card player in the game. But also, you keep bad players in the game. So you should be able to come back home and replay every hand that you played that night, who won and who lost. You should keep a running tab in your head. So if there's a really good loser who loses big every week, and he's a contributor to your income, you want to keep him in the game no matter what. So, for instance, you may let him win the last hand. If you get into a face-off late, you may throw some money back at him, so he feels like, "Ah, if we'd only played another hour, my luck was changing."

Now if there's a good player, fuck him up. Sit next to him, fart, be disagreeable with him, call him up and say, "The night's been changed from Thursday to Wednesday." Get him out of your game, because he's going to take money out of your pocket. If you're a true poker player, you're reading men's souls and finding the losers among them. The last line of his book is a great one: "I am no longer a professional poker player because I found to be successful at my business I was spending my life surrounded by losers." And there is an absolute cynicism about that. And that's what any good trial lawyer does: takes that absolute poker logic and ability to read what a person wants. "Well, what this person doesn't want is for it to drag through court. And he absolutely has the case, my guy doesn't have a case in hell." Maybe it's a divorce case and the guy's wife is suing him, she should absolutely get the thing. But she's only got the heart for like one or two appearances in court. "We'll drag it out and she'll take anything. We put her through a year of this and make her life miserable and we're calling her home, we're calling her work, she'll give up, she doesn't have the balls that you have. And her lawyer doesn't have the balls that I have."

To what extent do you apply poker logic to filmmaking in terms of getting a sense of someone you're working with, what drives them, what their weaknesses and strengths are?

I always think of it not as poker but as handicapping, like the guy at the track who handicaps the horses. That's what I tend to do as a director if it's an actor I haven't worked with before. There are actors who work from the outside in, there are actors who work from the inside out. There are actors who are only good in the first couple of takes, there are actors who are only good after they get some warming up. Well, I'm going to have all these actors in the same scene sometimes. Mary McDonnell and Alfre Woodard work different ways. Alfre said, "Just tell me what you want. I'll even ask you for a line reading every once in a while. Specifically tell me what to do, I'll find a way to make it my own." Mary McDonnell wouldn't let me finish a sentence. I would get halfway through the sentence, she would say "got it" and walk away. And she would have gotten it. But she had to complete the sentence for herself for it to work for her. When you've got actors who have a different rhythm as far as what take they're good at, you have to find that out very quickly and you shoot over the shoulder of the guy who needs some warm up. You don't put his face on camera yet. So the other guy gets to do his good stuff in the first three or four takes and then you turn around and this guy's had three or four takes and he's up to speed. Or, if it's going to be a two-shot and it's not going to go back and forth, I may say, "Okay, while so-and-so's still in the dressing room, I'm just going to act the other part and we're going to play around with the lighting and the blocking for a minute." And I'll get the actor up to speed.

Couldn't you tell the other actor to hold back for the first couple of takes?

Not if it's a two-shot. Then you're wasting film. You want to get them on the table when they're both hot. When there's an actor I haven't worked with before, and there's a big scene, I want to do it in a master shot or in just two shots. But I need this scene to really move along. And I don't know the rhythm of this actor. There are some actors who are very good and they really listen and they really react to what's said, but they need time to do that. If you make them go any faster, it gets a little blurred. So, if you've got that kind of actor, you're going to need to cut away, you're going to need to do coverage. So you can speed the pace up to where you want it later on. You can't just say, "Faster, faster, faster," they're not going to respond.

Another aspect of the conception of Shannon is that he's another example of someone who worked inside the system and now he's trying to work outside the system, bringing it back to the theme of independence.

Well, he's an insider but at the same time an outsider and a very typical protagonist. Faulkner's most interesting people are insiders but outsiders. So they know the South, they know the county, but they're somewhat alienated from it, they've been away to school or something. They don't quite feel like they can lose themselves in it anymore even though they don't want to live anywhere else. So there's a little bit of alienation, at the same time they really understand how the machine works. It's a useful character. It's a good way to have a character who isn't a total neophyte, the way the guy in *Brother from Another Planet* is. Joe Morton's character in *City of Hope* is that guy who's an insider, but he's been made an outsider because he's classed himself out of the neighborhood, so he's somewhat vulnerable with his dealings with his constituency. He takes a certain amount of shit when he goes to that community center.

Jamey Sheridan as Shannon and Jenny Lewis as Shannon's
daughter in "Shannon's Deal."

What kind of input did you have? Starting with the pilot, were you involved in casting?

Yeah, I'd say, "Here's a list of people I think would be wonderful." The problem with casting is that they always want the series to run ten years. So I was looking for guys to play Shannon who were forty, and they said, "But if it runs ten years, then he'll be fifty! How can we have somebody who's fifty on TV?" They were talking about Peter Coyote at one point. The people they got who I recommended were Liz Peña and Richard Edson. I said, "I hope you can get somebody this good," and they tried them and they listened to me and they made the deal. I was very happy with a lot of the other choices.

For all that the series had going for it, it's hard to imagine where it would have gone after a certain point.

Yeah, how long could it run, because I told them, "Basically, every week there's going to be a moral dilemma." They asked, "Couldn't somebody pull out a gun? Couldn't there be more jeopardy?" I answered, "Well, his soul is in jeopardy." They even had one episode in the second season where he falls off the wagon and gambles again, which was nice. I gave them some ideas for shows, and then other writers went and ran with them. I think I gave them the idea for "Sanctuary." The writer did a really nice job with the episode called "Art." That's the one where the guy gets caught stealing a painting, and he was supposed to be stealing it for the mob for an insurance scam, but they give him the wrong address so he gets caught. It's really funny. That was one where I gave them the basic idea for it. I haven't even seen them all.

The second year I didn't give them any ideas, I just said, "You don't need me anymore, you've got a lot of good writers." And they said, "We'd really like you to be a consultant." I asked, "How little can I do?" And they asked, "If we get in trouble, will you help us get out of a corner?" And so there were three or four episodes where they called me up and said, "We're in a bind here. Can you do something?" Sometimes I'd do a little writing, other times I'd just talk story with them on the phone. But it was pretty much Stan Rogow's series at that time. One of the great things that Stan brought to it was Wynton Marsalis. We were saying,

Series regular Richard Edson and Jamey Sheridan in
"Shannon's Deal."

"Let's have a different kind of music for this. We can't really have the usual detective music. What has the mood of this guy?" We started talking about jazz and Stan brought up Wynton Marsalis. Stan did a really good job. TV is a tough world.

Were you tempted to direct an episode?

I would have had to join the Directors Guild for one thing. But it's like commercials or rock videos. When you make a movie yourself, it's almost a year, between writing, producing, directing, editing, and doing publicity to support it when it's done. Plus in between, in stolen moments, writing all these other screenplays for somebody else, each one averaging four drafts. You just don't have time to take two weeks out and prep for and direct a TV show. If you're doing the pilot and setting the tone, there is quite a bit to do creatively. I have friends who are doing "NYPD Blue," "Homicide," and "New York Undercover"—the style has been set. Directors are brought in and they're traffic cops to a certain extent. They have to be good but the DP and the actors keep the style in their heads and the director is just the person who gets it done.

CHAPTER 8

Los Gusanos, City of Hope, and Passion Fish

Your previous novel was published twelve years before Los Gusanos. *How do you know if something's going to be a film or a novel?*

Usually a subject says to me, "This is what it is." But with the novels, it's usually how many points of view I'm going to get into to feel like I'm telling the whole story. I'd say in *City of Hope* there's three or four people whose points of view we truly get into for a while, and then we go to the omniscient point of view. In *Los Gusanos*, we're really in maybe twenty to twenty-five people's points of view, seeing the world through their eyes, sometimes seeing an incident we've already seen through a totally different point of view. And that's part of the style of the book, which is to say, how you feel about these historical events depends upon where you were standing in the room when it happened.

Generally, in a movie I think an audience can deal with three or four. There's what I always call the omniscient point of view, which is the wide shot of the house on Halloween night, then the antagonist's point of view, which is over the edge of the chainsaw, and then the protagonist's point of view, which is inside the closet as the chainsaw rips through it. Usually you can't ask an audience to get into many more viewpoints than that without them disassociating from the movie.

Isn't it also related to how you disclose information? In Los Gusanos, *a hundred pages in it's still not apparent where the narrative's going, although there are clues. You can't predict where we're going to be in the next chapter. Whereas in a film, you can't keep an audience in the dark for that long.*

For about twenty minutes at the most. And even then, usually you have a couple of teasers. If you think of a thriller, there's usually a murder before the credit sequence. You don't see the face of who did it. A monster movie, you see somebody going "Aarghhh!" but it may take fifteen to twenty minutes to actually see the giant ant. You don't necessarily read a book all at once, there's a different relation to time.

What was the process for getting Los Gusanos *published?*

The day before we left for Cincinnati to shoot *City of Hope* I sent *Los Gusanos* out to six publishers with my cover letter because I didn't have a literary agent at that time. So I was negotiating with the various publishers while I was in Cincinnati.

Your interest in Latin America goes back as far as your short story "Old Spanish Days" in the mid-1970s. Why have you gravitated towards this in your recent work?

I've always been interested in those things that separate people, although they seem to be living parallel lives. You're walking down the street with someone, and does the fact that they speak a different language mean that they think differently? If so, how differently? For instance in Japanese, if I were explaining *Mountain View* and I said it was a piece Maggie's sister did, they would ask, "Older sister or younger sister?" They don't conceptually have a generic idea of sister—they only have older sister or younger sister. So the language in some way shapes and is shaped by how they see the world. One of the ideas I was trying to get at in *Lone Star* is that race is an illusion but culture is very real. The genetic difference between people of different races is so tiny and is a predetermination to almost nothing, it's a very bad indicator of who that person is. But if you look at culture, it's a much better indicator of who this person is going to be, how they might react to a situation. I grew up around people of other cultures, mostly people speaking Italian. There's the mainstream culture you see in movies and TV and books, and then you have these subcultures or parallel cultures. I'm always interested in the tension between a mainstream and parallel culture and how they differ, how cultures mutate and where that border is. Where's the hard edge and where's the soft edge? Sometimes it's sports, sometimes it's music that seems to be the place where the most interaction is happening. There was a time when the idea of an Anglo and a Saxon walking down the street together and not killing each other was strange, but now we have Anglo-Saxons.

But Los Gusanos *isn't really about cultural assimilation?*

It is in the sense that you have these people who are living in America and, depending on their generation and background, they've either unpacked their bags emotionally and mentally, or they haven't. There are those who say, "I am a Cuban and I am an exile and that is all I will ever be." It's thirty years later and the characters have either said, "Okay, that's that," or they haven't. And the main character is like a born-again Christian. She was very young when the Bay of Pigs happened and she could have just said, "Well, that was my parents' deal," she feels this void and being a Joan of Arc warrior in this old cause fills it, almost with the purpose of gaining status in her father's eyes, to become a "son." That happens—people find they're hungry for something to fill their life with, to give themselves to. It may be the Moonies or a political cause or something really good, but they have that hunger.

What drew you to Cuba?

Cuba is very much metaphoric. We still have a blockade on Cuba, not for any practical reason but because it's metaphoric. I was raised a Catholic and the big political and religious metaphor of the time was between Catholicism and Atheism, Democracy and Communism. In this hemisphere it all came down to this one little island that had always considered itself the most North American of Latin America. The people of Havana thought of themselves as the most cosmopolitan. They weren't *gringos*, but they weren't Puerto Ricans—that kind of attitude. There's an old Latin American joke told about Cubans and Argentineans: How does a Cuban commit suicide? He climbs on his ego and jumps off. As I got to know more about Cuban history I was interested in the fact that it parallels our history, just the dates are different. We both had revolutions against colonial powers, we both had slavery for a long time. We had our civil war, and Cuba was still having theirs—a long, protracted one. The United States, the modern capitalist country, is one of the players. And there are these people who, within a family, might have been on different sides, just like in the American Civil War. I've always been interested in how the personal and the political affect each other, and on a small island, so much of this stuff was very personal. Families knew each other. It was, "Well, Fidel didn't get killed in jail because his father was a wealthy plantation owner and he knew somebody, so Fidel had a pretty good time in jail, much better than anyone he's ever arrested." And there was a Latin American tradition of students flirting with the Left and getting in trouble, and then some of them became minor politicians and only a few of them ended up becoming hardcore revolutionaries. It's interesting that somebody might have the analysis to say, "This order we have now is oppressive," and join the rebels, but there might be some point that they will not go beyond because of something personal—because their father's ranch gets taken away, or they're Catholic and somebody nationalizes the church's land. That's personal.

The structure of the book is unusual—it's the least narrative-dependent novel you've written.

There is a small linear story in there, which is like a Graham Greene story, and that was the throughline on which I hung what I thought was the real story—this mosaic of where all these people are coming from and how they got where they are now. Most of them are exiles, even the CIA guy, exiles from how they thought things would turn out, how they started thinking the world was going to go. And each of them acts or doesn't act, joins this conspiracy or doesn't, for their own reasons. And those are personal as well as political. So you have a political movement and there are people with a very dry analysis, but what are they overcoming? Franklin Roosevelt was from Hyde Park: he never won his own town, they were rich Republicans, he was considered a class traitor. He was a very cunning, crafty politician, he wasn't some saint who dropped down from the skies in his wheelchair, but what made him see beyond his class? I'm interested in what makes people transcend the border of what you would expect of them.

Along with the prismatic effect of all the different points of view in each chapter, there's a recurring technique of dropping the reader in media res and forcing them to figure out what they're in the middle of.

If the story does not have a driving plot, you want some kind of feeling or emotion, and to a certain extent you want the reader to be jogging a little to catch up—but they're in the action already, or in some kind of emotional state with a character. I'm trying to get the reader to pay a little bit more attention because I'm trying to take them somewhere where they don't necessarily know what's happening—it's not a genre that's going to fulfill its genre expectations. But eventually all the evidence is there, I don't leave people without the evidence.

Do you see any cinematic influence on your writing technique? For instance, in the transitions and ellipses between events and moments?

Certainly when I started my novels got called cinematic, and when I started making movies they got called literary. Movies have influenced book writing in rhythm more than anything else. The physicality of movies, the ability to set a scene fast using one detail, is something that probably started in pulp or genre fiction, and that has become a tool that all fiction writers have. People have seen and read so many stories that they don't need every detail.

The title of the book translates as "The Worms," but that image seems to signify a number of different things.

It's kind of like Thomas Pynchon's novel *V*, where there is a woman whose name changes but it always begins with a *V*, and then there are these side stories where *V* has different meanings. It's a metaphor I use several different times and it means different things in different contexts. The first is that the leader of the country of their birth called these people worms for having left. How do you take that? As, "Yes, I'm a coward, I fled," or as a point of pride, "Yes, I'm a *gusano* and I'm proud of it," making a little sign with your finger? That's where it began. And then with the guy with internal worms it's one thing, the idea of being a parasite is another—is that a bad thing to be or is that the only subversive position possible?

What kind of research did you do?

I read probably fifty books, and I must have read, oh, twenty Cuban novels, mostly in Spanish, that I found by hook or by crook, to get a feel for the culture and the history. I saw [Tomas Guitierrez] Alea's movies, which I really liked, and a few films by [Humberto] Solanas.

Did you go to Cuba?

Yeah, but I actually wrote most of the book before I'd been there. I tried to go a couple of times, but it was not that easy to get there. Spent a lot of time in Little Havana over the years, talking to people, getting people's stories. In 1980 I got an assignment to write an article for *The Atlantic* about the Mariel boat lift, so I got to go into the Orange Bowl where they were keeping people who were coming in. My Spanish wasn't that good then, so I stumbled through conversations, and finally this guy came up who spoke pretty good English and said, "You may say you're a journalist and have this card but people are not going to want to talk to you because they're afraid that what they say may be held against them getting on the other side of the fence." The guy started interpreting for me but the problem was, being Cuban of course, he just started arguing with them about their answers. The story didn't get published, they decided it was too sights-and-sounds and they wanted something with more statistics in it.

What contact if any did you have with the politics of the Cuban exile community?

I think I've been debriefed by a couple of people, just casually. Not in relation to the book, just in relation to asking questions in certain places. I've certainly had conversations with Cuban people in the arts where I got the feeling, "Well, wait a minute, that's not a question they want to know, they have to file a report saying whether this artist is or is not sympathetic to the revolution." This is not so much recently but when I first started I met a Cuban, who was an attaché to something and an artist in New York, who went back to Cuba every once in a while, and you get in a conversation and you say, "He doesn't seem that interested in those last three questions."

You use untranslated Spanish dialogue extensively in Los Gusanos. *Is that in the service of realism?*

One of the things I wanted to get at is that there is a whole community of people who live in Miami but do almost all of their business with each other. Some don't speak any English in a given day, even if they can speak it. It is an absolutely enclosed community that you can live within. I worked in a sausage factory in Boston where I was one of three guys who spoke English, and most of the guys had been there for thirty or forty years and the only English they spoke was stuff they saw on TV, so they'd be speaking in Italian and then they'd say, "E poi Mannix shoots da guy dead."

   The community they lived in was Italian, not Italian American. I wanted to give that feeling. I'd seen various other strategies: Hemingway got into the very Castilian thing of "thee" and "thou" for the formal use of *usted*, but it didn't feel like human speech to me. Then there's the one where you have people say a bunch of things in English and then they say, "*Verdad?*" Or they say, "*Que pasa?*" and the rest of it's in English. I wanted the feeling that sometimes some of the characters are going to be on the outside looking in, including the reader. I want the reader to sometimes say, "I don't understand what they're saying," because many of the characters are in that situation. Sometimes I'd type Spanish sentences and then look at the context and say, "Okay, if you really want to know what's being said here, can you tell?" There are only a few cases where you can't. Usually I'll pose a question in Spanish and answer it in English, and from the answer you get what the question was. Or do the opposite. I used a lot of cognates, words that are spelled almost exactly the same in both languages. It was important for me not to have the Spanish be in italics because italic has an emotional content for me—this is not normal.

What inspired City of Hope?

I had thought of making something like *City of Hope* for years and years. It's the only movie other than *Secaucus Seven* where I

Tony Lo Bianco and Joe Morton in *City of Hope* (1991).

did no research at all. I've just lived in places like that my whole life. After I'd written the first draft, I thought, maybe things have changed a little so I started reading the *Jersey Journal* and the *Hudson Dispatch*, and every day for a week there were three headlines right out of my script. So it's based on Albany, Atlanta, East Boston, Hoboken. The importance of it being a smaller city is that in New York City, if something's a big story, it's national news and the national media get into it and refract what happens just like they did in the O.J. trial. Whereas city politics in Detroit only have to deal with local press, which doesn't refract it as much. I wrote it very quickly, in a week or two, and I didn't change it much, we just went off and made it.

Was City of Hope *partly a response to* Do the Right Thing, *addressing many of the same concerns, and was "Hill Street Blues" an influence?*

Sure. In the case of *Do the Right Thing*, which I liked quite a bit, I felt like this is a complex situation seen from one block. From the point of view of that block, cops might as well have dropped from outer space. And I felt like some of the cops were one-dimensional. Many of my older relatives are cops. I know and care a little bit more about where they're coming from. And they don't say, "Let's get in the car and beat some black people up." I want you to tell me where they're coming from, and also what they're getting.

In *City of Hope* I wanted the feeling that the cops were part of the fabric of this city. I was up for jury duty recently in Jersey City and they asked, "Do you have any relatives in the police force?" and half the people called said, "Yes." It's not that the cops are somebody separate, you know them.

I remember being in a college political science class on the city and we were talking about the police as an organization. It was rare for me to talk in class but I started talking about my grandfather and other relatives who were cops—and it was like I'd come from outer space. All these other people said, "Oh, jeez, you really know a cop." I thought everybody did. My personal dealings with cops doing their jobs had never been very good—they were the guys who cornered you and asked you a lot of questions about things you might or might not have done. One of those scenes in *City of Hope* comes from a personal experience where one day I was playing basketball with a bunch of white guys and the cops came and very politely asked if anybody knew anything about someone who was selling musical instruments or who might have broken into a store, and then it was, See you later fellas. And later in the day I was playing with a bunch of black guys and the cops came and it was, Okay, which one of you sons of bitches broke into the store? They had a totally different attitude.

In New York City, cops and firefighters pretty much get the same pay. Everybody likes the firefighters—the firefighters are easy-going guys, kind of nice to be around, and the cops have this kind of edge to them. And the question is, is it that the edgy guys choose to be cops, or is it that after three years of being a cop, you become that way? Whereas after three years as a firefighter, you take a laid back, longer view of it, and when you show up everyone is happy that you are there. If you're a cop, and you walk into a neighborhood, everybody tenses up and hates you. Just because of your uniform.

I thought *Do the Right Thing* was a great microcosm, *City of Hope* is an expanded microcosm. Spike did a great thing, which was to get it down to that block. It was influential in my thinking, but this is a story I've been thinking of doing for twenty years, about all the levels of the city, and how it's connected. "Hill Street Blues" is unavoidable. I liked that show, but I didn't get to see it very much. I am not a regular TV watcher. But what I liked about the style of "Hill Street Blues" was that it was much more realistic about the way police work—you don't just have one case. Something comes up on a case that happened two weeks ago—that's ancient history. There's not that dramatic focus on one thing. And that's more than a physical style.

Was it hard to finance?

Larry Estes was running Columbia–Tristar Homevideo and he had a mandate to make a bunch of pictures because one of the first things he invested in was *sex, lies and videotape* and it had made a lot of money. I had met him on the set of *Little Vegas* because he had financed that picture. Maggie went and had a meeting with him and said, "We think we can make it for three million dollars very quickly," and he said, "Great." That was that—one-stop shopping, terrific. And we agreed that we would look for the right distributor later on.

Vincent Spano and Anthony John Denison in *City of Hope.*

What made you think you could shoot something of this scale for as low as three million?

We were very lucky. We got the weather we needed, we had really good actors and crew. It's a very ambitious movie to shoot in five weeks. We were able to shoot in forty different locations in thirty days. That's really tough. We often had a company move in the middle of the day and we still got it done. I think I ended up throwing a couple of lines one way or the other so we didn't have to carry an actor for an extra week.

And night shooting is expensive, but we didn't change anything from night to day. Shooting in mastershots, while they take a lot of doing, once it's shot, you save time in the shooting and the editing. We would cover one eight-page scene in a morning. I wrote the transitions in the script, the term I used was "trade." I would have a conversation going, and then the stage direction would say, "And we trade and follow these two characters. And these are the first lines that we hear, and these are the first lines that we see on camera." Very much written in the script.

And it was very much a conceptual thing: "This is how I'm going to keep from having to cut between this business and that business. And these are the things that I want to link." We did a lot of prep before we even got to the day of shooting. I would go to the locations with Bob Richardson with a video camera, some production assistants, and a script and we would have them read the parts and walk — "Let's see how far the dialogue takes us from this office on this set. Does it get us to the stairs? Oh, it gets us halfway down the stairs. Well, that's the point where I want this other character to come in, so that's where we're gonna pick up this guy and go over here." So we worked out the shots before the actors even showed up. So Bob would say, "I'm going to have a problem lighting this unless we have a cut here or somebody to block a light right here or somebody to pop up with a reflector board and pop down behind the bar." To the point where there's a very long mastershot of the bar that I'm in, and I'm basically standing at the bar watching the little video-assist, and when I saw it hit a certain character I knew I'm about to come onscreen so I put it behind the bar, looked into my drink, looked over, did my scene, and then they went past me after about five lines with Vincent Spano where we insult each other a little bit, and then I followed the camera to watch the rest of the scene. We had worked things out to that point.

It's an energizing thing for actors to be able to do it in one, to know it's not going to be cut into little pieces. I told the actors, "Yes, you wander off camera, but you have to wander off camera with the energy and knowledge of what you're going to say next, so that if the camera followed you we would have a story. Each one of you, no matter what your piece in the puzzle is, we have to feel like that's a story worth following. And the movie could be about just that." There's a lot of pressure on the last guy. We had one long scene in City Hall where the last guy who had dialogue blew his line—and it was a really good take. I would shoot until I had two that I liked and then that was that. So we had a much shorter editing period because I knew that in a two-hour-and-ten-minute movie I had a half hour to forty minutes worth of master-shots, where you pick the one you like the best, cut the slates off and go to the beach—you just cut eight minutes. In post, on a good day, maybe you cut five minutes. There were a few nights when Bob Richardson said, "Next time you make a low-budget movie, please write a low-budget script." But we shot it in five weeks.

The look of the film was going to be hard-edged, not a lot of pretty light, which you could do fast, so you don't have to hang a lot of stuff. I wanted hard, directional light that was invasive, sometimes it even invades the head. There's a shot with Joe Morton where he's backlit so hard that it actually starts to eat away at the outline of his head. I knew Bob was fast from working with him on *Eight Men Out* so I knew we could make it in five weeks. It wasn't nearly as hectic as making *Brother from Another Planet* because we were working with all experienced people instead of relative newcomers.

What were you trying to express through this camera style, beyond the functionality of keeping things flowing?

Basically that these people don't know it, but they're all connected. We know they're connected because we see them in the same frame without a cut. But the characters all think, "Oh, it's us and them. We're over here and they're over there. How can something that they do affect me?" When in a small city like that—absolutely. When people were asking me about that, I often used

Jace Alexander, Todd Graff, and Vincent Spano in
City of Hope.

the example of "Okay, it seems like a personal decision to send
your kid to a private school if you live in New York City or
Boston. But it absolutely affects the fact that the public schools
suck now." Too many of the people who should be, or could be,
staying and fighting to make those public schools better are saying, "Nah, I'm not sending my kid into that," even though they
went to public schools. It's not just a personal decision, it's a political decision.

*Why did you open the film with a tight, canted close-up of Vincent
Spano's face, and then have the shot right itself slightly?*

One of the things you worry about when you're doing those big
mastershots is losing any personal point of view. So I wanted to
start in this guy's head—you hear construction noise, which is
kind of like a headache. I wanted to start with him and then gen-
eralize. So you're right in the guy's face and he's talking about his
personal problems and then without a cut you're kind of wandering around in the world. You say, "Who's this guy? He's very

unhappy, there's something a little off-kilter here." There's something wrong with this picture, and something unbalanced about this guy's life. And then you get into, "Oh, he's at a construction site and he's not happy with his job and in fact his father runs the site." All the way down till he meets his friends, you get a lot of information about him, but you are also starting to get other information, and you lose him for a little while, and you see a city councilman talking with the guy who runs the construction site. So you get a little bit of that background, but then you get back to him. It's a way of saying this is one of our main characters, giving him an intro, but then that first shot is like the whole movie. We're going to spend a lot of time with this one guy, he's kind of the protagonist, but then here's this other guy who might be the protagonist, plus there's this whole social world around them. It's like the opening of *The Howling,* which tells you the kind of movie it's going to be. To me every movie is its own world.

This is the first time you shot a film in the 'scope aspect ratio. Did that present new problems or challenges?

Even though the city is usually not thought of as a horizontal thing, Bob's idea, and it really made a lot of sense, was we're going to be doing all these mastershots with a lot of different characters and we were going to be trading two people talking in the foreground for three people who were coming up the hallway in the background, so we use Panavision wide screen and we can have all five people on screen without sacrificing image size. And without panning to find people, we would be able to just hold. And it wouldn't feel too crowded. And one of the things you don't want to do with a 'scope movie is pan, because it makes you seasick to watch it if you pan fast. We would make slight adjustments in the blocking and start to see the people who were about to become the story in the background. And then we talked about, "Okay, it's going to add a couple of pounds to the steadicam. Because we're definitely going to need some steadicam in this, we'll do as much as we can on the dolly." But Bob's a hard-ass with his crew, so he said, "Well, what the hell. He'll be in good shape when the movie's over." I think our guy had to check into a hospital.

How did the film's structure and style affect your approach to pacing and dramatic emphasis?

Each of the films has its own rhythm. *Eight Men Out* and *Matewan* are set within a year of each other, but they have very different rhythms. The rhythm of *Matewan* is the rhythm of a mountain ballad. And it's very dissolve-y and slow and has some of the feeling of the seasons. Whereas *Eight Men Out* is the dawn of the Jazz Age, so it has a much faster rhythm. Even the montages are percussive. *City of Hope* opens with this industrial-strength rock and roll and the sound of an elevator. It's relentless from that point on. Rather than fast cutting I have the trading. Information and story just keep coming at you. It's not quite Oliver Stone, but it is an in-your-face kind of movie. There's not much relief in it. In some of the other movies, I actually will do something just for relief. In the baseball scene in *Matewan*—bad shit is going to happen fairly soon, but we have to have a time where things look hopeful before the audience goes under again. It's almost like a drumroll to prepare you for the fall. There's no drumroll of wonderfulness in *City of Hope*. There're little snatched moments.

What's the narrative throughline for the film?

There are two throughlines, two guys who are having these parallel crises—Vincent Spano's character, Nick, and Joe Morton's character, Wynn. Their lives cross in three or four different places but they never meet. There's an interview with Allan Dwan where he talks about trying to eliminate anybody who's only connected to the story by one strand when you have a big cast. I kept that in mind when I was writing, so the person that Joe Morton has to ask a favor for, his wife's brother, ends up being the night security guy in the store when the guys break into the place, but then he has a nice long scene with Vincent Spano on the basketball court. So he's connected in two or three places. It's fairly rare that there's a guy who has a day player scene. The two mentors, the old mayor and the mafia guy played by Lawrence Tierney are one-offs, but you figure their influence is still on the city. And then I realized I had more than two guys; there's the Tony Lo Bianco character. So I had these nice arcs for these characters.

The history of immigration in this country is that that first generation barely made a living but their kids are going to finish high school and do better than they did. And then there's the Tony Lo Bianco generation who bust their butt and make the compromises they have to make and they get somewhere. And then within two or three generations there are these guys who say I don't want to work as hard as Pop did, I don't want to waste my life kissing the asses of these politicians and mafia guys—I want to write songs or whatever it is they want to do. Then you know you've made it in America. Vincent Spano's arc was dealing with that—he's disaffected when we first meet him; he's inherited certain assumptions in a world that he doesn't like. He thinks his father is very corrupt but he didn't know how hard it was to survive when his father was a kid. So to a certain extent he sees through the bullshit but he's on shaky ground because he grew up in a different world than his father did. And his father made all these compromises and now the check is coming due.

And with Joe Morton's character the arc is this guy who is a representative for his people, but how clean can he stay? Is there any way to stay honest in politics? One of my theses with that is that it's as easy for a politician to be disappointed in his constituents as it is for his constituents to be disappointed in the politician. When you see the arc of a politician, very often they start out as reformers, and there's a certain belief that the people are good and want good things and if he can reform the system and deliver services to people—you're a public servant. And by the end they can be really horrible, cynical, Richard Daley kind of people who say, "Ah, you hand the people any kind of shit as long as you do this, this, and this—they'll eat it up." The scene where Joe Morton visits the old mayor on the golf course for him is kind of, "Is this the ghost of Christmas future? Is this who I become if I start making compromises and do I have to do that?" And the old mayor is not totally cynical. He says, "I did some good stuff and this is your job, you can make progress. You've also got to play ball sometimes." Whereas the total cynic is Lawrence Tierney's character, this mob guy, who's saying, "This is the way the world works." I always felt the New Jersey state motto should be "Hey, what you gonna do?" which is what my character echoes.

Angela Bassett and Joe Morton in *City of Hope*.

Of the three characters crises, Nick's seems to be the most emotional and psychological.

He's younger and it's personal and he doesn't know who the fuck he is and eventually he's so extremely unhappy that he's putting himself in physical danger for no good reason, and that's his way of acting out—so he's the least focused. Both Tony Lo Bianco and Joe Morton are players, they can try to pull things off in the world. Lo Bianco's character blows it and Morton's saves the day by finding a third way—he's lucky, he dodges the bullet. Vincent Spano's character doesn't know any way to make the world work for him.

The father/son relationship also functions as a kind of microcosm for the pressures of social obligation and alienation.

Yeah, and between Joe Morton and his constituents.

The film is as much about family as society.

Yeah, and you run back and forth. One of the things that I wanted to get into is that small-city politics is always personal. Even in

Los Gusanos—Cuba was a small enough country—it was personal, not just ideological. One of the main theses of the film is that it's one thing to expect, on a national level, people to be good politicians and do things for reasons of principle. On a small-city level it's, "If we lose the mayoral election, your uncle Louie loses his job with the city and he's such a fucking loser he's never going to find a job that pays that much. Your cousins aren't going to go to college." That's a hard thing to ask somebody to do, to do something on principle when it's going to hurt their family. That's what society asks people to do all the time.

What was your conception of Asteroid?

Asteroid was always meant to be somebody who had hooked onto a metaphor for what he saw around him and that metaphor was mass media and mass marketing being the god of the time. So the things that he says are catchphrases that you hear in advertising: "Money talks, nobody walks," "Why settle for less when you can have it all?" He's always looking at TV and hooking into what I think of as the carrot that's always in front of you, the way the boys who mug the guy are when they're looking at the video machines and sneakers. In this country if you're poor you have this constant media thing going around you reminding you that you should have these things and that there's probably something wrong with you if you don't—so there's this rubbing in that you're not with the program. And I wanted there to be some kind of chorus—I do some of it with radio ads and billboards, but I also wanted it personified in some way. So he's intoxicated by mass media, like someone walking around India talking about Vishnu.

In terms of David Strathairn's performance, did you have a specific pathology?

It's almost like autism crossed with Tourette's syndrome. The autistic part keeps him from seeing the things he doesn't want to see, the warm, human things and sentimental connections with people. The Tourette's is that he has to express the metaphors. No matter what you say to him, he'll find a way to turn it into his obsession. I told him, "You hear something, you see something, but these are the messages that are getting through."

So what's the significance of him hearing and taking up Tony Lo Bianco's calls for help at the very end?

It nailed the coffin shut. At that point Tony Lo Bianco is kind of asking for help from the world and from above, and all he's going to get is an echo. They could yell back and forth for another five minutes, which they do—I cut before they ran out of gas. It's a fairly bleak ending and it's similar to *Lone Star* except that *City of Hope* is like a snapshot; it doesn't go back into the past. It's right here, right now, boom—there's the American city and these problems. And because it was a snapshot, it was less hopeful, because it was a very bad period. We did screenings and got people who were city workers and cops and people who worked with the homeless to come in and talk about their city after they had seen it. In each city we would get a different response. In L.A. what was amazing was that except for the people down in Watts and one or two more radical councilmen it was like, "Oh, we don't have those kinds of problems, that's an eastern urban problem." And you'd say, "Oh, what about Watts?" and half the people we talked to who were city officials said, "Well, that's not part of L.A." I said, "Well, yes it is." This was before the L.A. riots. It was interesting, the reactions I got were very much the same as those we got for *Baby, It's You*, where some people said, "So they stay together, right?" I said, "You wish, but no." With *City of Hope* people said, "Where's the hope in the movie?" The title can be taken literally or ironically because it's a film about believers and cynics. If Joe Morton says, "I want to make this a city of hope," you believe him. If the mayor, who is a cynic, says it, it's ironic. A city of hope according to him is a city where you take everything that's not nailed down and leave the blacks and Hispanics to fight over what's left. That's patronage politics when it goes bad. It's the same movie—it's a litmus test. How do you see the world? I can understand why you feel like it's pretty hopeless, if you look at the big picture. And that may be a Rorschach test for people who see this movie.

How do you feel about Wynn's "triumph"?

Well, it's a very mixed triumph. He does get people mobilized, they go to City Hall, they win one little battle, and that's it. His only triumph is that he's very lucky he got out of it that time. You've got to feel good because he doesn't sell out, he finds a way not to, and he's learning a little skill. But you've also got to feel, how long is he going to be able to survive doing that? He's learned two things: He's done his first political favor, he's gotten his wife's brother a job, and he's done his first finesse, where he's found a way to not commit himself to either side because he was going to lose votes if he went one way or the other. So he's turning into a politician, which is not necessarily bad, that's what his job is. You just hope that if he's in office another eight years or he becomes the next mayor that he's able to hold on to a little bit of his soul and his ideals. There is still some hope with him; he is not a totally corrupted character but he's got to get his hands dirty.

Passion Fish is a film that keeps the audience off-balance for a while. It doesn't tell you up front what you're going to be watching. It's almost abstract in comparison with the materiality of City of Hope's concreteness.

I had the idea for this movie since I was in college and saw *Persona* and I kept looking for a place to put it. I had worked as an orderly for years and was always interested in the women I worked with who were also visiting nurses and had private patients. What always interested me about it was these were mostly pretty tough women who had kids and their husbands weren't in the picture and they were working midnight shift with me and pretty much the private home patients did what they wanted to. They were in charge. If you're a patient in a nursing home, you're not ordering people around. Or, if you are, they'd probably just leave you there in your own puddle of pee. So these were women whose uniform at our job said, "I'm the person in charge." When they went and worked in a private home, that uniform said, "I'm like the maid." It was one person and their family paying them to do this kind of thing and unless the patient was non compos mentis and was really out of it and they were alone with them, if the

Alfre Woodard and Mary McDonnell in *Passion Fish*.

guy wanted a cherry soda, you went down to the corner and got him a cherry soda. You could complain about it, but that was your job, to be a companion, to be a maid, to be the person who did the medical care, to sit in the room, to watch the same TV show if that's what they wanted to do. So there was this incredible loss of power. And I started thinking about power relationships and how this was a strange one because one person was in power because he was healthy and could walk around and the other person was powerful because he was the one who had economic power and signed the checks. And what a weird up-and-down thing that could be, that there were moments in the day when the person who was the poor mother of three kids, who had to have two jobs just to get by, was the powerful one. Because she could walk and the other person couldn't. My idea was like *Persona* where there was a woman in a wheelchair in some kind of power struggle that could turn out friendly. And I always felt in the American version, they would be different races, the woman who was pushing the woman in the wheelchair around would be black. In my experience in hospitals, that was pretty much the story.

And the catalyst for me to make the movie was a place that would make you come out, that there was something you would come out for, a place and a culture that was seductive in some way. We were traveling with some Australian friends, doing a tour from Austin through Louisiana in a van, to listen to music. We hooked up with Jimmy MacDonnell who has this zydeco band Loup Guru. We went to see Buckwheat Zydeco and Jimmy at a Mother's Day show in Lafayette and Jimmy said, "Oh, you shouldn't go to a hotel tonight, you should stay with my parents. It's on the lake." We stayed at this lake and I woke up in the morning and I said to Maggie, "This is the place where that story about the woman in the wheelchair has to happen." Once I had that place the movie started taking shape and we ended up shooting there. Louisiana's not the kind of community where you can lock yourself away without somebody coming and asking if you're okay. There's still a personal thing there. It's not anonymous, which can be claustrophobic, and I'm sure it was for May-Alice when she was younger. People know your business. People know

Alfre Woodard, David Strathairn, and Mary McDonnell
in *Passion Fish*.

if you come to church or not. But for her, it means there is no chance to hide. If she stays in New York, she could be one of those people in an apartment who you never see again, who just sends out for things.

The film is mainly about May-Alice and Chantelle's relations to the physical world around them. And May-Alice hasn't been looking. When you're looking at TV you're not looking at anything else. She's closed the blinds. She's on the lawn for two seconds and then the nurse carries her in. She doesn't go out after that. But then she's starting to resee something that she ignored and wanted to get away from when she was a kid, which is why I had her get back into photography. And eventually that leads to her coming back to the world, hoping to be happy again. And when we meet her, she has given up on that possibility, she just wants to not feel pain. And that's pretty much what Chantelle has just come out of, which is a serious drug thing. And she doesn't want any complications, she doesn't want to get involved with Sugar, she just wants to stay even keeled and maybe her father will give her her kid back. And she starts getting sucked out into life again.

Race remains a subtext—it's not manifest, until outsiders come in.

Exactly. One of the points of having them be of different races is that in that relationship, race is usually expected to be the big separator, yet it's not that big a deal. When they get out in the world it's a big deal. In that house, the power relationship is not about black and white, it's about "I'm able-bodied and you pay my check." So the power struggles are all about that, to the point where Chantelle wins by leaving May-Alice on the lawn and May-Alice wins by getting Chantelle to come back and say, "I need this job." So they have leverage over each other. I usually don't do cinematic in-jokes, but it was on purpose that the movie they watch together is *What Ever Happened to Baby Jane?*, which is these two women in a house doing numbers on one another. But I also felt like it would be more of a comedy. What I wanted was the audience to identify with a character who wasn't necessarily likable, to spend some time with her before she got into that power relationship. Having had a lot of SCI (Spinal Cord Injury) patients and knowing the stuff they went through when they were first in-

Mary McDonnell in *Passion Fish*.

jured from depression to anger back to depression, and who were considered good candidates for rehab and who weren't, I knew that basically, any problems that you had before you were hurt, you still had. If you were an asshole before you were hurt, you're an asshole in a wheelchair now. If you were a person who didn't have that many problems, you now had this physical problem but mentally you might be able to get past it because you had some strength going into it.

My other big thing was the idea of limits and I very much wanted it to be about two women who were forty, running into these walls. There's a connection between *Baby, It's You, Return of the Secaucus Seven,* and *Passion Fish. Baby, It's You* is about being twenty and that first inkling that not everything is possible, that not everything is going to turn out the way you wanted it to. She says, "I don't love you," and he says, "Why not?" The idea that there might be a ceiling is so new to those kids. *Return of the Secaucus Seven* is about being thirty and this recognition that the world is not going to turn out the way you wanted it to and you're going to have to deal with that. They're still very hopeful and idealistic, however, they just know it's going to be an uphill climb. *Passion Fish* is very much about being forty and having hit unpassable ceilings. They're people who have to realize that not only is the world not going to end up the way they wanted it to, their lives are not going to be what they hoped them to be. The one woman is not going to be Meryl Streep, she's not even going to be able to have a baby, and the other is not going to be able to be the fun-loving party girl she always wanted to be, she's going to have to buckle down and do these responsible things that may be as boring as taking care of some rich white lady, because she's got a daughter to take care of. I'm fascinated by America where so much of advertising and the American psyche is about no frontiers, manifest destiny, the sky's the limit. What happens to people who hit that ceiling? Then what do you do? That's what "Shannon's Deal" was about.

Is that something you've experienced?

Sure. With things other than movies so far. Certainly all my kid dreams were of being an athlete. And at a certain point you realize, "Jeez, not only am I not lucky enough to get to be the center

Alfre Woodard in *Passion Fish*.

fielder for the Pittsburgh Pirates, but I'm not good enough. There are people better than me and no matter how hard I work I'm not going to be that good. Now what do I do with that?" Not a huge thing, but something I had to deal with. I wasn't as smart as I wanted to be at certain things. I really liked biology and science and I got to a certain point where I realized that with the kind of intelligence that I have, I could never be a doctor.

What's the significance of Rennie's passion fish story?

He is saying you have to hold this in your hand and wish for something. These are two women who haven't been wishing. As a good Cajun he's probably making it up at the moment.

Did you make it up?

Yeah. But there's a lot of things like that in Cajun lore—reading the entrails of fish, stuff like that. During that trip they both hook into it. May-Alice shows it more than Chantelle does, but she has this strange, great time that she never expected to have before. And if she decides to pursue this thing with Rennie, it's this impossible relationship. He's a serious Catholic and you don't just leave your wife and kid, and she's paralyzed from the waist down. So this is not a marriage made in heaven. But what is possible is that they're actually going to have a pretty good relationship—and to a certain extent she's the perfect woman, because he can go over to her house and his wife isn't going to be jealous. Because she believes, "This is a woman who's not a woman anymore, she's paralyzed from the waist down. What kind of threat could she be?"

Is there actually a fish called "passion fish"?

No, we made up the name. And we didn't have a name for the movie for the longest time, it was just called "The Louisiana Project." All I could come up with were nasty, facetious titles like "One Walks, the Other Doesn't." We had a contest; we had the local junior high school sending us titles; we had the crew writing things. "Passion Fish" was one of my possibilities and I think two other people on the crew also suggested it.

What approach did you take to the material stylistically?

I wanted the audience to take the trip with May-Alice into that depression. I talked with the cinematographer, Roger Deakins, about the light, that we would start in this very clinical light of the hospital. We don't really see anybody else's face, it's very much May-Alice struggling, and it's very frustrating, but there's this hard light on it, there is no escaping, she can't lift herself up, there's no darkness, there's nowhere to hide, and that's what I wanted for the opening. But the minute she gets to her house, the frame starts getting tighter and tighter. We started putting more and more layers of curtain on until finally the only light, in that room in that montage where all the caretakers come, is the TV set and we're in very tight shots on people. I wanted to get to the point where the audience is shriveling up with this woman, rolling up in a ball, and she's got her two drugs, television and wine, and she's anesthetizing herself. And then Chantelle comes in and the first thing you get is light coming in. It's like a vampire movie at first. We let it be hard; you almost expect little holes to appear in May-Alice. And one of the first things Chantelle does is drag her outside and dump her on the lawn and she's squinting. The first time you see Chantelle alone up in her room, she's weeping too and you know she's got some heavy-duty stuff—and there are these two unhappy women in this house.

Was there a deliberate strategy to film the characters in single shots and separation initially, and then at a certain point start putting them in two-shots?

That's allegorical grouping and I started doing more of that about the time of *Matewan.* Think of a Western—*High Noon*—Gary Cooper against everybody. You can do it in a fairly mechanical way, but I think it does add up. You can have somebody in a shot with other people but, for instance, when May-Alice is in a shot with other people for the whole beginning of the movie, you don't see their faces. She's so isolated, she's like the little girl at the beginning of *The Secret of Roan Inish*, in that she's in her own world. They're in their world and they don't really see into hers and she doesn't have any time or energy to see into theirs. So I really wanted to keep those two women as isolated as possible from each other for as long as possible. When we got them outside, a lot of what we wanted to do was tie them to their background. Antonioni is famous for allegorical architecture: one character will have a volcano next to her and the other will have the peaceful sea next to him in the same shot. I don't quite do it that metaphorically, but I did want May-Alice, and Chantelle too, but mostly May-Alice, to start to get tied in with that land, because she's starting to have some kind of connection to it. Which is one of the reasons I had them not in the living room, but out on the lake at the end.

Why did you choose to have so much fluid camera movement in the film, most of which isn't informational or narrating?

I wanted some of the sensuous quality of the music and the land and the colors down there to get into the movement. In that montage of caretakers, at the same time it's getting more dark and claustrophobic and May-Alice is just not leaving her couch, it starts to get more and more static. Then when they get outside, there's much more emotion. It's a very dissolve-y kind of country: you've got the Spanish moss hanging down, the trees don't even have hard angles, there're rivers that are very sinuous. You get into that a little bit with the zydeco and then that trip at night on the mudboat with Rennie is very lyrical and sensuous. And I just wanted that feeling to be part of what was invading their lives. A reawakening of not necessarily sexuality, but sensuality.

Then the other thing I wanted was to be in the arena with them. Sometimes May-Alice is moving, sometimes she's stationary. Sometimes Chantelle is moving. And I wanted the camera to have the ability to not necessarily watch them static. It's so personal and so intense sometimes that you really want to get in their faces. And to do that you're going to have to move if either one of them moves, instead of cut, cut, cut. So often what I wanted the camera to be was the referee at a boxing match, where you keep moving as the referee so that your angle isn't blocked. We would work it out after the actresses worked out how they were going to move. I was playing more with the idea that their relationship was always in flux. It's a teeter-totter of power and they have their moments where they just butt heads and they have their moments where they both make each other miserable and they even have some

moments together that are really nice. The first moment occurs
when the two sisters, who went to Catholic College, come over
and May-Alice gets Chantelle to act a scene with her. She just says,
"My injections," and Chantelle picks it up and really does a nice
acting job.

And that's not the end of the movie, they have other problems
after that, but that's the first time they play together. And that
changes the flux. So we tried to schedule everything so I had more
time with the actresses and they had more time with each other.
Rather than saying, "We're going to do this until you hit it once,"
I would keep going back to them and saying, "We've got an interesting thing going here." I'd take Alfre to one side, and once again
to use the boxing idea, I'd get her in the corner. "This time I want
you to be more aggressive." And then I might go to Mary and say,
"You're really feeling vulnerable here. If she pushes, you might
break." And just see what happens, play with that dynamic a little
bit more. And in playing with the dynamic I'd say, "Don't move
any different, but you push more." And neither would know what
the other was doing. And the great thing about those two actors
is, they're real actors. If somebody does something in the frame
with them, they're going to react to it. They're not just going to
play the same notes they hit before. So it was always very dynamic
between the two of them.

*Acting is itself incorporated into the film's thematics, which exam-
ine the relation between real life and daytime soaps. What were
you trying to get at there?*

I wanted to play those two elements against each other. Here's
somebody who's been in that soap opera world of misery and
that's been her profession and she's never been stuck in it for real.
That's the irony, as in *Secaucus Seven*, which takes on the form of
a soap opera. You could almost make a soap opera out of it, and I
guess they did. What was that TV show? "Thirtysomething." I
never watched it, but people watched it religiously, like a soap
opera. The main thing about the world of the soap opera is when
you don't like a story you can change it. So the actresses say, "Oh,
the next season they decided I would be a bad girl instead of a
good girl." And when the producer comes back to ask May-Alice
to return to the show, she's not just going to be in a wheelchair,

she's going to be blind too. You can just do that with a snap of your fingers. And people disappear and they die and they bring them back. "Okay, we'll just change the story"—there is something in that that is juvenile and wonderful and false, the way that only a soap opera can be, that lets the audience and the actors out of real commitment. There is also a style of acting in soap operas that lets you out of real commitment. People die all the time in soap operas and the actors stay at pretty much that same emotional level. There's no grief on a soap opera. I've had actress friends who were fired off soap operas because they were acting too realistic and they were told the American public, or the people who watch soap operas anyway, don't want the camera on you while you're feeling real emotions because it's too scary.

So in a way, I wanted to play May-Alice's real, heavy shit against that lack of commitment. And when you're paralyzed, you are committed. You are there. Soap opera work is a way of avoiding commitment because it's good money, it's a good job, and you can tell yourself you're still an actor. May-Alice had all these dreams about being a movie actress and doing real work and when the actresses visit, everybody rolls their eyes and says, "Oh, yeah. Haven't we all said that?" But if you don't value it the way that May-Alice didn't value it, you're always going to be fooling yourself a little bit, and you're always going to be somebody who specializes in relationships with people you don't really care about that much because then you can't get hurt.

As a writer you have a natural sense of humor that you put to use in the scripts you write for other people but largely avoid in your own films. Passion Fish *is the first film of your own that has a comedic side. And yet you're also trying to maintain a certain level of realism. What's the relationship between them?*

It is a comedy, in that it's not a tragedy. Or it's a melodrama, which I guess is somewhere in between. Occasionally there is humor that the character isn't trying to generate. When the two old high school friends come to visit, some of what happens is kind of funny, a little bit satirical. And the same thing with the soap opera actresses—the character played by Sheila Kelley, who's spouting the phony Faulkner I wrote for her, and Nancy Mette's character, who goes into a whole speech about the anal probe.

David Strathairn, Alfre Woodard, and Mary McDonnell
in *Passion Fish*.

Which to me is the metaphor for life and limitations. And that
speech is about being a trooper and doing it as best as you can, if
that's what you've been handed.

Humor is a very tricky thing. Because *Passion Fish* is a movie
about a woman in a wheelchair, it could really be grim. And one
of the things I like the most about people, especially Americans, is
their ability to come up with gallows humor, to be humorous in
very, very difficult situations. I'm always interested in using humor
the way I'm interested in using violence, to tell you something
about the characters. So in *Return of the Secaucus Seven* one of
the things you should notice is that when the men and women separate they talk to each other in different ways. The women talk directly about their problems with each other. The men tend to give
each other humorous shit, tease each other, make jokes, and then
when they actually have to work something out, they do it on the
basketball court, in a physical, indirect way with this smash between J.T. and Jeff.

In the genre movies I've written for other people, for them to be
interesting and have any kind of perspective on themselves, they
have to have a sense of humor. I'm real careful in a movie with

tone. You can blow the tone of something very quickly. And you can blow it by being too serious in some cases. For instance once you set the tone of violence in a movie, if you change it you can really knock people out of the movie and they can't watch it anymore; for example, if you've been having comic violence and all of a sudden somebody's shot right in the head. I think that was the purpose of a guy getting shot right in the head in *Bonnie and Clyde*: "Wait a minute, whoa. That was direct and nasty. We're in a whole new world here." This isn't just lighthearted anymore, we've taken the tone and we've darkened it and we can't lighten it again. If there's a sense of humor in what I do, I usually ask, "Okay, does this character have a sense of humor or not? And what kind of sense of humor is it?"

One of the funniest lines I've ever written was in *Lone Star* just after Charlie Wade blows the guy's head off and the deputy says, "You killed him," and Charlie says, "You have a talent for stating the obvious." Now that was part of Charlie Wade. He had this really mean sense of humor that he uses to get people to fight with him. So it's about character. It's not necessarily that the audience is going to laugh.

Why have your films from City of Hope *on all dealt with recovery, coming to terms, or reconciliation?*

Redemption. One thing is, I'm dealing with older people. *Baby, It's You, Return of the Secaucus Seven*, even *Lianna* are about fairly young people. The characters in *Eight Men Out* are kids. That's part of the reason they get into what they get into. I don't know if I would feel like making another kid movie.

That's not strictly true though. In The Secret of Roan Inish, *the protagonist is the little girl. It's about the family but it's very much about children, and yet it's still dealing with those issues.*

To a certain extent, with the grandparents it is. But I think that seeing the world clearly and figuring out what you're going to do about either the world's limitations in regards to you or your limitations in regards to the world is a huge part of life. In the Catholic religion, and I think you see it in Scorsese's movies sometimes, which are more Catholic than mine, you need temptation and occasions of sin in order for you to be a good person. If everything was fine and there were no temptations, you wouldn't sin, but it wouldn't count for anything. You have to be tested. I think when you're talking about character, many of the themes, even in "Shannon's Deal," are about characters presented with these moral choices, or moments where they get to show a lot of character or crap out on themselves. And that's the victory. So it's an arena of drama that interests me more than who shot who and whether the hero escapes at the end. *The Fugitive* was extremely well made, but it doesn't have a big character shift in it. There are some nice turnabouts, but it's really about "Can this guy clear his name?" I guess there's character in that he just doesn't give up, but he's a hero after all.

CHAPTER 9

The Secret of Roan Inish and Lone Star

Is The Secret of Roan Inish *your "finding your roots" film?*

Not really. Being Irish wasn't a big part of my youth. Being Catholic was, but that's a totally different thing. This is a story that Maggie had read when she was ten years old, and she remembered it for years and years and would tell me, "There're not enough movies for kids. We should make this thing." Finally I read it and I said, "You're right. This is a really neat story." So I wrote it in the two weeks before we went to Louisiana to shoot *Passion Fish*, so that while I was editing *Passion Fish* Maggie and Sarah Green, her partner, could go look for locations in Ireland. Rosalie Frye's novella was set in Scotland. She's an illustrator too; some of the shots in the movie are right from her illustrations—the shots of the little girl lying in the flowers or looking down at her grandfather or when she's in the boat and the seals are popping up around her in the fog. At the very end of the movie you see some of her illustrations at the bottom under the credits. During World War II she was a coast-watcher on the coast of Scotland. And she never saw any submarines with her binoculars, but she saw a lot of seals. And she asked if there were any stories about them and they told her the story, which exists both on the Irish coast and in Scotland. I set it in Ireland, because besides being a little more familiar with Irish history and culture, one of the things that I did get from the Irish Americans around me growing up and in Boston was that so many American songs are about going on the road, going to a great place, while Irish songs very often are about loss, they're about leaving something behind. That sense of Ireland being this island that's obsessed with loss—their national sovereignty, their language, their sons and daughters, and a certain past, seemed to me perfect for this particular story, which is about the loss of an island and a way of life. And is there any way to go

Jeni Courtney as Fiona in *The Secret of Roan Inish* (1994).

back to that world? Scotland has its own preoccupations, but the loss isn't as heavy.

If the characters are looking back on a lost way of life, it isn't an idealized one.

There is a fantasy children's movie in *Roan Inish*, but finally there is also this very realistic core to it. The kids win not by finding the secret ring or the magic passageway. They win by going and busting their butt, and committing themselves to a very hard life. They've said, "We're going to live on this island where there's no running water, and we have to work to even earn that right." That's a tougher message than what's generally in your average fantasy/children's movie. The grandmother is saying, "It's so hard," and the grandfather is saying, "There's not too many women who would come to this island and accept this life of tough work." At the same time they are lost in the new world. There's nothing for the little girl there. And the grandparents, because they are as old as they are, they're just on borrowed time and have lost their animus by being away from that island. So there isn't anything golden about it. That's why I have the two kids do so much work. They work in the book, but I made the sequence much longer and gave them more heavy physical labor to do to get those cottages in shape. The kids had fun doing it too, because they only had to do it for a couple of takes and then stop. And then the art department took care of the rest.

I didn't change a whole lot from the novella. I wanted to give it a little bit of an edge, so I invented the character of Tadhg, who John Lynch plays. I had heard of the sylkie myth before. I felt like a lot of the information this little girl is getting in this story is pretty heavy stuff and it's not necessarily that cool to be related to the sylkies; there are fishermen who think it's bad luck to be related to them. So I wanted the story that she gets about her background and the sylkie woman not to come from the congenial old grandfather but from somebody who was a little threatening. And I thought of *Treasure Island* where you have this kid who is among these adults who do not necessarily always have the kid's best interests at heart. In the case of Tadhg, it's not that he's going to do something bad, but he's a little menacing and upsetting—he's crazy.

When I started working on the adaptation, I started thinking

"What do I really like about this story?" One of the cool things is it's great to read aloud, and I started thinking of the oral tradition versus what we now have in this country, which is a media tradition. In oral tradition, stories are passed on by word of mouth, generation to generation, and they connect you with your ancestors, and who you are as a people. They are often creation myths, or "How we came to this place." Very often they are also very practical—the stories about the sea not only tell you legends about your ancestors, they tell you, "If you see this kind of sky, get off the water fast. Or if you see this condition there's going to be a lot of mackerel around." And those are things you need to know to survive. Native American oral history is often the same.

So oral tradition is partly about keeping history intact, but it's also an instruction manual for life.

Yeah, but only within its context. If you change the context it doesn't work anymore. So in this place where we have always lived, this is how things work. And these stories tell us that how somebody say twenty generations ago dealt with it, is still a good way to deal with it. There's not that connection between you and your own history with a media tradition. It's a little like religion in California: "Well, I'm tired of being a Buddhist, I think I'm going to be a born-again Jew. But only the parts I like, not the dietary stuff, because that's a pain in the ass." And then maybe a year from now you'll be a Sufi. Whereas religion in an oral tradition society is hooked into the nature around you, who you are as a person and a race, what your name is.

The oral tradition very much shapes Roan Inish's *narrative approach—the stories provide the little girl with a framework and references.*

I played with different ways to present that oral storytelling. One thing I didn't do is a whole lot of fast cutting. I realized early on that this is a movie kids will like if we can ever get them in the door, but the kids who are going to like it the most are the kids who are read to, not the kids who only sit in front of the TV and watch Saturday morning stuff that has a lot of fast cutting. We may get those kids back, but we're gonna lose them for a little

The Secret of Roan Inish.

while, where kids who have been read to will chill and look at the nice pictures, but they'll really be listening to the story. There are different strategies for different stories. So there is one story that consists of pictures with narrative voiceover, there is somebody telling a story without any pictures, there is the beginning of narrative over pictures and then the narrative goes away, and the pictures continue and the narrative comes back right at the end. In one, the guy introduces it and then there's no dialogue at all, just a montagey, impressionistic thing with music, when the kid floats away. The pictures that you were seeing were the pictures imagined by a ten-year-old Irish girl who's never seen a movie or a TV show, and so I wanted them to be somewhat fantastic. She doesn't even have a book with pictures in it to illustrate it, so she's extrapolating what the thing looks like from the words. Each of those stories changes the depth of Fiona's contact with her world. So the first story she hears is the one about Sean Michael, which is about the sea and its two-faced nature, but at the end of that danger is a domestic situation—just as at the beginning of the movie, Fiona is a little girl on this ship in the raw sea, but then she walks up in this huge green expanse and there's this nice cozy grandmother with the tea.

The first story Fiona hears suggests British colonialism is partly to blame for the erosion of the oral tradition, referring to the policy of forbidding the use of Gaelic in school.

That's something I brought in that wasn't in the book. I wanted this thing about Irish culture. Gaelic is not widely spoken there, but you still see it in signs, there's still this little connection with the world that came before. I found that to be a good metaphor for Fiona and the way she was living now with the world that came before, when seals and people were more symbiotic, when they lived a natural life and made their living off the sea. And also, just as you said, this is when they lost that language. When I did the research for *Roan Inish*, I read a bunch of autobiographies by writers who grew up on the Aran Islands. Almost all of them were written in Irish first and then translated into English and they were very poetic. When I went to Ireland with the script I had several people look at it, including people who were from Donegal and people who were older and remembered the thirties and forties, and asked them, "Would your grandmother or your father say this? Is this too archaic or too modern for when I'm setting it, right after World War II?" But also, the Irish-speaking people, including one guy who was the head of Irish-speaking television on the coast, would say occasionally, "This locution here, you've obviously got it from a book translated from the Gaelic. We don't say that in English. That's a direct translation from the Gaelic." For example, "Oh, they were cold poor." Well, you say "cold poor" in Gaelic, but by the time it got to English it was "dirt poor." It was an interesting thing, thinking about a bridge to the past being that language.

Another thing that gets established in that first story is this idea of speech having some kind of power, that utterance can be dangerous. The pivotal moment at the end is when Fiona finally tells the grandmother what she told everyone else.

And also direct utterance—you have to deal with it, you have to look someone in the eye, you don't couch it in a story or a metaphor. Irish is so metaphoric, when you say something direct it really means something. It's why I gave the little drumroll before Sean Michael finally speaks to the schoolmaster—you've been

hearing the other guy's voice and then all of a sudden—Boom!—
you hear this Irish curse.

*Is your conception of the mythic elements of the film—the sylkie
in the story, the way natural forces of the sea and the seals and
gulls behave both in the stories and in the main body of the film—
literal, as in* The Howling, *or a projection of Fiona's imagination?*

What you're seeing in the film is a conscious conspiracy between
the sky and the wind and the waves, the water, the seals and the
gulls, to take this child and keep him alive until these people come
back and hold up their end of the bargain. No, it's not the way
she's seeing them. There are scenes where someone's telling her a
story and we see how she would imagine the seal and everything,
but within the story, yes, the seals bring the little boy back, and
that's not a story she's being told. And the gull comes down and is
just watching, kind of supervising the whole thing. The waves get
choppy just when they need to throw Jamie back on shore. There's
a storm brewing and it waits until they get in the cottage and then
it lets loose. I try to give the audience a hint in the very first
scenes—the first point of view that you get is from underwater,
and then you come up and you see a boat. So the establishing
point of view isn't Fiona's, we get that later when she looks up and
sees the gull. The establishing point of view is the seal's, and the
last thing in the whole film is the seal on the rock. And also you
look over the seal's shoulder—if a seal has a shoulder—at Fiona,
from the seal's point of view. It was really important to me, and it
seems very simple, but that was the hardest shot in the whole
movie. Basically that's me trying to give the audience a hint that
there's a consciousness operating here. They're interested in this
girl for some reason.

*Another important shot is when the camera pulls back from Fiona
and Jamie at the fireplace to include the other characters. What
were you trying to get at with that shot?*

It was wide over their shoulders, toward the fire. Until that moment it had been Fiona and Jamie up by the fire and then turning
back to the grandparents and the cousin who hadn't believed her.

Jeni Courtney in *The Secret of Roan Inish*.

She's hooked into Jamie and finally the grandfather says, "Look at us all here. Who'd of believed it?" It's almost like a shot through the window at the whole family. We couldn't pull that off, so I just went back. They are together, they're going to keep trying to live there as a family unit. A strange one, not one that's going to be able to reproduce itself, but they've made that commitment.

Why did you choose Haskell Wexler to shoot this one?

Mainly because he's very good and he was available. But specifically because Haskell's really good with natural light and firelight from candles or fireplaces. Also, on the Donegal coast the Irish weather changes every hour. I knew how good Haskell was at making everything match and appear seamless. So I went back to what we did with *Return of the Secaucus Seven*—the call sheet would have three different scenarios on it. This is the sunny day scenario: if we had any sunny weather, Boom! we're right into Jamie being taken away. We got four sunny days in a row where we could shoot all that stuff. And then here is the nice but cloudy day scenario, and here is the really funky, about-to-rain-really-hard scenario. We had to be prepared for all three. And Haskell was able to do variations within each of those and match them. So he was the perfect guy for me.

What do you think the sylkie myth represents?

After I made it, people started sending me the chapter from *Women Who Run With the Wolves* that's about the sylkie myth. I think that a couple of things are going on there. One, I think people are part animal and so many of the early myths from so-called primitive people are about those animal parts of you. Native American myths are often about coyote people or crow people. You try to have the attributes of the things you eat and the things that are fellow hunters. If you eat the deer you try to take its swiftness. If you hunt the same things the coyote hunts you try to have its cunning.

I think there're also a huge number of myths all over the world about the animal you hunt being your brother, about the spirit of seals and the spirit of man being brothers at one time. Then one of the brothers walked on land and the other stayed at sea. We don't kill an animal, it's our brother—brother seal has sent us some food. So after we kill a seal we always thank them in some way. The Native Americans do the same thing with deer. It's the spirit of deer who has sent us some meat because it knows we're hungry. But that spirit is never touched, only this one that was sent to us as a gift, and we had to work for it a little, but it is not an enemy.

The second point is there are many different versions of the sylkie myth, and the heavy one is where her children try to follow her into the sea and they all drown. But I think almost all of them end with, "And he never hunted a seal again." People who were hunting seals were killing them for the oil because they probably didn't have a big enough boat to go kill a whale and couldn't afford whale oil. Seal meat was pretty awful so the seal was basically dumped. But nobody could afford guns, so they usually were tracking these seals in caves when the tide was going out and bludgeoning them to death with clubs or shovels or killing them with harpoons. Seals have big, very human eyes and I think that some of what was happening, was hunters and fishermen having some residual feeling of, "Oh, that looked so human when it looked at me." I think there was some little bit of guilt for killing this

Chris Cooper as Sheriff Sam Deeds in *Lone Star* (1996).

human-eyed creature, but also maybe a little embarrassment at being people who still had to hunt seals. You were living pretty low on the hog if you were wearing seal-skin shoes and using seal oil to light things. So I think the myth has a couple of meanings. And I think there was a time when we lived closer to nature; in fact we lived so close to nature that our ancestors were seals. We're half-seal and half-person.

Fundamentally, you've always talked about your work in terms of storytelling. Lone Star, *even more than* The Secret of Roan Inish, *seems on one level to be an examination of the role of storytelling in people's lives and in the shaping of society.*

Yeah. You know, history has the word *story* in it, and I think the main thing I was thinking about in writing the movie was: "What do we need history for? What do we use it for?" And that's history both in the kind of larger social sense of "Remember the Alamo," but also personal history. You know: "Mom made me do it," "If only my brother had been nicer to me, I would be a happy person today." And at what point do we say, "Okay, you can't blame history," or, "You can't take credit for history." At the end Chet says,

"My father says you have to start from scratch and pull yourself up from there," which isn't true. Nobody does that. Everybody starts with some kind of handicap or advantage, and that's their personal history. And it's also their group history. I was interested in the way those two interact: both the personal, and the social and group history. But also, "Is there escape from that?" I'm always interested in responsibility and when we expect people to just be responsible for themselves.

Lone Star is about discovering the truth behind the legend, and the power that such legends exert over a community's sense of itself, yet it's also a reworking of a classic myth, the myth of Oedipus.

I wanted that idea that you have to be careful of what you look for, because you might find it.

It's an interesting double movement—the narrative keeps moving further back in time while also moving forward in time. Sam talks about his story being over, yet he is actually constructing a story and becoming its narrator.

Very specifically what that was about is that both Pilar and Sam are people who are on the verge of either accepting that they blew something or something was blown for them. In Pilar's case, she married this guy, she had his kids, and he died. And so, where do you go from there? You know, you're almost forty. With Sam, he is forty, and he wasted this marriage to this crazy, female football fan. And he's realized, probably only a couple weeks after taking it, that, no, he doesn't want to be sheriff, that that was something he had to deal with about his father, not something he wanted to do. And the question is being asked constantly through it, "Are you doing something that's about you or is this something that's about living up to the legacy that's been left to you?"

That double movement you were talking about—Sam is trying to deal with a father who is dead. Pilar almost accidentally finds out about a father who she didn't know was her father. And Joe Morton's character is trying to deal with a father who's alive. There are these parallel things. Sam is the one who is going back into the past, he's the one who's digging the deepest in a way. On the other hand, Joe Morton's son is looking for roots. But he's got the live museum, he's got the grandfather there. So, okay, "Where do I come from? Did it just start from scratch like my father said or is there something behind it?" So he goes back and he finds his grandfather. And it was very purposeful that the grandfather is into Seminole Indian history and that their big talk finally is in front of a museum exhibit. It's about roots. There is a positive side to remembering that stuff. On the other hand, you have a last line in the picture, "Forget the Alamo," which I once considered having be the title of the movie. There is an extent to which romantic love is antisocial. Not marriage, which is very social, that's when you make it public, and say, "Okay, we're going to follow certain rules. We're now allowing the rest of the community into our relationship." It's why a lot of people get along fine until they get married. It's a social contract whereas romantic love is automatically antisocial. So when they say, "Forget the Alamo," they have to say, "Forget what society thinks, forget society's stories. We are going to do this thing together." They can't stay in Frontera, around her mother and other people who know eventually, the thing is going to get out. So there is also the sense that sometimes what you have to do is just forget history, you have to escape it.

At the end there's a real attempt to deny some of society's taboos— not just incest but also interracial marriage.

You can do that on a personal level, but probably not on a social one. There are interracial couples, but it's not something that is generally accepted in society, either by black or white people. You can have black friends, but that doesn't mean that black and white people are getting along. That's individual accommodation, which is very different from what society is doing.

Do you agree with Otis when he says, "Blood only means what you let it"?

Everybody takes what they want to. Once they get to that point of maturity, they say, "This is going to mean what I want it to mean." Being black can be this huge point of pride or of pain. It can be something where you say, "Well, other people may have a problem with this but I don't, I'm going to go on with my life, and I'm going to try to have it not be about race as much as I can.

Eddie Robinson and Ron Canada in the Seminole museum
in *Lone Star*.

Now, that doesn't mean that other people are going to allow me to
have it not be about race. But me personally—I'm going to live my
life as a human being. It's a fact. It's not a quality of my character." It's the same thing with, "My father was the sheriff of this
town." At some point you have to decide, "How much am I going
to let that mean to me?"

*Do you see the father/son dynamic in the film as a metaphor?
Father/son themes run through much of your work. Is it something which particularly resonates with you?*

It's not a big bug for me. I think it happens in life so much that it's
almost not a metaphor—just what is. There are those metaphors
that are so close to what's going on they go beyond being metaphors. I remember talking with Kris Kristofferson about the plot
and he wasn't involved in the father/son story. He was talking
about how to him the three sheriffs represented three generations.
He was saying, "This could be the generation, this could be the
story of some Israeli colonel saying, 'I was a warrior so my son
could become a poet.'" In America you could have the generation

who says, "Look, I may be a hard-ass, and I may be an asshole, but I want my children to live in peace, so I'm going to kill all the Indians and all the wolves." And then you have the next generation who says, "Well, I'm still going to be in charge, and I'm not going to feel bad that Dad killed all the Indians. But I'm going to make life a little easier for them. I'm going to go to the reservations and make sure that they get their government handouts." The third generation is the one that says, "Oh my God—we were so terrible, killing all those people. Look at how we've treated them. My grandfather was an asshole. My father was an asshole."

However, you also have the guys who want to go back to their grandfather's way of thinking. And that's what that school meeting is about—all these different people in the pot. From the Pat Buchanans saying, "This is a white, Christian nation and we are in a holy cultural war to keep it from becoming multicultural and to keep our workers working and fuck everyone else," to the people who want to say, "Forget the United States. We live in the world. We're part of the world community. And human beings are the tribe." There're so many gradations between those views in American society right now. I'd say that's because we've been around a certain amount of time. If you went back a hundred years, you wouldn't have found that last gradation. You would have found people who said, "Well, Jeez. Do we have to kill all the Indians? Can't we just put them on reservations?" and that would have been a Liberal. The Conservative would have been the guy who said, "No, we need a Final Solution. We have to kill every last one of them, because they are expensive to maintain." It's almost not metaphoric, as I was saying. It's so literally what went on.

How did the subplot with Del and the army base emerge in the writing?

I wanted to have these three communities, where we were basically in a part of Mexico that somebody had drawn a line underneath and made into America, but the people hadn't changed. So, the Anglos got to run things, but it was still basically a Mexican town. And where do the blacks fit into that? Well, they're kind of mercenaries in this case. A lot of that thinking came out of the Gulf War. I saw, time after time on television, black men and women being asked, "So, what was your part? Why are you here?

Kris Kristofferson in *Lone Star*.

Matthew McConaughey in *Lone Star*.

What do you think of this war and everything?" And time after time I heard people answer, "This was the best job I could get."

And then I started seeing those who were officers, and then there was Colin Powell. And then I saw a lot of interracial couples who were married and in the army. And I realized, well, here is what used to be, only a few years ago, one of the most racist and retrogressive parts of society—maintaining the status quo—being the institution where even though it's about going and killing other people, there seems to be a certain degree of equal opportunity. Or if not equal, better than in the free market. If black people are saying, "This is the best job I could get," and they feel like there's some chance for advancement, that's much better than they feel like in the free market.

I started thinking about the Buffalo Soldiers, the Negro-Indian scouts, which I actually knew a bit about before I started writing this, how, yes, they were part Indian, but they were there working for the white people against other red people. How there comes that point where, yes, you can move up as long as you're willing to be the mercenary or the hired gun. In Batista's Cuba, many of his hitmen were black. That started to fascinate me. Here's a strange thing that history has done in this country. It has said, "We're going to do this and that on the surface about equal opportunity," but because the army finally is a part of society that we can control to a certain extent, because people have to take orders, all of a sudden this becomes the place where black people can make a life for themselves. And it's more controlled than regular society. There's that line when Del's talking to the private, and she says, "Outside it's just chaos." And he's thinking, "My life would have been me coming into the bar at night where people are fighting and killing each other and divorcing each other."

I knew the social aspect first—I wanted the ruling class that was having to give up the reins. I wanted the people, the Mexicans in this case, who are taking over the reins. And then I wanted there to be this mercenary class, the blacks. And then I started thinking about who the representatives of those classes were going to be, and I wanted more than one. In each of those groups, I wanted to also have a personal story that was important. So, the driving narrative is about this murder mystery, and the black people would be an enclave, one small neighborhood in an army base, which is this artificial little world, and you really knew when you were in that section of town. And then I basically had the idea, "Well, what if it's not just this guy who's seen it all and owns the roadhouse, but he has something to deal with, which is a live son."

It's curious that the subplot is more moving than the main plot.

One guy's dealing with a father who's dead—it's history and there's something always slightly removed about history. I try to make it a little less removed—in the transitions there's no cut or dissolve. I tried to make it immediate, in the same place. But there's nothing we can do about history. We can learn what really happened, but we can't change it. His father's dead. He can't change that relationship. He can change how he feels about it, but he's not going to have that scene with Dad or anything like that. And the same thing with Pilar. Both the person she thought was her father and the one who really was are both dead. But the one person who can is this bar owner who has a son, and they've had this chilly nonrelationship for years and now they have to deal with each other. So that's got to be more moving, because it's immediate.

What's the significance of the long scene between Sam and his ex-wife, Bunny?

One of the things is that we have been doing all of this poking in the past about Sam's father, but Sam was a kid when that was happening. Sam is the protagonist, the one leading us through the plot, but I noticed as I was reading it myself that so many of his lines are just simple reactive lines—he's asking questions. He doesn't have any huge speeches. I tend not to do those big Paddy Chayevsky speeches for the main characters. I'll often give them to a secondary character, and they may be more thematic than anything else. In *Passion Fish* it's the "Anal Probe" speech, which is a metaphor for life, and for limitations. That scene with Bunny serves two purposes. One is metaphoric: This is a woman who has not escaped the past. It's clear that the weight of her family and their money doomed the marriage. The two of them came into it carrying this shit on their backs that made it impossible. He was still in love with another woman and he was still dealing with his

Eddie Robinson and Joe Morton in *Lone Star*.

father who wasn't there and was eventually dead. She was still dealing with her father who was very much there, and who gave both of them very little room to breathe. And you imagine that she has this incredible, fierce loyalty and love for her father that's also a fierce hatred. And some of that was, we've seen that Sam was this kid who was ripped out of this Romeo and Juliet thing, but then what did he do? Well, what he did was he tried to go to a totally different world. And he couldn't make it, because history wouldn't leave him alone and the weight of society was waiting for him there. And it wasn't his father, it was her father. There's still a chance for Sam. He and Pilar at the end of the movie are basically embarking on a second life. Bunny is someone who's not going to have one. She is absolutely trapped in that room. You can see her thirty years from then—same person, the room is just messier.

One of the thematic links between the different strands is the idea of needing to belong to some group, which is also very moving.

Especially in the United States, which is not a traditional culture. Never was.

And her tribe is the Dallas Cowboys.

Absolutely. But it's a very artificial thing. Sports are timeless in a way. Besides being such a Texas thing, they are somebody else's drama. Every year there is another NFL, another Super Bowl. They are so vicarious, it just seemed like a great metaphor for somebody who can't live their own life because it's too painful. There are all these subcultures in America that you belong to because there is the illusion of, and sometimes there really is, choice in America. What do you choose to belong to? Have you chosen? If people choose to be macrobiotic and they belong to that, that becomes what they are about. They choose to be a Crip or a Blood if they have more limited options. But there are choices that are more responsible and more personal, where you actually take care of somebody else and have to deal with somebody else and have to affect and be affected by the world. And then there are choices that are totally vicarious. With May-Alice in *Passion Fish* it would be to watch soap operas and live their soap opera lives with them, and many people have made that choice. Their strongest emotional lives are on television.

Is Bunny's name intended to echo Sam's father's name, Buddy?

Well, not so much. It's just that you try to characterize people through their names. And the name "Bunny" is a diminutive, a child's name and a nickname. She's someone who's still, at least in her relationship with her father, infantilized. It's a bit literary, and it's a bit wasted. At one point I was thinking of having some of Sam's old campaign posters in Bunny's garage, until I realized he wouldn't have had them up there, and the slogan for his election campaign for sheriff would have been "One Good Deeds Deserves Another." And the deeds of the father are visited on the son. That's very literary. He is who he is because he is kind of a buddy to a lot of people, a crony. In the same way, Pilar is solid like a pillar. And Mercedes eventually has mercy. You give a feeling to people through their names, especially the ones you only see for a little while.

The final moments of that scene are interesting. Sam tells Bunny, "You look good," and she says, "I like it when you say that, Sam."

It implies a kind of agreed deception, a mutually convenient denial of reality.

It's also one of the moments where Sam is most like Buddy. Think of how Buddy ran the town. There was a lot of deception, a lot of, "Well, we both know it's illegal, but it's not hurting anyone. So I'm going to look the other way." Which is kind of like saying, "You look good, Bunny." Instead of saying, "Honey, you're a mess. Get yourself to a shrink." In the rest of the movie Sam is the guy who doesn't want to come to an accommodation, doesn't want to cut anybody any slack. He's the Grim Reaper kind of guy, who says I want all the facts on the table, and I don't care who it hurts. The second time he acts like his father is at the very end of the movie. He says, "Well, that's the truth. But who is it going to do any good? It's one of your unsolved mysteries."

Does it represent growth in his character?

Yes, to a certain extent because he was so extreme in the other way. He's not going to become Buddy—he's not going to become a corrupt sheriff. He's still a man of principle. But there is that point where being a certain kind of man of principle becomes just being a weapon. Buddy's feeling is, "Yes, there are all these statutory laws, but my job is to help people in this town live without fear, so if they are doing something that is statutorily wrong, but I don't think is messing anyone up—I'm not going to bother." There's something more mature about that, than, "These are the rules and we're going to live in a Calvinist universe. And any time there's any infraction, I'm going to nail you for it." Reform administrations and reform politics are often very Calvinist.

Is the derelict drive-in movie theater where Sam and Pilar meet at the end another manifestation of the need for a community? Did you intend to invoke the collective experience of movies?

Yeah, that's where people came together. Like in Bogdanovich's *The Last Picture Show*, it's the place where all the kids met and our society was created. To a certain extent what I wanted that to be is, "Okay, this is where we were torn apart. The last place we were together." I wanted the sense that they are looking at the

Elizabeth Peña and Chris Cooper in *Lone Star*.

screen as if something may come up, but the screen is wasted. There are the ravages of the past. So in that last image, I wanted both the sense that they are going to go forward, something could be projected on that thing. But they're not the fourteen-year-old kids that they were. They've had some damage. Things have fallen away. They're different people. But that doesn't mean that their love is dead.

What was the film being shown in the flashback? It looked like a Corman "women in prison" movie.

It was *Black Mama, White Mama*, which was an AIP movie that Jonathan Demme actually has story credit on. It was one of those Filipino jobs. It was basically *The Defiant Ones* in a women's prison. Pam Grier and Margaret Markow—they're handcuffed together and they escape. Once again, it may be a little literary, but it's about people of different races being chained together whether they want to or not.

Of all your films, this has the most complex use of point of view— we get overlapping perspectives of events in the flashbacks, and often one person begins telling Sam a story and then somebody else finishes it, talking to Sam from a different time and place. Why those extreme yet almost imperceptible shifts?

For any history that you read, you have to consider who's recounting the history. How do they see the world? What's their agenda? Because *Lone Star*'s involved with history, I wanted people to get that idea that the answers Sam is given are always going to be influenced by the person who's giving them. "This is where I was in the room, this is what I saw." "This is me being the hero of the story." Sometimes they're lying. Or lying to themselves. But always keeping to that idea that this is not what happened—this is how I remember what happened, like *Citizen Kane*, in that one keeps getting a more complete picture of Kane because different people know different sides of him. I wanted there to be that guide who starts you into the story, and then you get into it, and you live it immediately, but I wanted there to be that little residue of somebody watching. So when we see Eladio Cruz killed, we cut away to the guy who started the story, hiding under the bridge. And that's where his story is coming from—a witnessed murder. At the end, Otis introduces the story. It starts with him and the poker game and Charlie Wade coming in, but when we come out of it, Hollis is also telling the story—we start changing points of view within the telling of it. When you see the close-up of the gun firing, the one which kills Charlie Wade, there's one shot shooting left and there's another shooting right. Two people, different points of view. If you're one guy, it's an eyeline problem. Whose point of view is this from? So let's do it two ways.

Did you attempt to change the style of the film depending on whose subjective state you were depicting?

Yes, according to who they are and according to their emotional state. Within each of those stories, Sam is always the listener, but there are different strategies. Sometimes the voice comes in at the beginning and a different voice picks it up at the end. So the point of view changes. But I also wanted the emotional state of what was being told. The first one that we see is kind of a tall tale. It's a guy bullshitting with his friends at a table, and so I wanted that to feel like a Western. Because when Hollis the mayor tells the story, he is going to embellish it and make it into a real showdown. And so the shooting of it was a little bit more strict, very much the same cuts and lines you would get if it were a Western showdown. And it had all the fetishistic items: the guns, and the hats, and the badges. Whereas in the last story that's told, it is very impression-istic. There are no lines anymore. We don't hear what Charlie Wade is saying when he's telling Otis to go. We know the kinds of things he would be saying. The scene where Eladio Cruz is mur-dered, we go from this very close-up imagination of what is going on to these wide shots, which is the guy under the bridge. He's guessing what happened and what was said close-up, but he was basically seeing from a distance. So it's not literal, but I wanted each one to have a different emotional content. Some of that emo-tional content would be the emotions of the person who's telling the story. It was also for some variety in the movie, so that every story isn't the same. Certainly you always try to evoke what you want the audience to feel. How claustrophobic do you want them to be? How distanced do you want them to be? How close do you want them to be? How much of a surprise do you want it to be when Charlie Wade shoots the guy? How much tension do you want to evoke, even though it's the past? You want the audience at a certain emotional state when they come back to the present and there's Sam taking this thing in.

The fluid visual transitions between past and present suggest something like magic realism.

I wanted the past, those stories about his father, to be so much more present than when you play the harp and do the lap dissolve. Sam is still about the past, because as quiet as he is, he is still an other-directed individual. He carries his father thing with him, mostly in a resentful way—he has to live under this guy's shadow. Same thing with the transitions in *City of Hope*—they were all written as well. You don't cut to another part of the room, you are brought there by the camera. A cut is very much a tear. You use a cut to say there's a separation between this thing and that thing. And so in *Lone Star*, I didn't even want a dissolve, which is a soft cut.

What motivated the canted camera angles in Lone Star? *For instance, the opening shot of the scene where Mercedes is sitting in her yard drinking?*

It's usually about the emotional state of the character, because I don't have much time with them, because there's a lot of business to take care of. That particular shot says, "This is supposed to be someone who's home relaxing; she's making herself a cocktail and she's got nice music on in the background—but there's something off about her life, something unbalanced and unsettled."

Why does the scene where Sam drives to see Pilar have such a lyrical, abstract tone to it?

It's like the nighttime boat ride in *Passion Fish*. It has some of the same otherworldly, lyrical mood. This is the part of Sam's life that he still has a chance to change, the part that if he does it right, is outside of society. I wanted something about what's going on inside him, which has got to be very hopeful, purely emotional. This is their own little world of two; you don't see another person—this is what the relationship used to be. It has its own light. There's more dissolves than anywhere else. It has a different kind of music. It is a kind of time-out for Pilar and Sam. And that's what you hope a personal relationship can be.

The wide-shot of them in the empty restaurant alone with the jukebox, echoes the final shot of the film with them at the drive-in.

The jukebox holds some of their past. The song they play, "Since I Met You, Baby," or "Desde que conosco," is also playing on the jukebox when Del walks into Otis's place, a different version of it. That's very subtle, but that's how different cultures use the same song. It was a song that was a hit on black stations, and then it was the first hit for Freddy Fender, the first Hispanic rock-and-roll guy. He took rock and roll, black music that was becoming used by white people, and brought it to Latin America. I don't know whether anybody would have picked that up.

Why did you call the film Lone Star?

It has an immediate visceral impact and then a historical reso-
nance. Sam is very much the loner in this Western tradition, trying
to bring justice to the situation, as far as he's concerned. A wrong
has been done and he's going to right it, even if it costs his father's
reputation. It's kind of like *High Noon*—the man against the
town, that's how he sees himself. By the end, what you hope is that
he doesn't see himself that way anymore. He's starting to reinte-
grate himself in society. "I've got to leave you people alone with
your legend." Very literally, Texas was the Lone Star State before
they were part of the Union, after they had kicked the Mexicans
out. They were a republic. Because they had their eye on becoming
part of the United States, they said, "We'll be the Lone Star. We're
the individual who is eventually going to join the society." One of
the reasons why I chose Texas for this thing is because the state of
Texas has a compressed history that is like a metaphor for the history of the United States.

*How do you approach the interplay of foreground and back-
ground characters in a film like this?*

When I write, having been an actor, one of the things that I do
is go through and play every part, and ask, "Is there a three-
dimensional character here? What are the connections between
this character and the rest of the story, and can I have more than
one connection between this character and the rest of the story,
thematically and just in terms of plot?" In your average Hollywood movie there are two leads and everyone else is basically an
extra—in mine the secondary characters start moving forward and
become primary. It's like the way that I mix sound—if you're in a
bar, and it's noisy, the background sound is mixed up closer to the
foreground sound, which makes it a little harder for people who
don't hear very well. I'm not the only person who does it that way;
Robert Altman and Martin Scorsese do it that way. The secondary
characters have got to have their say. Even if he doesn't get a lot of
air time, the guy who stands up in the school board meeting and
says, "Hey, we stole it fair and square, buddy. Winners get to write
the history," well, he's got a point. And you can't make him one-
dimensional. Every once in a while when watching an otherwise

interesting movie, all of a sudden there are, let's say, these cops and they're one-dimensional. Just the bad guys. And that's very, very useful for an action/adventure movie. In *Los Gusanos* one of the characters is a political torturer. He does terrible things to people. And that's his job. I was interested in what the guy thinks and what could possibly be going through his head. And so I did a lot of reading about it, accounts by people who used to do torture. What do you have to think of yourself to be able to do this? What does being that person do to you?

CHAPTER 10

Men With Guns

Did you consider calling it Hombres Armados?

Well, having done *Los Gusanos* and having seen the wince on the face of the people at HarperCollins when I said, "Oh yeah, I don't want to translate it," to help the distributor out it really should have an English title.

But don't they wince when you tell them it's subtitled?

I felt I wasn't going to buy it if it was in English, if it was a bunch of people walking around Latin America speaking English with Latin accents. And the main character himself has people interpret for him the whole time. Once he gets out of the city, he says, "Nobody speaks Spanish here. What's going on?" Well, guess what? You're a foreigner in your own land when you go to this part of the country, and that's very true in Mexico and Guatemala where there are large Indian populations.

What are you trying to evoke with the title?

What you hope is that the title sets something up in the minds of the audience. It's something that's mentioned several times in the movie. People keep saying, "Who did it?" "Men with guns." Eventually it's clear that it doesn't quite matter which side they're on, they still mess up your life. Half the movies or books ever written could be called *Men With Guns* and it would be appropriate. The title is very blunt and simple and has a generic quality and there's a generic quality to the movie's setting. We're careful not to say where it is—I want the story to have some of that generic, universal feeling. The title is the first thing people come across, the thing that they know before they see it. It doesn't have to be, "Oh, I

Sayles and Federico Luppi on the set of *Men With Guns/Hombres Armados* (1997).

know exactly what this film's going to be." It's almost more emotional than informational in some ways, sometimes the rhythm of the title is more important. *The Return of the Secaucus Seven* was an ironic title—these people are back but not in the way that they were before. The sound of that was more important to me.

So the title suggests that all men with guns stand for the same thing in the end?

To the person who's on the other end of the gun. It's civilians who suffer the most casualties, usually, not just from guns and mines but from being uprooted. Huge civilian casualties in almost every historical war. It's very rare that you get the whole populace up in arms about something. Generally it's, "These people are fighting and I hope we don't get caught up in it." If they really have all the information and think it out, they may have good reason to join one side or the other, but they usually don't, they just say, "God, there's a storm brewing and I hope it doesn't come through our village." And when it does they have to make these life or death decisions without enough information. In the story Padre Portillo tells, the villagers are just these guys growing their corn and all of a sudden the army shows up out of the blue and says, "Either these five guys and the priest are dead or we slaughter the whole village." What do you do? There's no arguing with that.

Yet the villagers' response is not what you'd expect—they're very rational and pragmatic about it.

They don't act in what we think of as an ordinary Western reaction, which is that they would fight or they would run. Think of any Western: "Our backs are against the wall, we'll turn to the Magnificent Seven." The mindset of the most orthodox, traditional village is that you lose your soul, your connection to the past and the future, if you lose your land. There is a holy connection to that place and that way of life. If you go to the city and get a job in a restaurant or end up begging on the street, you've lost your soul, even if you're still alive. If you wander around from place to place as an itinerant laborer, you've probably lost your soul. In the Christian ideal, it doesn't matter where you are.

The village almost functions as a single entity or organism, as if the individual is only meaningful as part of the whole.

With certain groups that's both a religious and a political structure—there'll be a group of elders who are always the first to talk about things, but the whole village is involved. In the West decision making is usually more hierarchical but there's also this idea that your individual life is not so connected to a place or even to a group.

What was the point of departure for this film?

It's somewhat based on experiences that the parents and uncles of a couple of friends of mine had in Latin America. What interested me was that in both experiences they were very intelligent guys who were worldly in some ways but they didn't know or want to believe the extent to which the people that they were ostensibly working for were sponsoring them in bad faith and did not want the people they were trying to help to have a better life, they wanted them poor. That lack of curiosity, that willing innocence led to them getting people involved in things that got them killed. From that basis I got into this idea of somebody who thinks their legacy is one thing and then discovers it's another altogether.

Were the people in these two cases American or Latin American?

Half-and-half. One was an agronomist for the Rockefeller Foundation, and the other was a doctor in Guatemala City who got involved in a UN program. One of the good things about their programs was that they said, "We're not going to come in here and tell people how to do things, we're going to give people knowledge and send them back to their villages." In both cases the local people that they sent back to their villages were considered subversives by the government because they were making people more self-sufficient, which meant that they weren't available to go pick coffee beans or do whatever the slave wage gig was that the country's power structure wanted them to do. You could find the same story in any developing country. There are these two opposing views—the PR idea that the government puts out, that we're doing things for our citizens, and then the economic reality, which is that other forces really don't want people any smarter. It's a tension that's still present in the U.S., though not in an overtly genocidal way. There is this idea that everybody's equal and entitled to good education; but there's also this very strong idea that there are winners and losers and that you don't want your children and your people to be losers. And so without thinking about it too much people support government policies or a way of thinking that makes sure that, "It's fine if those kids get a good education, but my kid is going to get a better one, because he's going to be a winner. And only a few kids can get into Yale, so let's make sure we don't bend over backwards too far to make sure that everybody can get into Yale. After my kid's in—yeah."

Given that you sympathize with the idealism of the progressive, how pessimistic do you feel about the conflict between progressive and antiprogressive social agendas?

I sympathize with it but I think it's just much more complex than most people want to think. No matter what you do, any kind of contact is going to change that more protected culture, and not

Federico Luppi as Fuentes in *Men With Guns/Hombres Armados*.

Men With Guns.

necessarily for the better. That was the point of Peter Mathiesson's *At Play in the Fields of the Lord*. A subtheme in *Men With Guns*, because of all the different languages, is that one of the ways you keep your culture unchanged by the outside world is to make it hard for other people to understand. If you discourage learning Spanish and people going out and coming back with information, you're just as guilty, if that's the word to use, of a kind of willed ignorance as the people in the city who don't really want to know about you. It defends your culture by keeping it pure but it doesn't do a whole lot for it in terms of surviving in a world where the other side has more guns and technology than you and has figured out a way to suddenly own the land you used to own. One of the things I'm getting at again is that there is a price for knowledge. People don't want to know for a good reason—because if they do know, either they have to be more cynical than they like to be, or they have to take responsibility for what's going on. If Fuentes were to have gone back to the city having seen the results of what the army had done in a few of these places, it would be tougher for him to stick his finger up the general's butt or have a casual conversation anymore. You have to ask, "Who is this guy, and what's his responsibility for wiping this village out?"

What function does the American tourist couple play in this scenario?

They are absolutely liberals. They know a certain amount, but knowing them and having them be part of your life and be at their mercy is a very different thing. For me, they are what America is to Central America—since the Monroe Doctrine, which basically said, "Anything that goes on in this hemisphere, we want to control." The U.S. has done many things in Latin America but none of them have been to make those people more self-sufficient. During WW II there was the Good Neighbor policy because Argentina and Chile had a lot of ties with Germany and Italy. We got very friendly with Mexico and partly created their golden age of film by cutting off the Argentinians, not giving them any more Kodak film, so the Mexicans' competition disappeared. It usually hasn't been gunboats, it's usually been market manipulation and manipulation of governments and elections. During the entire genocide period in Guatemala in the seventies and eighties, American tourists could still go to Lake Atitlán, and they might have heard vague rumors about this but they were like Teflon, nothing stuck. The tourists in the film are pretty nice people, and they know more about what's going on in the hinterlands of this guy's country than he does. However it doesn't affect them, it's not their lives, they float on a sea of money.

And yet they're also almost oblivious to the dangers around them and are the safer for that.

There they are in guerilla territory. But every once in a while something does happen to a tourist and it's a huge deal in the U.S.: "My God, how could that happen?" It's the poorest part of the world, things happen—whether it's coming from the airport in Miami or turning down a wrong street in an L.A. neighborhood. And it's shocking that that world and their world could intersect in that way.

Did you go to Guatemala to research the script?

I talked to a lot of people and I had done some research for a cable movie project that never happened called *Sanctuary* that was about the Sanctuary movement in the eighties. So I was fairly well versed in it as far as the history and I traveled in Guatemala when things were really calming down. One of the people we traveled with was a Miskito Indian woman who had had a local political job under the Sandanistas and gone through a tough time in the Contra wars. She felt that what was going on in Guatemala was very much like what happened at the end of the Sandanista regime, which was that there were two opposing sides and that left 80 to 90 percent of the people out of the conversation. The people were not consulted. Guatemalans would say, "Well, the guerrillas had some good ideas, but they didn't necessarily represent us. And the army certainly didn't represent us." And now they have an agreement with the U.S., which was usually funding one side or the other. In Nicaragua it was the Contras, in Guatemala it was the government. Very often the accords were seen as happening because there was a recession in the U.S. and we had less money to give them to go kill each other. One journalist in Guatemala said the choice for the army was: drink less beer or kill fewer Indians and they chose to kill fewer Indians. Their lifestyle was going to go—they were going to have to climb up those mountains, not have helicopters to fly them to the top. It wasn't worth it so they said, "Yeah, maybe we should talk." That to me is the negative part of that Teflon thing—it didn't really cost the U.S. anything except cash to keep things the way they were in Guatemala, which was our most successful coup.

Why did you not identify the film's setting as Guatemala?

When people hear about genocide, it shocks them for a few seconds and then they just say, "Well, those are the kind of people who kill everybody." For a while it was, "Anything could happen in Uganda, but it couldn't happen in Zaire." Then there's a moment of shock when it happens in Zaire and then people say, "Well, of course, it's Zaire, what do you expect?" I didn't want people to have the click-off reaction: "Well, of course, it's Guatemala. They're very primitive there, even for Central America."

What was the arc of the film, given that it's a road movie?

Some of it is just geographical. I wanted the story to start in the city where life seemed pretty normal and nobody was getting shot. When we were scouting I was looking for a glass and plastic city with tall buildings, central high plains, some hilly mountain country, and then starting to climb into the deep mountains where people can hide out. So there's a geographical movement. In the music I'm trying to get a pan-Latino feeling, with very urban genres like merengue and rap in the beginning of the movie, then cumbias, which are a little more country-like, and then by the end of the movie we're into much more indigenous music. And it's not all from one country, so when we go through the cane fields it's a very African-Caribbean sound so that we could be starting in Buenos Aires and then going to Venezuela and then to Cuba and maybe ending up in Bolivia in the high mountains. And I wanted a kind of progression in the horror. At first it's a story that's told to him and you imagine things. Then it's a story that's told to him and then illustrated. And he starts meeting the people themselves and finally it's a story that's happening to him.

*What's behind the storytelling framework? The film begins with
an Indian woman telling her daughter the story—and then what
we see from then on is what happens to Fuentes until finally he
arrives in the mountain village where the mother and daughter
live.*

When I was learning Spanish I read a lot of magic realism books.
One of the interesting things about magic realism is that people
have certain powers or certain things happen to them that are
supernatural, but it doesn't help them get out of their situation.
It's very unlike the rash of American movies in the last seven or
eight years with angels or ghosts in them, where usually that connection with the afterlife saves somebody's life or wins the ball-
game through intercession, like in *Angels in the Outfield*. In the
Latin American stories, there are these powers—but you're still
fucked at the end of the story. To me, what that gets at is that for
indigenous cultures that are still orthodox, in a spiritual way what
they have is very valuable; it keeps them together and gets them
through life, but practically it doesn't help them at all. So this
woman has certain cognitive powers, she can see Fuentes coming,
she has a certain prescience—but she didn't see that mine in front
of her. She wasn't prescient enough to see that cold fact right
where she put her foot down. So the mother telling the story
seemed like a good metaphor for people who have this extra spiritual thing that sometimes is a disadvantage because it separates
them from what's going on in the world. People on both sides
envy what the other one has. In America there's this videostore
mentality about religions: "Isn't it wonderful that these people
have this spirituality and this connection with the land?" But you
only take it so far, you don't commit yourself to it. But the minute
the troops show up and say, "These five people have to die, and if
they die then we'll trust you and your children can enjoy this land
in the future," well, the person who's committed to that world
view would say, "Okay, it's a bad deal but that's the only deal I
can imagine, because all those generations of the past expect me to
hold up the deal the way they did." Whereas the American who's
just dipping his toes into that religion says, "Okay, wait. Let's
switch religions."

Is the film in some sense a spiritual allegory? There's the priest who's lost his faith and this soldier who's lost his soul and Fuentes' journey seems on some level a spiritual journey towards death.

Yes and no. Whether the movie is spiritual or not, it deals with people who are wrestling with that themselves—what is there that's practical and what is there that's spiritual and do I believe in spiritual things? And, in the case of the doctor, "If I don't, how far does this humanist thing take you?" And when do you get off that boat? When it becomes inconvenient? How much are you willing to pay for that? Generally, only the people who are most committed to some kind of spiritual life are willing to go all the way, like the Indians. When it really comes down to that awful situation of, "Either I do this or I die," most people will get off the boat. Fuentes doesn't know that about himself yet. The priest has been tested and he failed and he knows that about himself. The doctor has never been tested. He has never been put in that situation and he's not really put in that situation in the movie. But he takes risks just to know and by the end of the movie he takes responsibility. He's not heroic. And I don't have much time in the beginning of the movie to put you in his world and give you an idea of where his mindset comes from. His son-in-law is much more cynical and he's of the power structure mindset; he's a player in that he's closer to the dirty end of what goes on, but the doctor is like a mercenary for the power structure.

Why do you introduce Fuentes with him inserting a finger up the general's rectum, giving him an examination?

Well, it's a kind of intimacy with the power structure, but he doesn't really know what they're like. He can get that close to power, that's what he's grown up in, everybody has their mindset, so he's more likely to buy what they say. That's why I'm so interested in community. The way that the human mind develops is that there's all these generic capabilities—Bruno Bettleheim says that all humans are born with a capacity for language and if they aren't put in a culture that has a language, if they're isolated for some reason, they'll invent their own. There's this need that wants to be filled.

Federico Luppi and Dan Rivera Gonzalez in *Men With Guns*.

I also feel that a culture creates a box that gets filled with your attitudes and there are boxes of different sizes. If you live in a very orthodox small community that doesn't have much to do with its neighbors, you may have very deep knowledge about certain things like corn and the seasons and the spiritual life and historical past of your people, but that box will be very small as far as the rest of the world is concerned. If you're an American and you've traveled a lot, there are things outside your box even though it's a bigger box—and one of those things is the emotional knowledge of powerlessness. There's an assumption that because we're Americans, not too many bad things happen to us. Nobody from the country in the film would wander into those hills except Americans or maybe Germans, who have that kind of confidence—which is a kind of ignorance. There's a kind of assumption that things are going to turn out right because they've watched as much TV as they've watched and things have pretty much turned out alright before. Whereas for somebody in the same country who has not had that kind of life, their box includes the emotional knowledge that you can really get hammered. It may be that they're much more cautious than they should be and that holds them back because their box got tightened by the knowledge that

"Jeez, I got creamed when I was twelve, my father lost his job and shot himself." It could be a personal one or it could be cultural—it could be that it's 1956, I'm black, and I live in Alabama—and even if things change, you're going to carry some of the size of that experience, the borders of what you can hope for, what you can think, how your mind is set up, how you see a situation.

I always talk to actors and people who want to direct about how you send different characters into the same exact situation; literally each object has a different value to it. Some things they don't even see, other things are definitely important. That's one aspect that interests me about community—what that community gives you that makes you strong but also makes you blind or ignorant because the community didn't want to or couldn't deal with certain things.

Do you see the end of the film as offering hope?

Through Fuentes's eyes, there is a kind of freedom to this place, where even as primitive as it is and as poor and hungry as they're going to be, at least there are not men with guns telling them what to do and shooting them if they don't do it—or shooting them anyway, even if they do do it. I decided since we'd spent a lot of time with these characters, we'd try to give them all a beat in this final scene and have it be between them and Fuentes and their own consciences. The person who needs that open air the most is Graciela, Domingo needs the responsibility of doing something for somebody else, and the kid is just along for the ride. If he gets bored there he's going to try and find somebody who's going down into the world and he may very well end up being a career soldier because that's the best deal he's seen, and unlike Domingo he was not brought up with a religious background, he can't sin, he's a stray looking for the best ride he can get.

Do you believe in what Cerca del Cielo represents—a kind of true freedom from oppression?

People tend to have those religious or personal goals: If only I could lose fifty pounds—that state of being is their state of hope. If only I get to be vice president of the corporation, then I've got it made. The composer's nephew from Tijuana said, "So Cerca del

Federico Luppi and Dan Rivera Gonzalez in *Men With Guns*.

Cielo means the United States, right?" I said, "Yeah, for some people it is." For those Indians you see in the street at one point it was Mexico City—close to heaven. But you look at Cerca del Cielo and what Domingo is saying about it and you realize, Yeah, they're free as long as they don't have a decent standard of living, as long as they don't cut any of those branches down and actually grow food. So they're free to starve. The minute they start to try to stand up on their own two feet and try to be a town, live the life that they lived before, they're fucked. So it's a very mitigated freedom, and some of it is, Yeah, everything has its price and the price isn't fair. And if you don't know or chose not to know, you're surprised when the bill comes.

Has that been applicable for you in terms of your career?

They haven't been heavy emotional things. You get less sleep, you have to work harder, you don't pay people as well, you make compromises of scale and visuals in order to tell the story that you want, you almost always notice a better way to do something or a way that you would rather do something, but you do it the way that's okay and works for that moment, probably more often than somebody does who's working with a larger budget. And you could get three million dollars more if you cast this actor, and they would only cost you one million more, so there's two million dollars more that you have to make the movie—but the actor's not right for the part, or the actor's going to be calling the shots. I'm not a perfectionist but there's things that I wished I could do all the time but, well, it's not going to happen. Even people who make mainstream films with bigger budgets have to make some of those decisions, they just don't have to make them quite as often. I've worked much harder than I would have liked to have worked. I can work hard but I'm not a workaholic, it's not like I wake up in the morning and say, "Oh Jeez, I've got to work until I drop today," but sometimes I've had to do that, just to write enough screenplays to make enough money to get myself back into a position where I can finance or be one of the major investors in our own movie. I've had to jumpstart the momentum of getting people to invest in our movies once in a while.

What have you been writing lately for the next push?

I did some drafts on *Mimic*, about giant mutant cockroaches in New York. It was a really good basic story and I did things to improve it and then Miramax brought in four other writers after me because they were in production and they were changing this and that. But finally it was still a movie about giant mutant cockroaches and people in situations of peril and I did not change that basic story, so I actually asked not to get credit. They had done most of the work already and it was based on a short story somebody wrote and I'm not one of those people who think I should try for credit just in case I get it. I'm also adapting *Gold of Exodus* for Castle Rock. It's a nonfiction book by Howard Blum, who used to work for *The Wall Street Journal*. It's about a couple of archeological adventurers in the eighties who went to find the real Mount Sinai, which unfortunately was in Saudi Arabia, a place you can't get a visa to visit. I still owe a draft or two on a science fiction movie called *Brother Termite* for James Cameron, which is based on a book set in the year 2005 about how the aliens have in fact been in the White House since the 1950s, running things from behind the scenes, and they've only just come out of the closet and people aren't too happy about having them around and things are coming to a head between the little bulb-headed guys and the humans. It's nice writing for him because you can write anything and he'll figure out a way to do it. The original novel has a lot of good ideas; it's the best kind of science fiction, it really makes you think about things. The aliens are like a group phenomenon, not an individual phenomenon; they're like termites or ants, or cells in an organism—but the ones who've been hanging out with humans have been corrupted and started to individualize. And I'm doing an adaptation of a Darryl Ponicsan novel for Sydney Pollack called *Tom Mix Died for Your Sins*, about the old cowboy star. You never know with these things if they'll happen because both Pollack and Cameron are guys who juggle a lot of future projects.

What was Men of War, *which you wrote?*

It went straight to video, apparently, I think, because Miramax would have had to pay me $50,000. They bought the film. Stan Rogow brought me in to write it at Atlantic Releasing back when that company existed. I wrote it under the title *A Safe Place*, and the company went under. Eight years later I got a call from Arthur Goldblatt, who worked for the bank that was handling the bankruptcy. He was in charge of looking at the stuff that they owned to see what was worth anything and he read this and then years later became an independent producer. The first ten minutes don't have anything to do with my script, and then it settles down and for one of these movies it's actually not bad. The basic idea was a bunch of mercenaries who are sent to lean on the natives of an island to get them to sign a paper to give up the mineral rights to their island. The mercenary leader decides these people need protecting and the group breaks into two factions. It's actually some of Dolph Lundgren's best stuff. He's pretty good in it, and the action is not bad. The director is Perry Lang, an actor who was in *Eight Men Out*, *Alligator*, and some other things I've written. His first film was *Little Vegas*, which I acted in, and the lead was Tony Denison, who is also in this film.

As a veteran independent filmmaker, what's your reading of the rise of independent film as a phenomenon?

I look at it as a combination cultural and economic phenomenon. Right about the time we got into the game, maybe a year or two before home video and cable really started, we were really going into this weird vacuum where repertory theaters were starting to die, the same way drive-ins had. Around the beginning of the eighties video pretty much killed off repertory. In those theaters, there were some people who were committed to staying outside the Hollywood system; they didn't want to become a manager for Loews, they wanted to keep their theater going. So some of them, even by the time we got there, had started experimenting with open runs of foreign movies, a Truffaut movie, a Fassbinder movie, whatever, in an open run, and they were doing so-so. They were hanging on. At the same time, the generation that came just before me had been exposed to foreign films, so you get guys like Martin Scorsese and Francis Coppola who bring a kind of European sensibility to American subject matter. The movies started looking different. They also brought a more adult treatment of sex and violence and politics to the movies. So that started, I think, building an audience that was interested in stuff that Hollywood was not that interested in or likely to continue to turn out. Every once in a while they would turn out a couple of interesting movies that dealt with those things, but mostly their business is mass culture and mass culture usually is not successful if it takes too many risks.

So it was this time when our movie and *Northern Lights* and *Heartland* and Claudia Weill's movie *Girlfriends* came out and got good press and had pretty long, successful runs. What started was the beginning of an audience that didn't ask, "This is an American movie, I haven't heard of anybody in it, how good could it be?" They would treat it like a foreign movie. So for the first couple of years I think our films were basically foreign movies. We were part of what those theaters that had been rep theaters at one time were now showing. And they had some good successes. Then about 1983 or '84, filmmakers started realizing that the movies that really got a long run were not the subtitled movies, but movies that were English language. American, Australian, British, and sometimes the odd Canadian movie. That's when I think the small distributors started looking very specifically for English language films. That meant them saying, "Let's pay attention to these people making independent American films." Jim Jarmusch had some success; a couple of other people entered in. It started to build a little momentum. I think the heyday of subtitled films started to wane about 1984 or '85, and since then, the percentage has gone down for subtitled movies.

And once video became a fact of life, it provided a new revenue stream not just for the studios, but for independent filmmakers.

Absolutely. Especially in the late eighties, when the video curve was still going up and nobody knew where the ceiling was going to be. You started to have video companies saying, "We can finance pictures." It doesn't happen much anymore, but there was a three- or four-year window when we got two of our pictures financed by video presales. Certainly more than half the people who see our movies don't see them on a big screen, which is too bad. I work with really good cinematographers and the movies are great-looking on a big screen, much better. They have more emotional impact and there's more visual information.

What does "independent" mean to you?

I think there're two ways to view an independent. One way is to ask if the financing is officially independent. And that doesn't mean much to me. In *Variety* terms, Carolco is an independent. If it's not a major studio, it's an independent. My personal view has always been that independent filmmakers do what they do because there's a story they want to tell. Not because they're thinking in market research terms, or because they just want to get a picture made so they'll accept any actor and script changes they don't think are good ideas just because they want the ride. Or they're willing to say, "Maybe I'll make this movie in three years, but I'm not going to make it under these conditions, because at this point we're destroying everything we set out to say." I don't know any of these guys especially well, but I've met Spike Lee and Martin Scorsese and I'd say they're pretty independent-minded. Oliver Stone pretty much does what he wants to and tells the sto-

Sayles and Dan Rivera Gonzalez on the set of
Men With Guns.

ries he wants to. And nobody could make a Tim Burton movie but
Tim Burton, so studios leave him alone. I would call those guys independent, more independent than somebody who gets their
money from a shoe manufacturer who says, "Yeah, but change
this, this, and this and my daughter has to be in it."

*And what do you make of the fact that there is now a thriving
independent scene with its own economy, which wasn't the case
when you started out? There were people trying to do things by
themselves, there weren't festivals or magazines or the support
structures that there are now.*

I think what's basically happened is that independent movies have
gotten to where fiction was when I first started writing. When I
first started writing fiction there was *Writer* magazine, which had
articles on "Punching Up Your Prose" and "How to Sell to the
Slicks," articles by people who were writing for *Dachshund
World*, as well as people who were writing various kinds of fiction. And there were workshops and retreats and the Iowa City
Writer's School, which was kind of the Sundance of writers. And

that while it was better to have connections, know an agent, know an editor, every once in a while, like I did, somebody could come through the slush pile. You could just send your shit in and there were still people who were first readers. Now if you go to the Independent Feature Project market, it is a slush pile. And most people who go now from companies who distribute movies are not the people who make the final decisions, they're the new people in the company, the junior people who aren't getting paid very well. And they're supposed to go and watch ten minutes of as many things as they can and then if it looks interesting at all they'll say, "Send us the cassette."

That's basically what the first reader did in fiction. There's going to be over a thousand movies sent to Sundance this year. Last year it was like six hundred. It keeps growing exponentially. Now, what you've got to figure is, the people I know who worked at *Harpers* or *Atlantic Monthly* got crates of books every week and somebody had to eventually read these things. I think movies are going to become more like that. As equipment gets cheaper, as the wherewithal, the ability to actually make a film, gets out there, as it's not a mystery anymore, every once in a while there's a story of somebody who came out of left field and got a three-picture deal and an agent and they're going out with Uma Thurman. There're going to be a lot of people trying to do it, but it's going to be like the novel world where most of them aren't going to be very good.

One big difference compared to ten years ago would be that now you can get almost any actor to take you seriously.

Ten years ago people didn't quite know who we were, now we continue to not know whether agents tell their clients we've offered them jobs. On *Lone Star* we had several situations where agents triple-booked their clients. They wouldn't sign a contract with us: "Oh, my client really wants to be in your picture, but we have a conflict." Which means they're going to go look for a conflict, they're going to go look for something that pays more than we pay, which is not hard to find, and so a week before we'd be expecting the actor to come we'd get a call, "Oh, that conflict's been resolved." And in one case we found out they had actually lied to two other productions, they had just kind of shopped their client around until they got the best price and then screwed two other productions. We continue to run into better known actors and actresses who say, "Gee, we love your work." And we say, "Yeah, it's too bad that part we offered you in *City of Hope* didn't come through," and they say, "You offered me a part?" Their agent didn't tell them.

In terms of the current scene, you've had films distributed by every indie.

Most of them are no longer in business.

If the whole scene were to collapse tomorrow, you'd still be able to make your films, presumably. But you are dependent on having distributors, at the very least.

Absolutely, we are always dependent. We've been lucky that we've been able to do it this far. We try to keep as little overhead as possible. So we've just been able to have the money coming in from old movies to pay for the office. Financing is still difficult. The people I respect most will say, "We don't think we can make any money on this, maybe you can some other way." Some also say, "Not this one. Not this script." But, to me, the good thing about it not being too easy is I'm not likely to make a movie I don't care that much about. Whereas you see people on a roll who make a movie because, "It's August and I haven't made anything in eight months." Sometimes I have to dip into my own pocket. I continue to have to invest in my own films. I am one of the investors in *Men With Guns*. I was the only investor at first. So we were able to get things like scripts printed and an office started in Mexico City. Sometimes I say, "This is little enough money, I can make this money back at some point and I don't have anything else I want to do with it. I'll just finance this."

When I started *Roan Inish* I said, "Okay, here's the money to get going on this thing. Let's try to get more money." We were two weeks into production and only my money had been spent. In fact, *all* my money had been spent and we were still plugging around for a deal, so we were over a barrel. So I still haven't made any money back on *Roan Inish*, even though, up to that time, it was our most successful grossing picture. So I'm willing to say, "Okay, I'll roll the dice again." I made this money making movies, whether as a writer, a director, or whatever, and I can lose it making movies. And eventually I'm going to crap out because you can't keep coming back to the table when the odds are not in your favor and not crap out once in a while. I still have the confidence that I can go and write movies for other people and make money. And I've done that before. That happened after making *Matewan*. I was down to zero and I just started writing movies again. So I don't sign three-picture deals, I don't take an advance when I write fiction, I try to make movies one at a time. And with each one, I look around for people who want to work with me this time around, who are still in business, who will answer my calls to distribute or finance it.

Filmography

As director and screenwriter

1979

The Return of the Secaucus Seven
Production company: Salsipuedes Productions
Producers: Jeffrey Nelson, William Aydelott
Unit manager: Maggie Renzi
Cinematography: Austin DeBesche (Duartcolor)
Editor: John Sayles
Music Director: Mason Daring
Cast: Bruce MacDonald (*Mike Donnelly*), Adam Lefevre (*JT*), Gordon Clapp (*Chip Hollister*), Karen Trott (*Maura Tolliver*), David Strathairn (*Ron Desjardins*), Marisa Smith (*Carol*), Carolyn Brooks (*Meg*), Nancy Mette (*Lee*), Brian Johnston (*Norman*), Ernie Bashaw (*officer*), Jessica MacDonald (*Stacey*), Jeffrey Nelson (*man*), Maggie Renzi (*Kate*), Maggie Cousineau (*Frances*), Jean Passanante (*Irene Rosenblum*), Mark Arnott (*Jeff*), John Sayles (*Howie*), Amy Schewel (*Lacey Summers*), Eric Forsythe (*Captain*), Betsy Julia Robinson (*Amy*), John Mendillo (*bartender*), Jack Lavalle (*booking officer*), Benjamin Zaitz (*Benjamin*)
110 min., 16 mm

1982

Lianna
Production company: Winwood Company
Producers: Jeffrey Nelson, Maggie Renzi
Cinematography: Austin DeBesche (Duartcolor)
Editor: John Sayles
Art Director: Jeanne McDonnell
Music: Mason Daring
Cast: Linda Griffiths (*Lianna*), Jane Hallaren (*Ruth*), Jon De Vries (*Dick*), Jo Henderson (*Sandy*), Jessica Wight MacDonald (*Theda*), Jesse Solomon (*Spencer*), John Sayles (*Jerry*), Stephen Mendillo (*Bob*), Betsy Julia Robinson (*Cindy*), Nancy Mette (*Kim*), Maggie Renzi (*Sheila*), Madelyn Coleman (*Mrs. Hennessy*), Robyn Reeves (*job applicant*), Marta Renzi (*dancer*)
112 min., 16 mm

1983

Baby, It's You

Production company: Double Play Productions, Paramount Pictures Corporation
Producers: Griffin Dunne, Amy Robinson
Associate producer: Robert F. Colesberry
Screenplay: John Sayles
Original story: Amy Robinson
Cinematography: Michael Ballhaus
Editor: Sonya Polonsky
Production designer: Jeffrey Townsend
Cast: Rosanna Arquette (*Jill Rosen*), Vincent Spano (*"Sheik" Capadilupo*), Joanna Merlin (*Mrs. Rosen*), Jack Davidson (*Dr. Rosen*), Nick Ferrari (*Mr. Capadilupo*), Dolores Messina (*Mrs. Capadilupo*), Leora Dana (*Miss Vernon*), William Joseph Raymond (*Mr. Ripeppi*), Sam McMurray (*Mr. McManus*), Liane Curtis (*Jody*), Claudia Sherman (*Beth*), Marta Kober (*Debra*), Tracy Pollan (*Leslie*), Rachel Dretzin (*Shelly*), Susan Derendorf (*Chris*), Frank Vincent (*Vinnie*), Robin Johnson (*Joann*), Gary McCleery (*Rat*), Matthew Modine (*Steve*), John Ferraro (*Plasky*), Phil Brock (*Biff*), Robert Downey Jr. (*Stewart*), Fisher Stevens (*stage manager*)
104 min., 35 mm

1985

The Brother from Another Planet

Production company: A-Train Films
Producers: Peggy Rajski, Maggie Renzi
Cinematography: Ernest Dickerson
Editor: John Sayles
Production designer: Nora Chavooshian
Art director: Stephen Lineweaver
Music: Mason Daring
Cast: Joe Morton (*The Brother*), Tom Wright (*Sam Prescott*), Caroline Aaron (*Randy Sue Carter*), Herbert Newsome (*Little Earl*), Dee Dee Bridgewater (*Malverne Davis*), Daryl Edwards (*Fly*), Leonard Jackson (*Smokey*), Bill Cobbs (*Walter*), Steve James (*Odell*), Edward Baran (*Mr. Vance*), John Sayles (*Man in Black*), David Strathairn (*Man in Black*), Maggie Renzi (*Noreen*), Olga Merediz (*Noreen's client*), Minnie Gentry (*Mrs. Brown*), Ren Woods (*Bernice*), Reggie Rock Bythewood (*Rickey*), Alvin Alexis (*Willis*), Rosetta Le Noire (*Mama*), Michael Albert Mantel (*Mr. Lowe*), Jaime Tirelli (*Hector*), Liane Curtis (*Ace*), Chip Mitchell (*Ed*), David Babcock (*Phil*), Sidney Sheriff Jr. (*Virgil*), Carl Gordon (*Mr. Price*), Fisher Stevens (*card trickster*), Kim Staunton (*teacher*), Anthony Thomas (*basketball player*), Rosanna Carter (*West Indian woman*), Josh Mostel (*Casio vendor*)
108 min., 35 mm

1985

Born in the U.S.A.
I'm on Fire
Glory Days
Music videos featuring Bruce Springsteen.

1987

Matewan

Production company: Red Dog Films, Cinecom Entertainment Group, Film Gallery
Executive producers: Amir Malin, Mark Balsam, Jerry Silva
Producers: Peggy Rajski, Maggie Renzi
Cinematography: Haskell Wexler (Duartcolor)
Editor: Sonya Polonsky
Production designer: Nora Chavooshian
Art director: Dan Bishop
Music: Mason Daring
Cast: Chris Cooper (*Joe Kenehan*), Mary McDonnell (*Elma Radnor*), Will Oldham (*Danny Radnor*), David Strathairn (*Sid Hatfield*), Ken Jenkins (*Sephus*), Kevin Tighe (*Hickey*), Gordon Clapp (*Griggs*), James Earl Jones (*"Few Clothes" Johnson*), Bob Gunton (*C. E. Lively*), Jace Alexander (*Hillard Elkins*), Joe Grifasi (*Fausto*), Nancy Mette (*Bridey Mae*), Jo Henderson (*Mrs. Elkins*), Josh Mostel (*Cabell Testerman*), Gary McCleery (*Ludie*), Maggie Renzi (*Rosaria*), Tom Wright (*Tom*), Michael Preston (*Ellix*), Thomas A. Carlin (*Turley*), John Sayles (*hard-shell preacher*)
133 min., 35 mm

1988

Eight Men Out

Production company: Orion Pictures Corporation
Executive producers: Barbara Boyle, Jerry Offsay
Producers: Sarah Pillsbury, Midge Sanford
Co-producer/production manager: Peggy Rajski
Based on the novel by: Eliot Asinof
Cinematography: Robert Richardson (Duartcolor)
Editor: John Tintori
Production designer: Nora Chavooshian
Art Director: Dan Bishop
Music: Mason Daring
Cast: John Cusack (*Buck Weaver*), Charlie Sheen (*Hap Felsch*), D. B. Sweeney (*"Shoeless" Joe Jackson*), Jace Alexander (*Dickie Kerr*), Gordon Clapp (*Ray Schalk*), Don Harvey (*Swede Risberg*), Bill Irwin (*Eddie Collins*), Perry Lang (*Fred McMullin*), James Read (*"Lefty" Williams*), Michael Rooker (*Chick Gandil*), David Strathairn (*Eddie Cicotte*), John Mahoney (*Kid Gleason*), James Desmond

(*Smitty*), John Sayles (*Ring Lardner*), Studs Terkel (*Hugh Fullerton*), Michael Lerner (*Arnold Rothstein*), Richard Edson (*Billy Maharg*), Christopher Lloyd (*Bill Burns*), Michael Mantell (*Abe Attell*), Kevin Tighe (*Sport Sullivan*), Clifton James (*Charles Comiskey*), Barbara Garrick (*Helen Weaver*), Wendy Makkena (*Kate Jackson*), Maggie Renzi (*Rose Cicotte*), Nancy Travis (*Lyria Williams*), Ken Berry (*heckler*), Danton Stone (*hired killer*), Stephen Mendillo (*monk*), Jim Stark (*reporter*), John Anderson (*Judge Kenesaw Mountain Landis*), Eliot Asinof (*Heydler*), Clyde Bassett (*Ben Johnson*), John D. Craig (*Rothstein's lawyer*), Michael Laskin (*Austrian*), Randle Mell (*Ahearn*), Robert Motz (*district attorney*), Bill Raymond (*Ben Short*), Brad Garrett (*PeeWee*), Tay Strathairn (*Bucky*), Jesse Vincent (*Scooter*)
120 min., 35 mm

1989

Mountain View

Production company: Alive From Off Center and WGBH
Executive producer: Susan Dowling
Producers: Susan Dowling, Maggie Renzi
Directed by: Marta Renzi in collaboration with John Sayles
Cinematography: Paul Goldsmith
Editors: Susan Dowling, Marta Renzi
Production designer: Sandra McLeod
Music director: Mason Daring
Cast: Thomas Eldred (*old man*), Jane Alexander (*bartender*), Jace Alexander (*son*), Fred Holland, Mary Schultz (*couple on porch*), Jim Desmond (*barfly*), Marta Jo Miller (*young mother*), Christine Philion, Nathaniel E. Lee (*newlyweds*), Cathy Zimmerman, Thomas Grunewald (*couple in truck*), Marta Renzi (*other woman*), Joanne Callum, Caroline Grossman (*girlfriends*), Doug Elkins, Chisa Hidako (*son's friends*), Sarah Grossman Greene, Irene Krugman, Caitlin Miller, Amos Wolff (*children*)
25 min., 16 mm

1990

City of Hope

Production company: Esperanza Inc.
Executive producers: John Sloss, Harold Welb
Producers: Sarah Green, Maggie Renzi
Cinematography: Robert Richardson
Editor: John Sayles
Music: Mason Daring
Production designers: Dan Bishop, Dianna Freas
Cast: Vincent Spano (*Nick Rinaldi*), Joe Morton (*Wynn*), Tony Lo Bianco (*Joe Rinaldi*), Barbara Williams (*Angela*), Stephen Mendillo (*Yoyo*), Chris Cooper (*Riggs*), Charlie Yanko (*Stavros*), Angela Bassett (*Reesha*), Jace Alexander (*Bobby*), Todd Graff (*Zip*), Scott Tiler (*Vinnie*), John Sayles (*Carl*), Bill Raymond

(*Les*), Maggie Renzi (*Connie*), Tom Wright (*Malik*), Frankie Faison (*Levonne*), Gloria Foster (*Jeanette*), David Strathairn (*Asteroid*), Anthony John Dension (*Rizzo*), Kevin Tighe (*O'Brien*), Josh Mostel (*Mad Anthony*), Joe Grifasi (*Pauly*), Gina Gershon (*Laurie*), Miriam Colon (*Mrs. Ramirez*), Daryl Edwards (*Franklin*), Jude Ciccolella (*Paddy*), Mason Daring (*Peter*), Lawrence Tierney (*Kerrigan*), Louis Zorich (*Mayor Baci*), Ray Aranha (*Errol*)
130 min., 35 mm

1992

Passion Fish

Production company: Atchafalaya
Executive producer: John Sloss
Producers: Sarah Green, Maggie Renzi
Cinematography: Roger Deakins
Editor: John Sayles
Music: Mason Daring
Production designers: Dan Bishop, Dianna Freas
Cast: Mary McDonnell (*May-Alice*), Alfre Woodard (*Chantelle*), Vondie Curtis-Hall (*Sugar*), David Strathairn (*Rennie*), Leo Burmester (*Reeves*), Nora Dunn (*Ti-Marie*), Mary Portser (*Precious*), Angela Bassett (*Dawn/Rhonda*), Sheila Kelley (*Kim*), Nancy Mette (*Nina*), Lenore Banks (*Nurse Quick*), William Mahoney (*Max*), Maggie Renzi (*Louise*), Tom Wright (*Luther*), John Henry (*Dr. Blades*)
135 min., 35 mm

1994

The Secret of Roan Inish

Production company: Skerry Movies Corp., Jones Entertainment Group
Executive producers: John Sloss, Peter Newman, Glenn R. Jones
Producers: Sarah Green, Maggie Renzi
Based on the novel *Secret of the Ron Mor Skerry* by Rosalie K. Fry
Cinematography: Haskell Wexler
Editor: John Sayles
Music: Mason Daring
Production designer: Adrian Smith
Cast: Jeni Courtney (*Fiona Coneelly*), Mick Lally (*Hugh*), Eileen Colgan (*Tess*), John Lynch (*Tadhg Coneelly*), Richard Sheridan (*Cousin Eamon*), Cillian Byrne (*Jamie*), Pat Howey (*priest*), Dave Duffy (*Jim Coneely*), Declan Hannigan (*oldest brother*), Gerard Rooney (*Liam Coneely*), Susan Lynch (*sylkie*)
103 min., 35 mm

1996

Lone Star

Production company: Rio Dulce/Castle Rock Entertainment
Executive producer: John Sloss
Producers: R. Paul Miller, Maggie Renzi
Cinematography: Stuart Dryburgh
Editor: John Sayles
Production designer: Dan Bishop
Art director: Kyler Black
Music: Mason Daring
Cast: Chris Cooper (*Sam Deeds*), Elizabeth Peña (*Pilar Cruz*), Joe Morton (*Delmore "Del" Payne*), Matthew McConaughey (*Buddy Deeds*), Kris Kristofferson (*Charlie Wade*), Clifton James (*Mayor Hollis Pogue*), Frances McDormand (*Bunny*), Miriam Colon (*Mercedes Cruz*), Jesse Borrego (*Danny*), Tony Plana (*Ray*), Stephen Mendillo (*Cliff*), LaTanya Richardson (*Priscilla Worth*), Stephen Lang (*Mikey*), Ron Canada (*Otis Payne*), Gabriel Casseus (*Young Otis*), Leo Burmester (*Cody*), Chandra Wilson (*Athens*), Eddie Robinson (*Chet*), Gordon Tootoosis (*Wesley Birdsong*), Oni Faida Lampley (*Celie*), Eleese Lester (*Molly*), Joe Stevens (*Deputy Travis*), Gonzalo Castillo (*Amado*), Richard Coca (*Enrique*), Tony Frank (*Fenton*), Jeff Monahan (*Young Hollis*), Damon Guy (*Shadow*), Dee Macaluso (*Anglo mother*), Luis Cobo (*Mexican American father*), Marco Perella (*Anglo father*), Don Phillips (*principal*), Tay Strathairn (*Young Sam*), Vanessa Martinez (*young Pilar*)
Film Extract: Black Mama, White Mama (1973)
135 min., 35 mm

1997

Men With Guns/Hombres Armados

Production company: Anarchists' Convention Productions/Lexington Road Pictures/Clear Blue Sky Productions
Executive producers: Jody Patton, Lou Gonda, John Sloss
Producers: R. Paul Miller, Maggie Renzi
Cinematography: Slawomir Idziak
Editor: John Sayles
Music: Mason Daring
Production design: Felipe Fernández del Paso
Cast: Federico Luppi (*Dr. Fuentes*), Damian Delgado (*soldier, Domingo*), Dan Rivera González (*boy, Conejo*), Tania Cruz (*mute girl, Graciela*), Damian Alcazar (*priest, Padre Portillo*), Mandy Patinkin (*Andrew*), Kathryn Janis Grody (*Harriet*), Iguandili López (*mother*), Nandi Luna Ramírez (*daughter*), Rafael de Quevedo (*general*), Carmen Madrid (*Angela*), Esteban Soberanes (*Raúl*), Ivan Arango (*Cienfuegos*), Lizzie Curry Martínez (*Montoya*), Roberto Sosa (*Bravo*), Maggie Renzi, Shari Gray (*tourists by pool*), Paco Mauri (*captain*), David Villalpando, Raúl Sánchez (*gum people*)
123 min., 35 mm

As screenwriter

1978

Piranha

Production company: Piranha Productions/New World Pictures
Executive producers: Roger Corman, Jeff Schechtman
Producers: Jon Davison, Chako Van Leeuwen
Director: Joe Dante
Screenplay: John Sayles
Original story: Richard Robinson, John Sayles
Cinematography: Jamie Anderson (Metrocolor)
Editors: Mark Goldblatt, Joe Dante
Art directors: Bill Mellin, Kerry Mellin
Music: Pino Donaggio
Makeup: Rob Bottin
Cast: Bradford Dillman (*Paul Grogan*), Heather Menzies (*Maggie McKeown*), Kevin McCarthy (*Dr. Robert Hoak*), Keenan Wynn (*Jack*), Dick Miller (*Buck Gardner*), Barbara Steele (*Dr. Mengers*), Belinda Balaski (*Betsy*), Melody Thomas (*Laura*), Bruce Gordon (*Colonel Waxman*), Barry Brown (*trooper*), Paul Bartel (*Dumont*), Shannon Collins (*Suzie Grogan*), Shawn Nelson (*Whitney*), Richard Deacon (*Earl Lyon*), John Sayles (*soldier*)
94 min., 35 mm

1979

The Lady in Red

Production company: New World Pictures
Producer: Julie Corman
Co-producer: Steven Kovacs
Director: Lewis Teague
Screenplay: John Sayles
Cinematography: Daniel Lacambre (Metrocolor)
Editors: Larry Bock, Ron Medico, Lewis Teague
Production designer: Jac McAnelly
Music: James Horner
Cast: Pamela Sue Martin (*Polly Franklin*), Robert Conrad (*John Dillinger/Jimmy Lawrence*), Louise Fletcher (*Anna Sage*), Robert Hogan (Jake Lingle), Laurie Heineman (*Rose Shimkus*), Glenn Withrow (*Eddie*), Rod Gist (*Pinetop*), Peter Hobbs (*Pops Geissler*), Christopher Lloyd (*Frognose*), Dick Miller (*Patek*), Nancy Anne Parsons (*Tiny Alice*), Alan Vint (*Melvin Purvis*), Milt Kogan (*preacher*), Chip Fields (*Satin*), Buck Young (*Hennessey*), Phillip R. Allen (*Elliot Ness*), Ilene Kristen (*Wynona*), Joseph X. Flaherty (*Frank*), Terri Taylor (*Mae*), Peter Miller (*Fritz*), Mary Woronov (*woman bankrobber*), Jay Rasumny (*Bill*), Michael Cavanaugh (*undercover cop*), Arnie Moore (*trucker*), John Guitz (*Momo*), Saul Krugman (*judge*), Blackie Dammett (*immigration officer*)
93 min., 35 mm

1980

Alligator

Production company: Alligator Associates, Group 1 Productions
Executive producer: Robert S. Bremson
Producer: Brandon Chase
Associate producer: Tom Jacobson
Director: Lewis Teague
Screenplay: John Sayles
Original story: John Sayles, Frank Ray Perilli
Cinematography: Joe Mangine
Editors: Larry Bock, Ronald Medico
Art director: Michael Erler
Music: Craig Hundley
Cast: Robert Forster (*Det. David Madison*), Robin Riker (*Marisa Kendall*), Michael V. Gazzo (*Police Chief Clark*), Dean Jagger (*Slade*), Sydney Lassick (*Lou Gutchel*), Jack Carter (*Mayor Ledoux*), Perry Lang (*Jim Kelly*), Henry Silva (*Colonel Brock*), Bart Braverman (*Thomas Kemp*), John Lisbon Wood (*mad bomber*), James Ingersoll (*Helms*), Robert Doyle (*Bill*), Patti Jerome (*Madeline*), Angel Tompkins (*newswoman*), Sue Lyon (*ABC newswoman*)
94 min., 35 mm

1980

Battle Beyond the Stars

Production company: New World Pictures
Executive producer: Roger Corman
Producer: Ed Carlin
Associate producer: Mary Ann Fisher
Director: Jimmy Teru Murakami
Screenplay: John Sayles
Original story: John Sayles, Anne Dyer
Cinematography: Daniel Lacambre
Additional photography: James Cameron
Editors: Allan Holzman, Robert J. Kizer
Art directors: James Cameron, Charles Breen
Miniature design/construction: James Cameron
Music: James Horner
Cast: Richard Thomas (*Shad*), Robert Vaughn (*Gelt*), John Saxon (*Sador*), George Peppard (*Space Cowboy*), Darlanne Fluegel (*Nanelia*), Sybil Danning (*St. Exmin*), Sam Jaffe (*Dr. Hephaestus*), Morgan Woodward (*Cayman*), Carl Boen (*First Nestor*), John Gowens (*Second Nestor*), Steve Davis (*Quopeg*), Larry Meyers (*The Kelvin*), Lara Cody (*The Kelvin*), Lynn Carlin (*Nell*), Jeff Corey (*Zed*), Marta Kristen (*Lux*), Julia Duffy (*Mol*), Eric Morris (*Pen*), Doug Carleson (*Pok*), Ron Ross (*Dab*), Terrence McNally (*Gar*)
103 min., 35 mm

1980

The Howling

Production company: Avco Embassy Pictures, International Film Investors, Wescom Productions
Executive producer: Steven A. Lane
Producers: Michael Finnell, Jack Conrad
Associate producer: Rob Bottin
Director: Joe Dante
Screenplay: John Sayles, Terence H. Winkless
Original novel by: Gary Brandner
Cinematography: John Hora
Editors: Mark Goldblatt, Joe Dante
Art director: Robert A. Burns
Music: Pino Donaggio
Special makeup: Rob Bottin
Cast: Dee Wallace (*Karen White*), Patrick Macnee (*Dr. George Waggner*), Dennis Dugan (*Chris*), Christopher Stone (*R. William "Bill" Neill*), Belinda Balaski (*Terry Fisher*), Kevin McCarthy (*Fred Francis*), John Carradine (*Erle Kenton*), Slim Pickens (*Sam Newfield*), Elisabeth Brooks (*Marsha*), Robert Picardo (*Eddie*), Margie Impert (*Donna*), Noble Willingham (*Charlie Barton*), James Murtaugh (*Jerry Warren*), Jim McKrell (*Lew Landers*), Kenneth Tobey (*older cop*), Don McLeod (*TC*), Dick Miller (*Walter Paisley*), Roger Corman (*man in phone booth*), John Sayles (*morgue attendant*)
90 min., 35 mm

1980

A Perfect Match (made for TV)

Production company: Lorimar Productions
Executive producers: David Jacobs, Lee Rich
Producer: Andre Guttfreund
Director: Mel Damski
Teleplay: John Sayles
Story by: Andre Guttfreund, Mel Damski
Cinematography: Ric Waite
Editor: John Farrell
Music: Billy Goldenberg
Art director: Tom H. John
Cast: Linda Kelsey (*Miranda McLloyd*), Michael Brandon (*Steve Triandos*), Lisa Lucas (*Julie Larson*), Charles Durning (*Bill Larson*), Colleen Dewhurst (*Meg Larson*), Clyde Kusatsu (*Dr. Tommy Chang*), Bonnie Bartlett (*Judge Greenburg*), Hildy Brooks (*Esther*), Alexa Kenin (*Angel*), Bever-Leigh Banfield (*Rhonda*)
100 min., 35 mm

1982

The Challenge

Production company: CBS Theatrical Films
Executive producer: Lyle Poncher
Producers: Robert L. Rosen, Ron Beckman
Director: John Frankenheimer
Screenplay: Richard Maxwell, John Sayles, Ivan Moffatt
Cinematography: Kozo Okazaki (Deluxe)
Editor: Jack Wheeler
Production designer: Yoshiyuki Oshida
Music: Jerry Goldsmith
Martial arts coordinator: Steven Seagal
Cast: Scott Glenn (*Rick Murphy*), Toshiro Mifune (*Sensei Yoshida*), Donna Kei Benz (*Akiko Yoshida*), Atsuo Nakamura (*Hideo Yoshida*), Calvin Jung (*Ando*), Clyde Kusatsu (*Go*), Sab Shimono (*Toshio Yoshida*), Kiyoaki Nagai (*Kubo*), Kenta Fukasaku (*Jiro*), Shogo Shimada (*Takeshi Yoshida*), Yoshio Inaba (*instructor*), Seiji Miyaguchi (*old man*), Miiko Taka (*Sensei's wife*)
116 min., 35 mm

1982

Enormous Changes at the Last Minute

Production company: Ordinary Lives Inc.
Producer: Mirra Bank
Directors: Ellen Hovde ("Virginia's Story"), Mirra Bank and Ellen Hovde ("Faith's Story"), Mirra Bank ("Alexandra's Story")
Screenplay: John Sayles with Susan Rice
Original stories by: Grace Paley
Cinematography: Tom McDonough
Cast: "Virginia's Story": Ellen Barkin (*Virginia*), David Strathairn (*Jerry*), Ron McLarty (*John*), Sudie Bond (*Mrs. Raferty*); "Faith's Story": Lynn Milgram (*Faith*), Jeffrey DeMunn (*Ricardo*), Zvee Scooler (*Pa*), Eda Reiss Merin (*Ma*), Fay Bernardi (*Mrs. Hegel-Shtein*); "Alexandra's Story": Maria Tucci (*Alexandra*), Kevin Bacon (*Dennis*), John Wardell (*Doc*), Lou Criscuolo (*George*)
110 min., 35 mm

1986

The Clan of the Cave Bear

Production company: Jonesfilm, Guber-Peters Company, Jozak Company, Decade Productions
Executive producers: Mark Damon, John Hyde, Jon Peters, Peter Guber, Sidney Kimmel
Producers: Gerald I. Isenberg, Stan Rogow
Director: Michael Chapman

Screenplay: John Sayles
Based on the novel by: Jean M. Auel
Cinematography: Jan de Bont (Technicolor)
Editors: Wendy Greene Bricmont, Paul Hirsch
Production designer: Tony Masters
Music: Alan Silvestri
Cast: Daryl Hannah (*Ayla*), Pamela Reed (*Iza*), James Remar (*Creb*), Thomas G. Waites (*Broud*), John Doolittle (*Brun*), Curtis Armstrong (*Goov*), Martin Doyle (*Grod*), Adel C. Hammond (*Vorn*), Tony Montanaro (*Zoug*), Mike Muscat (*Dorv*), John Wardlow (*Droog*), Keith Wardlow (*Crug*), Karen Austin (*Aba*), Barbara Duncan (*Uka*), Gloria Lee (*Oga*), Janne Mortil (*Ovra*), Lycia Naff (*Uba*), Linda Quibell (*Aga*), Bernadette Sabath (*Ebra*)
98 min., 35 mm

1986

Unnatural Causes (made for TV)
Production company: Blue Andre Productions, ITC Productions
Executive producers: Blue Andre, Robert M. Myman
Producer: Blue Andre
Director: Lamont Johnson
Teleplay: John Sayles
Story by: Martin M. Goldstein, Stephen Doran, Robert Jacobs
Cinematography: Larry Pizer
Editor: Paul LaMastra
Music: Charles Fox
Production designer: Anne Pritchard
Cast: John Ritter *(Frank Coleman)*, Alfre Woodard *(Maude DeVictor)*, Patti La-Belle *(Jeanette Thompson)*, John Vargas *(Fernando "Nando" Sanchez)*, Frederick Allen *(kid)*, Richard Anthony Crenna *(soldier)*, Frank Pellegrino *(Raul)*, Jonathan Welsh *(Dr. Lester)*, Luba Gay *(Rena)*, John Sayles *(Lloyd)*, Roger Steffans *(Golub)*
100 min., 35 mm

1987

Wild Thing
Production company: Filmline, Atlantic Releasing
Producer: David Calloway
Director: Max Reid
Screenplay: John Sayles
Based on a story by: John Sayles and Larry Stamper
Cinematography: Rene Verzier (Sona Color)
Editors: Battle Davis, Steven Rosenblum
Production designers: John Meighen, Jocelyn Joli
Music: George S. Clinton

Cast: Rob Knepper (*Wild Thing*), Kathleen Quinlan (*Jane*), Robert Davi (*Chopper*), Maury Chaykin (*Detective Trask*), Betty Buckley (*Leah*), Guillaume Lemay-Thivierge (*Wild Thing, age ten*), Robert Bednarski (*Free/Wild Thing, age three*), Clark Johnson (*Winston*), Sean Hewitt (*Father Quinn*), Teddy Abner (*Rasheed*), Cree Summer Francks (*Lisa*), Shawn Levy (*Paul*), Rod Torchia (*Hud*), Christine Jones (*Laurie*), Robert Austern (*Wiz*), Tom Rack (*Braindrain*), Alexander Chapman (*Shakes*), Robert Ozores (*El Borracho*)
92 min., 35 mm

1989

Breaking In
Production company: Breaking In Productions, Samuel Goldwyn Company
Producer: Harry Gittes
Director: Bill Forsyth
Screenplay: John Sayles
Cinematography: Michael Gibbs (Medallion Color)
Editor: Michael Ellis
Production designers: Adrienne Atkinson, John Willett
Music: Michael Gibbs
Cast: Burt Reynolds *(Ernie Mullins)*, Casey Siemaszko *(Mike Lefebb)*, Harry Carey Jr. *(Shoes)*, Sheila Kelly *(Carrie)*, Lorraine Toussaint *(Delphine)*, Albert Salmi *(Johnny Scat)*, Maury Chaykin *(Tucci)*, Stephen Tobolowsky *(district attorney)*, Richard Key Jones *(Lou)*, Tom Laswell *(Bud)*, Frank A. Damiani *(waiter)*, David Frishberg *(nightclub singer)*, John Baldwin *(Sam the Apostle)*, Eddie Driscoll *(Paul the Apostle)*, Melanie Moseley *(young woman apostle)*, Galen B. Schrick *(choir master)*, Duggan L. Wendeborn *(Faith House member)*, K. Gordan Scott *(counterman)*, Clifford Nelson, Roy McGillivray *(old men)*, Kim Singer *(anchorwoman)*, Charles E. Compton *(real estate agent)*
94 min., 35 mm

1989

Shannon's Deal (made for TV series pilot)
Production company: Stan Rogow Prods., NBC
Producers: Stan Rogow, Gareth Davies, Jim Margellos, Allan Arkush
Director: Lewis Teague
Teleplay: John Sayles
Cinematography: Andrew Dintenfass
Editor: Neil Travis
Music: Wynton Marsalis
Production designer: John Vallone
Cast: Jamey Sheridan (*Jack Shannon*), Elizabeth Peña (*Lucy Acosta*), Richard Edson (*Wilmer*), Jenny Lewis (*Neala Shannon*), Alberta Watson (*Teri*), Martin Ferrero (*Lou Gandolph*), Miguel Ferrer (*Todd Spurrier*), Claudia Christian (*Molly Tempke*), Ely Pouget (*Gwen*), Ron Joseph (*Det. Joe Menke*), Michael Bowen

(*Scotty Powell*), Eddie Velez (*Chuy Vargas*), Andrew Lowery (*Eric*), Stefan Gierasch (*Klaus*), Danny Trejo (*Raul*), Kevin Peter Hall (*card player*), Coco Mendoza, Russell Yip, Jesse Dizon, Brian Smiar

120 min., 35 mm

1990–91

Shannon's Deal (TV series)

Production company: Stan Rogow Prods., NBC
Executive producer: Stan Rogow
Producers: Gareth Davies, Jim Margellos; Allan Arkush (second season)
Created by/creative consultant: John Sayles
Cinematography: Stevan Larner; Michael Gerschman (second season)
Editors: William B. Strich, Stephen Potter, Conrad Gonzalez
Music: Wynton Marsalis (theme); Lee Ritenour; Tom Scott
Art director: James J. Agazzi
Cast: Jamey Sheridan (*Jack Shannon*), Elizabeth Peña (*Lucy Acosta*), Richard Edson (*Wilmer*), Jenny Lewis (*Neala*), Martin Ferrero (*Lou Gandolph*)
First season, April 1990–May 1990

Words to Music
Writer: John Sayles
Director: Allan Arkush
Cast: Michelle Joiner, Tanya Tucker, John Sayles, Iggy Pop, David Crosby, Stanley Brock, Joe Bratcher, Julius Harris

Inside Straight
Writer: Mark Rossner
Director: Allan Arkush
Cast: Dick Antony Williams, Ron Joseph, Michael Beach, Tisha Campbell, D. Scott Hoxby, Miguel Ferrer

Art
Writer: David Greenwalt
Director: David Greenwalt
Cast: Nicholas Miscusi, Marc Lawrence, Larry Hankin, John Michael Bolger, Mimi Craven

Custody
Writer: John Sayles
Director: Joel Oliansky
Cast: Lucinda Jenney, Jeff Perry, Bob Delegall, Frank Birney, Julianna McCarthy

Hitting Home
Writer: Tom Rickman
Director: Aaron Lipstadt
Cast: Ralph Waite, George Murdock, Ron Joseph, Nick Cassavetes, David Arnott

Sanctuary
Writer: John Byrum
Director: John Byrum
Cast: Robert Covarrubias, John Anderson, John Shepherd, Frank McCarthy, Monty Hoffman

Second Season, March 1991–May 1991
Bad Beat
Writers: Eugene Corr, Ruth Shapiro
Director: Eugene Corr
Cast: Darrell Larson, Mary Jo Keenan
Greed
Writer: David Greenwalt
Director: Allan Arkush
Cast: Whitman Mayo, Charles Lane, Stephen Tobolowsky, Juanin Clay, Tom Towles, Kurt Fuller, Ron Joseph
Strangers in the Night
Writer: Tom Rickman
Director: Tom Rickman
Cast: B. D. Wong, Victor Love, Clark Gregg, Steve Vinovich, Randle Mell, Dee Dee Rescher, Ron Joseph
First Amendment
Writer: Barry Pullman
Director: Allan Arkush
Cast: John Kapelos, Brent Hinkley, Stuart Pankin, Kimberly Scott, Sonny Carl Davis
The Inside Man
Writer: Corey Blechman
Director: Corey Blechman
Cast: Paul Whitthorne, Mark McManus, Julie Garfield, Michelle Forbes, James Lashly, Richard Roat, David Spielberg, Kimberly Scott
Matrimony
Writer: Kathy McCormick
Director: Betty Thomas
Cast: Michele Park, Barry Cullison, Cecile Callan
Trouble
Writer: Joan Tewksbury
Director: Joan Tewksbury
Cast: Michele Park, Barry Cullison, Cecile Callan

1994

Men of War
Production company: MDP Worldwide, Pomarance Corporation, Grandview Avenue Pictures
Executive producers: Moshe Diamant, Stan Rogow
Producers: Arthur Goldblatt, Andrew Pfeffer
Director: Perry Lang
Screenplay: John Sayles, Ethan Reiff, Cyrus Voris
Story: Stan Rogow
Cinematography: Ron Schmidt (Deluxe)
Editor: Jeffrey Reiner
Music: Gerald Gouriet

Production designers: Steve Spence, Jim Newport
Cast: Dolph Lundgren (*Nick Gunnar*), Charlotte Lewis (*Loki*), B. D. Wong (*Po*), Anthony Denison (*Jimmy G*), Don Harvey (*Nolan*), Catherine Bell (*Grace*), Tiny "Zeus" Lister (*Blades*), Tom Wright (*Jamaal*), Tim Guinee (*Ocker*), Trevor Goddard (*Keefer*), Kevin Tighe (*Merrick*), Thomas Gibson (*Warren*), Perry Lang (*Lyle*), Aldo Sambrell (*Goldmouth*), Juan Pedro Tudela (*Kalfo*).
103 min., 35 mm

Uncredited writing contributions

Love Field (1991) Jonathan Kaplan
The Quick and the Dead (1995) Sam Raimi
Apollo 13 (1995) Ron Howard
Mimic (1997) Guillermo Del Toro

Acting Credits

The Howling as morgue attendant (Joe Dante, 1981)
Unnatural Causes as Lloyd (Lamont Johnson, TV movie, 1986)
Hard Choices as Don (Rick King, 1986)
Something Wild as motorcycle cop (Jonathan Demme, 1986)
La Fin della notte (Davide Ferrario, 1989)
Untamagiru as U.S. Army officer (Go Takamine, 1989)
Little Vegas (Perry Lang, 1990)
Straight Talk as Guy Girardi (Barnet Kellman, 1992)
Malcolm X as FBI agent (Spike Lee, 1992)
My Life's in Turnaround as marginal producer (Eric Schaeffer, 1993)
Matinee as Bob (Joe Dante, 1993)
Gridlock'D as police officer (Vondie Curtis-Hall, 1997)

Fiction

The Pride of the Bimbos (Little, Brown and Co., 1975)
Union Dues (Little, Brown and Co., 1977)
The Anarchists' Convention and Other Stories (Little, Brown and Co., 1979) Home for Wayfarers, At the Anarchists' Convention, Schiffman's Ape, The 7-10 Split, The Cabinetmaker, Old Spanish Days, Bad Dogs, Hoop, Buffalo, Fission, Breed, Golden State, Tan, Children of the Silver Screen, I-80 Nebraska, 490-205.
Los Gusanos (HarperCollins, 1991)

Non Fiction

Thinking in Pictures: The Making of the Movie Matewan (Houghton Mifflin, 1987).

Published short stories and articles

"I Wanna Tell You a Story," *The Guardian*, Aug. 1, 1996

"20 Best Political Films," *Mother Jones*, May–June 1996

"How to Stay Independent," *Index on Censorship*, Nov/Dec 1995

"Above the Line," *Premiere*, Sept. 1994

"Keeping Time," *Rolling Stone*, Dec. 1993

"Peeling," *The Atlantic Monthly*, Sept. 1993

"Director's Cut: Punchy Delivery," *The Independent*, Nov. 29, 1991

"Maverick Moviemakers Inspire Their Successors," *The New York Times*, May 12, 1991

"Inside Eight Men Out," *Sport*, July 1988

"Treasure," *Esquire*, March 1988

"The Halfway Diner," *The Atlantic Monthly*, June 1987

"Pregame Jitters," *Esquire*, June 1986

Book Review, *Adventures in the Screenwriting Trade* by William Goldman, *Film Comment*, May–June 1983

"At the Republican Convention," *New Republic*, Aug. 2–9, 1980

"Dillinger in Hollywood," *Triquarterly*, Spring 1980

"Children of the Silver Screen," *Quest/79*, 1979

"At the Anarchists' Convention," *The Atlantic Monthly*, Feb. 1979

"Writing Dialogue," *Writer*, Jan. 1978

"Golden State," *The Atlantic Monthly*, June 1977

"Hoop," *The Atlantic Monthly*, March 1977

"Breed," *The Atlantic Monthly*, July 1976

"I-80 Nebraska, 490–205," *The Atlantic Monthly*, May 1975

Index